# White Nativism, Ethnic Identity and US Immigration Policy Reforms

D1525104

Analyzing US immigration and deportation policy over the last twenty years, this book illustrates how US immigration reform can be conceived as a psychological, legal, policy-driven tool, which is inexorably entwined with themes of American identity, national belonging and white nativism. Focusing on Hispanic immigration and American-born children of Mexican parentage, the author examines how engrained, historical, individual and collective social constructions and psychological processes, related to identity formation can play an instrumental role in influencing political and legal processes. It is argued that contemporary American immigration policy reforms need to be conceptualized as a complex, conscious and unconscious White Nativist psychological, legal, defence mechanism related to identity preservation and contestation.

Whilst building on existing theoretical frameworks, the author offers new empirical evidence on immigration processes and policy within the United States as well as original research involving the acculturation and identity development of children of Mexican immigrant parentage. It brings together themes of race, ethnicity and American national identity under a new integrated sociopolitical and psychological framework examining macro and micro implications of recent US immigration policy reform.

Subsequently this book will have broad appeal for academics, professionals and students who have an interest in political psychology, childhood studies, American immigration policy, constructions of national identity, critical race and ethnic studies, and the Mexican diaspora.

**Maria del Mar Farina** is an Assistant Professor at Westfield State University, in Westfield, MA. She completed her doctoral degree at Smith College, School for Social Work, in Northampton, MA, where she went on to become an Adjunct Professor and Assistant Director of Field. She is also a graduate of the MBA program at Western New England College, in Springfield, MA. She maintains a clinical private practice in Holyoke, MA, working primarily with the Latino community. Her work has been presented in the United States and Europe, including in Turkey and Poland, at the International Society of Political Psychology (ISPP), and in Italy, at Processes Influencing Democratic Ownership and Participation (PIDOP), part of the European Commission under the Seventh Framework Programme.

# Routledge Advances in Health and Social Policy

# White Nativism, Ethnic Identity and US Immigration Policy Reforms

## American Citizenship and Children in Mixed Status, Hispanic Families

**Maria del Mar Farina**

Routledge
Taylor & Francis Group

LONDON AND NEW YORK

First published 2018 by Routledge

2 Park Square, Milton Park, Abingdon, Oxfordshire OX14 4RN

52 Vanderbilt AVenue, New York, NY 10017

*Routledge is an imprint of the Taylor & Francis Group, an informa business*

First issued in paperback 2019

*British Library Cataloguing-in-Publication Data*
A catalogue record for this book is available from the British
Library

*Library of Congress Cataloging-in-Publication Data*
A catalog record for this book has been requested.

ISBN: 978-1-138-23437-6 (hbk)
ISBN: 978-0-367-43098-6 (pbk)

Typeset in Times New Roman
by codeMantra

To my daughter Katerina, who like many children in this country, is the American daughter of an immigrant woman.

# Contents

# List of illustrations

**Figure**

**Tables**

# Foreword

*Dr. Joyce Everett*

The release of White Nativism, Ethnic Identity and US Immigration Policy Reforms is both timely and uncanny. Timely because its release coincides with the dramatic shift in US policies affecting "the other" and uncanny because the book addresses an issue that is familiar to most Americans, but is at the same time a foreign issue that makes it uncomfortably strange. US immigration policy, especially those policies affecting Mexicans and American-born Mexicans, is an uncomfortable issue requiring more than a simplistic and short-sighted examination. Maria del Mar Farina's book provides a wide-sweeping appraisal of American immigration policy using multiple perspectives to assess why these policies focus on preventing "others" from entering the country. Before describing the key features of the book, a brief summary of the shift in American policies toward "the other" is warranted.

In November 2016, Donald Trump was elected the 45th President of the United States. Trump campaigned on a platform that reignited the public's fear of the "other". He pledged that he would build a wall on the border of the US and Mexico, that Mexico would pay for, and that he would temporarily ban the travel of Muslims from certain countries from entering the US. All with the intent of Making America Great Again! In the first 49 days of his presidency, he signed an executive order banning Muslims from seven middle-eastern countries from entering the US. He also signed other executive orders suspending the refugee program for 120 days and another authorizing the hiring of additional border patrol agents and ending the catch and release policies of illegal immigrants. The "other," mostly Mexicans and Muslims, according to Trump pose a threat to the US and therefore must be banished from the country.

Trump's election campaign exposed the deep-seated, unconscious fears a segment of the American public hold toward "the other," and his election as the President of the United States unleashed discriminatory acts against groups once considered as American as apple pie. The unfolding of Trump's efforts to appease his supporters through executive orders and other policies requires a much deeper and sophisticated appraisal of the underlying dynamics that led to his rise to power. Just such a careful and systematic analysis of the dynamic interplay of power and privilege is offered in this book.

White Nativism, Ethnic Identity and US Immigration Policy Reforms offers a systematic integrative and complex explanation of immigration policy reforms of 1996 and beyond using sociological, political and psychological theories. It begins by providing a conceptual framework based on critical historical discourse to carefully scrutinize social power relations. At issue is the manner in which inequality is produced, maintained and reinforced such that the construction of "the other" marginalizes and causes psychological damage to those perceived as "the other." What flows naturally from this examination of social power relations is an examination of what is the national and cultural identity of Americans. Similarly, this book examines what is American citizenship and on what basis is it bestowed, an issue that is directly related to immigration policies. Originally, it was White Anglo Saxon Protestant men, now referred to as "White Natives," who over time have become fearful of losing or facing a transformation of their American identity due to the increasing numbers of immigrants entering the country. Mourning the loss of what might be considered the ideal, "White Natives" resist the transformation or loss of American identity by designing immigration policy reforms that create barriers and/or restrict entry into the United States. But one must ask what happens when "the other" is an economic resource that most "White Natives" rely upon? What psychological processes explain the continued marginalization of "the other," especially American-born Hispanics? These and other profoundly provocative questions are explored in this book, leading to an examination of Hispanic children of immigrants and American-born Hispanic children's ethnic identity development, acculturation and sense of belonging in American culture.

Maria del Mar Farina's interest in these issues developed in 2009 during her doctoral studies at Smith College when she pondered the question of "why current immigration policy has attempted to keep 'the other' from entering the United States and why is 'the other' risking his/her life to enter at all costs a country that does not welcome him or her?" At the time Barack Obama was President and was perceived as a bright star, who would eradicate the massive deportation of Mexicans crossing the borders. Instead deportation rates went up substantially. In light of these events, Maria del Mar continued to pursue her interest in what motivated the raise of conservative immigration policies by using her dissertation to examine whether deportation reform policies enacted since 1996 affected the ethnic identity, acculturation and sense of national belonging of American-born children of Mexican immigrant parents. As chair of her dissertation committee it was a pleasure to work with such a competent and professional student.

She herself is an immigrant from Spain who came to the US to attend college and remained in the country thereafter. She is a trained social work clinician who has worked for many years with the Latino community, including with mixed status families and their children. Having grown up in a family that went through War World II, and a civil war, Maria del Mar is familiar with the effects of intergroup and intragroup conflict, displacement and migration. It is these experiences that add credence to the book and make it a significant contribution to the field.

Dr. Joyce Everett

# Acknowledgements

I want to express my gratitude to Dr. Vamik Volkan for his guidance and consultation as part of my doctoral dissertation committee, as well as for his encouragement to publish this book. Thanks also to Dr. Joyce Everett, who provided ongoing guidance, mentoring and encouragement to successfully complete my dissertation work. And to Dr. Joan Lesser, a valued mentor for many years now, whose encouragement and unwavering support guided my career path and made this book a reality.

# 1 Introduction

Social problems reflect dominant societal constructions that are historically informed and reproduced (Barusch, 2015; Jimenez, Pasztor, Chambers, & Fuji, 2015). Existing social policy analysis models taught in social welfare and social work policy courses depart from this perspective. Students applying these models learn to examine and contextualize specific social issues within the country's social and economic history. They review previous definitions of the problem, as well as the proposed and existing policies designed to address the social problem, and conclude with a discussion of the covert and overt effects of the social policy (Barusch, 2015; Jimenez et al., 2015).

These models, despite recognizing the constructivist nature of social problems, do not introduce students to any conceptual framework, such as critical discourse analysis (CDA) approaches, capable of systematically examining social construction processes. The models also fail to emphasize the importance of examining existing sociopolitical discourses, as related to a given social issue, to expose their hegemonic ideological premises (Reisigl & Wodak, 2001; Wodak, 2015). Political discourse analysis models have certainly emerged in other disciplines, such as in sociology (Fairclough & Fairclough, 2012; Van Dijk, 1997); yet, they have had limited cross-disciplinary influence, remaining largely outside of the scope and curriculum of social welfare and social work programs.

Likewise, the existing social policy analysis models do not explicitly consider individual and collective psychological processes that inform and support a group's conceptualization of the self and other. Yet, collective, largely unconscious, group processes give birth to group ideologies, which in turn reinforce constructions about the self and other (Tajfel, 1981, 1982; Volkan, 2013). These group, shared, psychological processes and their associated ideologies permeate the individual and group psyches, in what Layton (2006) termed the "normative unconscious" of a people. They also manifest in shared linking phenomena and processes, such as historical legends and myths that define, propel and reify the continuity of said group as collectively imagined (Volkan, 2009, 2013). Discourse analysis models, such as Van Dijk's (1997) sociocognitive discourse analysis model, have at times sought to integrate psychological processes as part of an integrated discourse analysis. However, they have done so from a social identity and cognitive perspective that neglects the role of affective experience and emotion in individual and group formation processes (Reisigl & Wodak, 2001).

This book introduces the reader to an integrated sociopolitical and psychological policy analysis model, drawing from existing social welfare policy models, critical discourse historical analysis (Reisigl & Wodak, 2001; Wodak, 2015), and psychodynamic individual and group collective processes. It provides a systematic and comprehensive analysis of the cognitive constructions, symbols, and affective social processes in which "social problems" are embedded. The integrated nature of this model fosters a complex deconstruction and analysis of social welfare issues and existing or proposed public policy remedies. In this manner, the policy's potential to exacerbate, ameliorate or prevent social inequality, marginalization, oppression and subjugation is fully uncovered. This analysis process ultimately results in the identification and development of new policy initiatives that are better positioned to address the complex, covert, social hegemonic ideological dynamics that have been reinforcing particular social inequalities.

## Conceptual framework

The integrated sociopolitical and psychological policy analysis model presented in this book is designed to answer 12 central questions:

1  What is the problem?
2  Why are sociopolitical debates focusing on the problem now? What is the sociopolitical context?
3  How is the problem defined? And, what are the dominant sociopolitical constructions of the problem?
4  What is the history of the problem?
5  Who is constructing the dominant definitions?
6  Who benefits from the existing prevailing constructions?
7  Who is being subjugated or dominated by the prevailing constructions?
8  What is the ideology that informs existing dominant sociopolitical constructions of the problem? And how does it manifest in the sociopolitical discourse?
9  Given the prevailing dominant sociopolitical discourse, what public policy remedies emerge as possible methods by which to address the problem? And, what are their overt goals?
10  What are the individual and collective psychological processes that produce the dominant ideology and its associated sociopolitical discourses about the problem?
11  What new public policy remedies emerge through the application of an integrated sociopolitical and psychological policy analysis model?
12  What are the micro level social work implications of the current policy?

This systematic analysis allows for a clear articulation of the social issue under study, its existing definitions and the associated sociopolitical discursive practices that are contextualized as part of a historical and ideological process. The model also expands the policy analysis a step further, since it studies and uncovers the collective intrapsychic affective processes that are linked to, and necessitate, the current dominant ideology. This model makes explicit the unequal power relations permeating a specific sociopolitical context and the ideological premises that fuel and perpetuate existing dynamics of dominance, subjugation, inclusion and exclusion. It concurrently examines the unconscious individual and group processes that facilitated the development and internalization of the ideology. In so doing, the policy's ideological premises emerge not as "products of," but rather as "constitutive" to, the dominant group's collective psyche and identity (Volkan, 1988, 2009b, 2013).

The last stage of the analysis explores these collective affective intrapsychic forces and the exclusionary social dynamics they have produced. In this final stage, the individual and collective unconscious dynamics that have intrapsychically delineated "what is me versus not me," or "us versus them" (Volkan, 1985, 2009b, 2013; Wodak, 2015) become clear and explicit. A successful integrative sociopolitical and psychological policy analysis, therefore, is designed to identify the group psychological processes that both necessitated and legitimized the dominant sociopolitical ideology, propelling its unquestioned social acceptance (Wodak, 2015). From an integrated policy analysis perspective, these societal, psychological, group processes of legitimization and thus, "common sense" normalization (Van Dijk, 1997; Wodak, 2015) need to be well understood and addressed. A newly developed social policy that is perceived as de-stabilizing to a people will not be accepted, unless the threatened aspects of the group's internal psychological identity, shared ideology, symbolic and cultural values have been recognized and progressively worked through.

## Policy analysis example: American immigration policy and deportation reforms enacted since 1996

Any focused policy analysis capable of exposing a policy's covert ideology and the group's psychological processes, fueling both the policy and existing sociopolitical discourses, requires a clear articulation and description of the social problem under study. To demonstrate the application, relevance and usefulness of the integrated sociopolitical and psychological policy analysis presented in this book, immigration policy reforms enacted since 1996, with a focus on deportation reforms, will be used as a case example.

The decision to focus this book on the analysis of immigration policy, with an emphasis on deportation reforms enacted since 1996, was primarily driven by the effects and human toll these policies have had on individual adult deportees, their mixed status families, and specifically on the American-born children of Hispanic immigrant parents. The other two influential factors behind this decision were the strong affects that permeate current immigration sociopolitical discourses and the ongoing national and global inability to address "the immigration problem."

The violence and aggression pervading current, global sociopolitical events between ethnic, national and religious groups have caused recent concern over the admission of "the refugee other," in Europe and the United States, particularly, over the admission of Middle Eastern refugees. This concern has been fueling the resurgence of anti-immigrant, White Nativist movements and sociopolitical discourses in which the terms "refugee" and "immigrant" are often invoked interchangeably both in the United States and abroad (Frum, 2015). The linguistic usage, and ensuing conflation of "immigrant" and "refugee," is most pervasive in sociopolitical discussions pertaining to the impending or projected racial demographic shift that threatens the United States' "White Native" critical mass representation (American Hispanics, 2015; Huntington, 2004b). These concerns are certainly not a new development and have been part of American history since the country's inception, emerging and re-emerging at particular historical periods of increasing immigration and internal racial conflict (Hing, 2004). The period between 1990 to the present constitutes a pertinent, contemporary example, as within the last 26 years, concerns over increasing immigration and internal racial conflict have been amplified by the war in the Middle East and the subsequent refugee crisis.

Since the early 1990s, and specifically since 1996, immigration policies began to focus both on efforts to secure the United States border with Mexico and on the implementation of new policies aimed toward interior enforcement. These policies were developed to facilitate the identification, arrest and deportation of the "foreign other," while also changing the grounds for deportation relief (Enchautegui, 2013; Hagan, Rodriguez, & Castro, 2011) and have significantly increased the number and rate of deportations. Since 2002 there have been 4 million deportations, and "close to 2 million since 2008" (Cave, 2013), often dividing mixed status families in a temporary, if not often permanent manner (Enchautegui, 2013).

Since the 1990s, the American sociopolitical discourse has continued to center on the "immigrant other" and on the policies designed to regulate this "other." Immigration policy has since become a highly politicized, contested and divisive national issue, used by politicians on the right and left of the political spectrum to legitimize their own political public platforms. However, what is often omitted from political rhetoric surrounding immigration and the immigrant "other," are the effects these policies have had on one of the most vulnerable groups within American society, children.

This book will illustrate how the permanent division of mixed status families has affected and will continue to affect the welfare of children, who in many cases are American-born children of the Hispanic immigrant "other." These children have had to endure significant financial and emotional hardships due to their families' mixed migratory status and the policies governing their permanency within the United States (Enchautegui, 2013; Fix & Zimmerman, 1999; Hagan, Castro, & Rodriguez, 2010). Of particular concern is that the number of children placed at risk by the existing deportation policies is only expected to rise. Reports by the Urban Institute (2010) indicate that in 2008, 20% of the children born in the United States were born to one immigrant parent; this percentage increased to 25.5% in 2015 (Migration Policy Institute, 2016). In a separate study, Fortuny and Chaudry (2009) found that "between 1990 and 2007, the number of children with at least one immigrant parent [had grown] by 8.2 million, accounting for 77 percent of the increase in children nationally" (p. 1), and 56% of these children were of Hispanic descent (Fortuny & Chaudry, 2009). In fact, and consistent with these statistics, a different study in the Economist's "Special Issue: American Hispanics" (2015) concluded that the recent Hispanic population growth in the United States could not be attributed primarily to immigration, but rather to increasing child birthing rates. The report also emphasized that if the American borders were to be closed "... and every unauthorized migrant deported... 48 million legal Hispanic residents [would] remain" in the United States (American Hispanics, 2015).

Immigration reform is expected to remain a highly contested and polarizing political subject, including deportation policies enacted since 1996. No bipartisan policy reform consensus has been reached to date, despite demographic population shifts and the effects of current deportation policies on an increasingly large number of mixed status families and American-born children. In an effort to end the political stalemate, in November, 2014 (American Immigration Council, 2016) President Obama implemented a number of executive orders to reform current immigration policies. These executive orders sought to develop a mechanism by which to regularize the migratory status of increasing numbers of unaccompanied migrant minors, arriving from Central America, through the expansion of the Deferred Action of Childhood Arrivals (DACA), while also seeking to expand the deferment of deportation proceedings to millions of undocumented immigrant parents of American citizen and lawful permanent resident children, through the Deferred Action for Parents of Americans and Lawful Permanent Residents (DAPA) (American Immigration Council, 2016).

Since their inception, these two acts were met with significant sociopolitical opposition from the state of Texas, as well as 25 additional states, which eventually joined together in a lawsuit against the U.S. government, United States vs. Texas, where they challenged the constitutionality of President Obama's executive immigration orders (for further information refer to American Immigration Council, 2016; and www.ice.gov). The Supreme Court heard this case in June, 2016, but was unable to reach a decision; instead, the Supreme Court remained in a 4:4 deadlock, which effectively stopped the implementation of DAPA and DACA's expansion indefinitely. The Supreme Court did not pronounce itself on the constitutionality of the acts, nor did it decide to strike them down (American Immigration Council, 2016; Benen, 2016; Shane, 2016). However, the Supreme Court's ruling effectively halted President Obama's executive immigration reform orders, preventing an estimated 5 million immigrants from regularizing their status and leaving them vulnerable to deportation orders (American Immigration Council, 2016).

The marginalizing and potentially destructive dynamics embedded within the current American immigration and deportation policies, and in the sociopolitical debates that surround them, are best captured by Aleinikoff and Rumbaut's (1998) discussion of public self-fulfilling prophecies. Within this context, Aleinikoff and Rumbaut (1998), quoting Robert K. Merton (1948), explain that any given societal group,

> responds... to the objective features of a situation... [and] to the meaning this situation has for [them]. Certain kinds of definitions of the situation... become an integral part of the situation and thus affect subsequent developments.... It is the social or public self-fulfilling prophecy that goes far toward explaining the dynamics of ethnic and racial conflict in the America of today.
>
> (p. 1)

Aleinikoff and Rumbaut's (1998) conceptualization of the social, group meaning-making processes, and the public self-fulfilling prophecies they can induce, is consistent with the theoretical underpinnings of the integrated sociopolitical and psychological policy analysis model. Hence, the integrated, immigration reform policy analysis presented in this book highlights the importance of two concurrent elements. First, the need to identify and explain the intrapsychic, collective social construction processes by which a dominant group, consciously and unconsciously, uses public policy as a legal mechanism for the production and reproduction of social dynamics of dominance, subjugation, exclusion and marginalization (Reisigl & Wodak, 2001; Van Dijk, 1997, 2000; Wodak, Cillia, Reisigl, & Liebhart, 2009; Wodak, 2015). Second, how immigration reform policy has served to create, confirm and reproduce the American, "White Native" group's expected self-fulfilling prophecy about "the other"; a White Nativist social prophecy related to "the Hispanic others" and their perceived reluctance and failure to assimilate (Huntington, 2004b). This White Nativist unidimensional construction of assimilation and the Hispanic other fails to consider the transactional effect between individual/group collective assimilation efforts and the host country's immigration sociopolitical context of reception in public policy development (Aleinikoff & Rumbaut, 1998).

The integrated analysis of American immigration and deportation policy reforms contextualizes current deportation policies as a legal process embedded in a complex, unconscious "White Native" intrapsychic defense system, aimed at averting the transformation and mourning of the "White

Native" cultural identity. An identity "White Natives" believe is under threat of transformation due to the increasing mass representation achieved by the Hispanic immigrant and the American-born Hispanic "other" in the United States (Huntington, 2004b; Swain, 2002, 2007).

Given the increasingly exclusionary, American social membership model reflected in immigration and deportation policies and the White Nativist ideology that facilitates their legitimization through historical racial, ethnic and national identity constructions (Berry, 2003; Tajfel, 1981, 1982; Van Dijk, 1997, 2000; Wodak et al., 2009), how are American-born children of Hispanic immigrant parents conceptualizing themselves? In other words, can American-born children of Hispanic immigrant parents, who have been born and/or raised in this country, feel a sense of belonging and/or emotional alliance/attachment to the United States when one or both parents, and/or other family members fear the possibility of deportation or have been deported; or when a large segment of their community lives under similar circumstances? How have immigration reform policies, enacted since 1996, impacted these children's ability to conceptualize an individual ethnic identity that is also comprised by a clear sense of belonging to the larger American society? Does the current sociopolitical discourse influence the acculturation process of these American-born, yet second-generation immigrant children?

This book will answer these questions by presenting an integrated sociopolitical and psychological analysis of immigration reform policies. It will also integrate a secondary, longitudinal data analysis of the Children of Immigrants Longitudinal Study, CILS (Farina, 2015) to support the analysis' conclusions. The longitudinal research study examines the evolution of the ethnic identity, assimilation processes and sense of national belonging of American-born children of Mexican immigrant parents in the United States between 1991 and 2003; a time frame overlapping with increasing White Nativist sociopolitical discourses fueling the current immigration reform policies.

## Part I: Sociopolitical framework

### *White Nativism, American identity and citizenship*

Chapter 2 introduces the reader to the sociopolitical conceptual framework used in the integrated policy analysis model. It begins with a brief discussion of critical discourse historical analysis (Wodak et al., 2009) and its relevance to the analysis of American immigration policy. The chapter proceeds by defining White Nativism (Huntington, 2004b; Swain, 2002, 2007), examining the ideology's influence on current immigration sociopolitical discourses and American citizenship constructions (Reisigl & Wodak, 2001). The sociopolitical analysis exposes the social dynamics of dominance, exclusion and marginalization implicated in the formation of a second-class citizenship, explaining their implications for the "Hispanic other" (Van Dijk, 2000, 2002).

Chapter 2 also engages in a critical analysis of globalization, capitalism and demographic change, partially informed by Wallerstein's world systems analysis model (Wallerstein, 2000, 2003) and by Huntington's (2004b) conceptualization of the American national identity. The chapter concurrently examines immigration policy reforms enacted since 1996, with a particular emphasis on the Antiterrorism and Effective Death Penalty Act (AEDPA) and the Illegal Immigration Reform and Immigration Responsibility Act (IIRIRA). The critical sociopolitical analysis explains how the current immigration sociopolitical discourse, influenced and informed by a White Nativist ideology, sought to prevent an "impending demographic shift" through the development and implementation of immigration policy reforms; thereby, exposing their White Nativist origins and their legal, exclusionary and subjugating aim.

The analysis deconstructs existing American citizenship definitions and immigration policy to reveal the exclusionary dynamics that pervade these legal mechanisms, linking these public policy tools to a White Nativist ideology. It explores, within this White Nativist context, the assimilation process of immigrant groups previously constructed as "non-white" and examines the intersectionality of race and culture, as well as its implications. The sociopolitical critical analysis makes explicit the covert, White Nativist, identity preservation mechanisms, where the selective social inclusion of "the other" operated to maintain the critical mass representation of the "White native group," re-buttressing their social dominance (Reisigl & Wodak, 2001; Wodak, 2015). The chapter's sociopolitical analysis shows that "White Natives" included immigrant groups, previously constructed as non-white, as part of their "White native" group, at a historical time when their critical mass representation and "White Native" identity were under threat from a possible transformation. The analysis concludes by comparing and contrasting the assimilation history of those previously excluded and marginalized groups to the case of the "Hispanic other."

## Part II: Psychological framework

### *Political psychology: individual and group identity*

Chapter 3 provides a brief introduction to political psychology, including its definition and applicability to the analysis of political social processes (V. Volkan, personal communication, February 22, 2014). It presents a political-psychological analysis and explains the psychological processes involved in the formation of ethnic and national identities, and in the symbolization of culture. It contextualizes each of these elements, not as external or peripheral to the self, but rather as constitutive and intrinsic to the development of an individual and group collective self (Applegate & Bonovitz, 2004; Erikson, 1968; Volkan, 1998, 2009; Winnicott, 1967). The analysis integrates Freud's (1917) conceptualization of individual mourning and melancholia, and explores large group, collective mourning, to examine the "threat" that the "Hispanic other" poses to the "White Native" identity and culture (Reisigl & Wodak, 2001; Van Dijk, 2001; Wodak, 2015).

The chapter synthesizes the key findings of the integrated sociopolitical and psychological analysis of contemporary American immigration policy and White Nativism. The analysis exposes immigration policy as an unconscious "White Native" intrapsychic defense system, embedded in and informed by a White Nativist ideology (Van Dijk, 2000, 2002; Volkan, 2009, 2013). This legalistic and political unconscious defense mechanism protects the "White Native" individual and group psyche from realizing that their cultural identity is being transformed and that this transformation cannot be stopped.

The findings of the analysis emphasize that efforts designed to avert the collective mourning of the "White Native" identity, as originally conceived, are damaging to the collective self of the group. The failure to accept the transformation of their "White Native" identity and symbolic intrapsychic internal and external representations, or cultural amplifiers (Volkan, 2009b, 2013), is also destructive because it prevents "White Natives" from engaging in a normal mourning process (Freud, 1967; Volkan, 2009b). This precludes their ability to achieve a more adaptive and integrated intrapsychic individual and group American identity.

The chapter concludes with a brief discussion of ethnic conflict and cultural contestation (Ross, 2007) in relation to immigration policy reform, highlighting the need to examine assumptions pertaining to the ethnic identity, acculturation and sense of national belonging of the Hispanic immigrant and the American, "Hispanic hybrid other."

## Part III: Integrated sociopolitical and psychological framework

### *Conceptualization of ethnic identity, acculturation and sense of national belonging*

Chapter 4 defines and explores ethnic identity, acculturation and sense of collective and national belonging, exposing the sociopolitical dynamics of power in which these conceptualizations are used and invoked. It makes their function apparent, both in maintaining the existing White Nativist sociopolitical dominance and in excluding and marginalizing the "immigrant other" specifically the American-born Hispanic children of immigrant parents—through immigration and deportation reform policy.

The chapter first defines and explores social identity, integrating Ross' (2007) and Tajfel's (1982) conceptualization of group identities, as well as the self-concept and its conceptual definitions (Markus & Kurf, 1987; Oyserman, 2004; Scheibe, 1995). It then examines the effects of the social context on self-concept constructions, particularly devaluing and stigmatizing ones, and their implications for the continuity of individual and collective group identities (Chandler & Proulx, 2008; Diehl & Hay, 2007). The chapter proceeds by defining and introducing attributional defense processes (Ashmore, Deaux, & McLaughlin-Volpe, 2004; Crocker & Major, 1989) as potentially protective to the individual and collective self-concepts when in a devaluing and stigmatizing context. It then engages in a discussion of the Hispanic paradox (Oppedal, Roysamb, & Heyerdahl, 2005), integrating the role of protective factors and defenses, used by "the Hispanic immigrant other," to explain this medical and mental health paradox. This discussion presents and explains the risks of de-contextualizing research, introducing an alternative theoretical conceptualization of the Hispanic paradox.

Chapter 4 also introduces various theoretical models pertaining to acculturation and their limitations. It examines the progression from unidimensional to multidimensional acculturation models, presenting and explaining Berry's multidimensional model (2003); and introduces and discusses segmented assimilation theory (Portes & Rumbaut, 2006; Portes & Zhou, 1993), including its implications for the contextualization of the possible acculturation paths followed by immigrant youth in the United States, particularly Hispanic immigrant youth. National identity and patriotism constructions, informed by Huntington's (2004b), Citrin and Sears' (2009) and Kosterman and Feschbach's (1989) conceptualizations, are then presented and examined within the sociopolitical context of the United States.

The chapter also engages in a discussion of national belonging through a civic engagement conceptualization. The discussion introduces multiple theoretical constructions of civic engagement, including Adler and Goggin's (2005) and Putnam's (1995, 2000) theoretical definitions. It also examines two components of civic engagement: electoral participation and religious affiliation and participation. Chapter 4 concludes by explaining how religious participation functions as a protective factor in mediating the adaptation processes of immigrants and their children to a host country (Putnam, 2005; Warner, 2007).

## Part IV: Integrated sociopolitical and psychological model: Application to American immigration policy reforms and American-born children of Mexican immigrant parents

### *Immigration policy and interior enforcement*

Chapter 5 presents a brief, sociopolitical historical overview of the inter-nations relations between Mexico and the United States, focusing on migrants, inter-nations conflict, war, occupation and loss. This brief overview makes explicit the historical inclusionary and exclusionary trends of American immigration policy from its inception (Hing, 2004).

The chapter introduces the reader to the Antiterrorism and Effective Death Penalty Act (AEDPA) and the Illegal Immigration Reform and Immigration Responsibility Act (IIRIRA), 1996. It integrates an analysis of the sociopolitical discourse that was unfolding as these acts were created, and their role in facilitating subsequent interior enforcement programs and policy reforms, examining the far-reaching effects of these two acts, i.e., increasing deportation rates, disproportionately affecting Hispanic immigrants, and the effect on mixed status families. The integrated sociopolitical and psychological policy analysis model is applied and illustrated in this section. It reflects the model's capacity to capture the complex, intrapsychic, group collective processes involved in identity formation and ethnic and cultural contestation. It also identifies their role in the development of exclusionary sociopolitical discourses, embedded in collective identity ideologies, that use public policy as a legal mechanism by which to protect the group's identity through the exclusion and marginalization of the "threatening other," i.e., the Hispanic immigrant other.

## Secondary study of the Children of Immigrants Longitudinal Study (CILS): White Nativism, ethnic identity development and acculturation

Chapter 6 introduces the research component of the book, which involves two interrelated studies: the original CILS (1991–2006) and a secondary longitudinal data analysis study of the CILS (Farina, 2015). The CILS was designed to study the adaptation processes of second-generation immigrant children in the United States (1991–2006), and it is the largest longitudinal study of this kind. The secondary study examines the longitudinal adaptation processes of American—born children of Mexican immigrant parents between 1991 and 2003 time period coinciding with a resurgence of White Nativism, increasing anti-immigrant sociopolitical debates, and the implementation of immigration policy reforms.

The chapter presents the two measures used to assess micro and macro levels of White Nativism in the secondary study of the CILS: the experiences of prejudice index and the perceived sociopolitical White Nativism index, and discusses their findings. The findings illustrate the children's progressive interaction with an increasingly White Nativist context, in which dynamics related to White Nativist superiority and immigrant inferiority are made explicit. The effects of the White Nativist sociopolitical context on the children's ethnic identity development are also discussed, showing that an increasingly White Nativist context produces an increase in the number of children who ethnically identify in a pan-ethnic manner. A transactional conceptualization of ethnic identity is developed and formulated in this section. This new conceptualization emphasizes the context-dependent and interactional nature of ethnic identity development.

The chapter proceeds by presenting the children's longitudinal acculturation pattern, along three dimensions: (1) linguistic acculturation; (2) culture, values and behavior and (3) ethnic interaction. The findings demonstrate the children's bilingualism, and their acceptance of some, but not all, of the cultural values and behaviors considered by "White Natives" to be "American." The chapter concludes by engaging in a conceptual exploration of acculturation informed by the sociopolitical and psychological analysis model.

## Secondary study of the children of immigrants longitudinal Study: National belonging

Chapter 7 first engages in an analysis of the children's sense of national belonging. It illustrates both the children's strong affective tie and primary attachment toward the United States, high patriotism, as well as a high to moderate level of civic engagement. It then proceeds to critically examine and operationalize White Nativist rhetoric that asserts that individual adherence to ethnic particularisms interferes with the development of a sense of national belonging.

The chapter also presents an analysis of the interaction between ethnic identity, acculturation, and sociopolitical White Nativism, and sense of national belonging. The analysis incorporates the findings of the secondary longitudinal study, deconstructing and exposing the conceptually flawed underpinnings of the White Nativist rhetoric surrounding ethnic identifications and particular acculturation processes. It de-problematizes ethnic identity and acculturation, and refutes their antithetical function to the development of an American sense of national belonging. This chapter also explores the relationship between ethnic identity and religious and electoral participation, and between acculturation and sense of national belonging. The analysis ends with a discussion of the direct and indirect effects of an increasingly White Nativist sociopolitical context on the children's sense of national belonging. The chapter concludes by providing a summary of the integrated sociopolitical and psychological analysis of American immigration reform policy and its implications for the American children of Hispanic, Mexican, immigrant parents and their mixed status families.

## Immigration policy reforms: Implications for clinical practice and policy development

Chapter 8 discusses the clinical implications of contemporary immigration policy reforms for American-born children of Mexican immigrant parents, connecting macro level social and immigration policy to micro level practice. The chapter proceeds to discuss future policy directions consistent with the findings of the integrated sociopolitical and psychological analysis of contemporary immigration policy reforms. This section links the secondary study's research findings to the proposed future policy directions. The chapter also explains the general usefulness of the integrated analysis model to social policy analysis. It highlights the model's capacity to examine the intended and unintended consequences of a policy, as well as the complex human psychological processes that inform its underlying ideology.

The chapter concludes by presenting a brief overview of the 2017, immigration executive orders issued by President Trump. This overview examines the implications of these new policy changes for mixed status families and their American children, with an emphasis on its long-term implications for the American society.

# Part I
# Sociopolitical framework

# 2 White Nativism, American identity and citizenship

## Introduction: What is critical discourse historical analysis?

The integrated sociopolitical and psychological policy model draws from critical discourse analysis (Van Dijk, 2000, 2001, 2002), specifically from critical discourse historical analysis (Reisigl & Wodak, 2001; Wodak, 2015). It is informed by some of the conceptual tenets of both approaches, and integrates them in conjunction with overarching concepts from social welfare policy analysis models and psychodynamic individual and group collective processes.

Critical discourse analysis, CDA, is defined by Van Dijk (2001) as "a type of discourse analytical research that primarily studies the way social power abuse, dominance, and inequality are enacted, reproduced and resisted by text and talk in the social and political context" (p. 352). The integrated sociopolitical and psychological policy analysis model, consistent with this definition, seeks to examine social power relations that produce, maintain and reinforce social inequality through the construction of an "other," and the political means by which this construction is enacted/implemented. In understanding the social and linguistic constructionist mechanisms that maintain or promote unequal power relations and social inequality, the integrated sociopolitical and psychological policy analysis model seeks to also identify how these specific sociopolitical processes can be addressed, ameliorated and/or resisted through policy development. The purpose of the model is to identify and expose obscured, subjugating sociopolitical ideologies, and the discursive, affective and sociocognitive practices that reproduce them. Policy changes and initiatives may then be successfully implemented that resist, ameliorate or eradicate specific forms of social subjugation.

Critical discourse analysis studies social discourse and discursive practices in which social problems are embedded (Barusch, 2015; Jimenez, Pasztor, Chambers, & Fuji, 2015). Within this context, discourse is defined as "a system of statements which constructs an object" (Parker, 1992, p. 5) and understood as being "located in time, in history, for the objects they refer to are objects constituted in the past by the discourses or related discourses" (Parker, 1992, p. 13). Critical discourse analysis, and the integrated policy model, examine the social discursive practices by which a certain "other" has been identified/constructed as "different from" the dominant group. This "othering" discourse, in turn, provides the basis by which the dominant group can "legitimize" the social exclusion of this "different other" (Aleinikoff & Rumbaut, 1998; Van Dijk, 2000; Wodak, 2015). The construction of "an other" does not only marginalize this "other," but has an organizing social function for the dominant group (Van Dijk, 2000). By defining "the other," a social group is also defining who they are; in other words, "they are" what "the other" is not (Derrida, 1984).

Linguistic, discursive practices, for example, that define "the other" as "foreign, ethnic, cultural, immigrant," give birth to the American "native" and to a collective "nativist group" (Wodak, 2015) that is defined as intrinsically different from the "non-native other" (Van Dijk, 1995; Wodak, 2015). The creation of the "American native" also ascribes power and rights to the "native," and can lead to social discourses and policies that further legitimize "American native" dominance and the concurrent marginalization and exclusion of the racial, ethnic, cultural, etc., "other" (Brodkin, 1999; Ferguson, 2007; Jacobson, 1998; Van Dijk, 1995). Legitimation is defined within this context as the "process of 'explaining' and justifying" (Wodak, 2015, p. 6). The process of legitimizing is achieved by specific ideologies that both explain and justify the social inequality, domination and subjugation of "the other." For example, the creation of the "American native" necessitates a White Nativist ideology that explains and justifies the "American native" social dominance and the subjugation of the "immigrant other."

Ideologies, as defined in critical discourse analysis and specifically from a sociocognitive approach, are belief systems shared by a particular group (Van Dijk, 2002). They are based on the group's shared cultural values, beliefs and practices, and provide the group with a "cultural common ground… [that] is non-controversial, commonsensical, and hence [understood as] non-ideological" (Van Dijk, 2002, p. 16). Ideologies thus shape the group's sociocognitive self-schemas and identity, both implicitly and explicitly, influencing and controlling the group members' social practices, while controlling and constraining how and what can be thought about (Parker, 1992; Van Dijk, 2002).

Van Dijk's (1995) sociocognitive discourse analysis of immigration, legitimization and policy captures well the hermeneutic, normalizing and hegemonic function of exclusionary discourses. The analysis highlights the ways in which "othering" discourses, embedded in an anti-immigrant ideology, foster in-group positive identity schemas, that shape, normalize and control how group members may come to think about both their collective self and "the other". Van Dijk's analysis (1995, 2000) further illustrates how the unquestioned acceptance of an anti-immigrant ideology can lead to its hegemonic reproduction. When this happens, the ideology operates as a matter of "common sense," reifying and legitimizing the social subjugation of "the other," as well as the in-group's dominance, based on positive sociocognitive representations of the individual and collective group's identity

(Van Dijk, 2000). Van Dijk (1995) illustrates this process when discussing anti-immigrant ideologies and the circular dynamics implicated in their production, legitimization and reproduction,

> if European [American] politicians and media attribute major social problems…to immigration and immigrants, they may thus influence the beliefs of large segments of the majority, and thus indirectly the models that underlie racist stories or discriminatory action of dominant group members, as well as other expressions of prejudice and resentment that may again be used by the politicians to legitimate political decisions on immigration restriction.
>
> (p. 22)

Van Dijk's critical discourse analysis model privileges individual and social cognition, de-emphasizing the influence of affective and sociohistorical processes (Blommaert & Bulcaen, 2000; Reisigl & Wodak, 2001) in shaping transactional schemas about a dominant group's identity and that of "the other" (Reisigl & Wodak, 2001).

The "context-sensitive, discourse-historical approach" (Reisigl & Wodak, 2001, p. 31) integrates Van Dijk's "concepts and categories (e.g. the notions of 'positive self-representation' and 'negative other-presentation')… but place[s] no emphasis on… sociocognitivism" (Reisigl & Wodak, 2001, p. 31). Instead, Reisigl and Wodak's discourse-historical approach "attempts to transcend the pure linguistic dimension and to include, more or less systematically, the historical, political, sociological and/or psychological dimension in the analysis and interpretation of a specific discursive occasion." (Reisigl & Wodak, 2001, p. 35). This discourse-historical approach also integrates critical theory to examine macro processes and discursive practices, thereby exposing their group-reifying, as well as subjugating and exclusionary, manifest and latent sociopolitical aims (Reisigl & Wodak, 2001; Wodak, 2009). Reisigl and Wodak (2001) identify four "discursive macro-strategies" (p. 43) by which to examine discursive macro processes, which have been incorporated in the integrated policy model:

1  Constructive strategies: used in the development and definition of a group's identity.
2  Preservative or justificatory strategies: they maintain the group's identity as a stable, fixed and thus real "entity."
3  Transformative strategies: used for the gradual transformation of the group's identity; and,
4  Destructive strategies: used to disassemble the group's existing identity construction.

This analysis approach historically contextualizes and makes explicit the latent intent of a group's specific discursive process and its ideological principles.

The integrated policy analysis model incorporates this historical approach to contextualize and deconstruct the collective social processes implicated in the production of social inequality. In so doing, it also makes explicit the intent of specific social policies; for example, whether a policy seeks to maintain, protect, or to dismantle, a group's hegemonic dominance and identity.

The subsequent sociopolitical analysis of contemporary American immigration reform policies, with an emphasis on deportation reforms enacted since 1996, will draw from a critical discourse historical approach to make explicit the White Nativist ideological underpinnings of these reforms. The analysis, also partially informed by Wallerstein's world-systems analysis model (Wallerstein, 2000, 2003) and Huntington's (2004b) conceptualization of the American national identity, will expose the internal contradictions of current immigration policy, as well as their potential to weaken and destabilize American society in a permanent manner.

## Sociopolitical analysis: Immigration reform

Contemporary American immigration policy, due to reforms enacted since the early 1990s, has sought to prevent the entrance of "illegal immigrants" into the United States, while also facilitating their deportation. These deportation reform policies have often led to the permanent division of mixed status families (Fix & Zimmermann, 1999; Preston, 2011a) due to parental deportation, and at times, to the concurrent departure of their American citizen children. These children, despite being American citizens by birth, appear to hold a "second class citizenship" (Rosaldo, 1997) that fails to protect their constitutional rights, rendering them "other," that is, different from "White Native" children.

Immigration reform did not become a source of social concern until the early 1990s, when the Hispanic other began to achieve a critical mass representation in the United States (Huntington, 2004a, 2004b; Swain, 2002, 2007). It was at that point that American "White Natives" began to feel threatened by the increasing presence of the Hispanic other and, in particular, by the presence of the Mexican other (Swain, 2002, 2007).[1] Although Hispanic, as defined by the United States Census Bureau, is a broad term used to refer to "A person of Cuban, Mexican, Puerto Rican, South or Central American, or other Spanish culture or origin, regardless of race" (United States Census Bureau, 2010, "Multiple Responses to the Hispanic Origin Question," para. 2), a closer scrutiny of its use within past and current immigration sociopolitical debates reveals a primary focus on a particular Hispanic other, the Mexican other, a group who constitutes the largest Hispanic subgroup within the United States due to Mexico's bordering status.

## Historical ideological context: White Nativism and being American

It is first necessary to ask who is an American before examining what it means to be an American (Spiro, 2008). Huntington (2004b) attempts to answer this question through a historical analysis in which the American national and cultural identity is traced back to the original cultural identity of the first settlers of the United States—White Anglo-Saxon, Protestant men or "White Natives." It is the "White Native," and an associated phenomenon "White Nativism," that is of particular interest in this analysis of immigration policy, given current sociopolitical discourses pertaining to impending demographic change, national incorporation and warnings related to a gradual loss of the "American culture."

Huntington (2004a) and Swain (2002) describe "White Nativism" as a recent American, "new white racial advocacy" (Swain, 2002, p. 15) movement that has gained force since the 1990s due both to the changing demographic composition of the United States and to the impact of globalization, which has resulted in the exodus of high-wage, non-skilled jobs overseas, increasing competition between white unskilled workers and immigrant workers (Huntington, 2004a; Swain 2002). Unlike previous white supremacist groups, such as the Ku Klux Klan or the Nazi party, "White Nativism" seeks to appeal to a different audience, a broad, white Euro-American mainstream audience, as reflected in the demographic composition of its members "Most are better educated, more articulate, and in many cases more appealing as human beings than the sorts of people that ran the older racist organizations" (Swain, 2002, p. 4). In addition, "White Nativists" advocate for race-preservation instead of racial supremacy, "affirming that culture is a product of race" (Huntington, 2004a, p. 41). They believe that impending demographic changes "foretell the replacement of white culture by black or brown cultures that are intellectually and morally inferior" (Huntington, 2004a, p. 41).

This definition of "White Nativism" makes explicit a dynamic of change and transformation that is often silenced within the debates of cultural pluralism and cultural diversity. Cultural losses are not only incurred by the nation-state or the immigrant other being incorporated into the capitalist world system (Wallerstein, 2003). The culture of the existing capitalist nation(s), also incurs some changes, and thus losses (Spiro, 2008; Swain, 2002). Huntington's words (2004a) also uncover a different discourse; not only is white culture changing, but it is also being perverted and replaced by something, brown, Mexican, other, that is perceived by "White Nativists" or by first class citizens as intellectually and morally inferior. It is no surprise that current sociopolitical debates in the United States, when questioning the demographic transformation of the country, have primarily focused their attention on immigration, immigration policy, and the impact of immigration on the current racial, ethnic, cultural and group national identity shifts (Huntington, 2004a, 2004b; Swain, 2002, 2007).

With the rising number of American-born children of non-native parents, contemporary sociopolitical discourses have increasingly advocated for more aggressive immigration policy reforms targeting this group of American-born to foreign others, including petitions to revise the Fourteenth Amendment of the American Constitution (Staff, 2015). This amendment grants the American citizenship to any individual born within American soil (Preston, 2011b), and thus to the American-born children of non-native parents. The integrative immigration policy analysis will primarily examine the effects of existing immigration policy reforms on American-born, Hispanic children of non-native parents, as they are a very vulnerable segment of American society, without a voice in the sociopolitical discourse. In fact, these children, as the analysis will illustrate, have been the recipients of the disowned aggression of American native citizens, due to the White Nativist efforts to preserve and defend their original culture, composition and identity from a transformation that is demanded by the capitalist global system in which the United States operates (Tani, 2015).

## Capitalism, change, national identity and White Nativism

With globalization, individuals are now more mobile than ever before, often residing outside of their birth country for a number of years (Spiro, 2008). However, globalization and its ensuing transnational dynamics are not the only forces influencing previously shared American national identity constructions. The number of children born to non-native parents has been increasing in recent years, particularly children born to non-American-born Hispanic parents (Huntington, 2004a). Since 1995, "immigrants and their children [have been] responsible for 90 percent of the population growth in the United States" (Swain, 2002, p. 85). Furthermore, between 2007 and 2008, 20% of the American native-born children were born to a non-native-born parent; and, of this 20%, 52.7% had a Hispanic non-native-born parent, who in 86.19% of the cases was of Mexican origin. Perhaps most relevant to this discussion about immigration, identity, change and mourning is that 99.66% of the children born to non-native parents had at least one non-citizen parent (The Urban Institute, 2010). Statistical projections suggest "racial and ethnic minorities will constitute at least 47 percent of the U.S. population…" by 2050 (Swain, 2002, p. 85). Given these demographic changes, is it possible to continue to conceive the American national identity and culture as static and unchanging? This is an important question that needs to be answered. Another important question is what it is meant by "American national identity and culture" in contemporary American sociopolitical debates and discursive processes.

## Resistance to change: American citizenship and immigration policy

Capitalism, globalization and its byproduct immigration, have raised and continue to raise complex sociopolitical and economic questions. For example, how long should the foreign other stay in a host nation? Should the foreign other ever be granted citizenship status? And what laws should govern the children born to these foreign others? Or as posited by Spiro (2008), "could a child be deemed a citizen at birth even if her parents could never be one?" (p. 13). These questions are of particular importance to "White Nativists" and conservative political factions within the United States since the foreign other, and specifically the Hispanic other, has continued to gain "territory" within the United States. The Hispanic other, not only accounts for over 10% of the children born in the United States (The Urban Institute, 2010), but also for three-quarters of the "illegal" immigration within this country (Preston, 2011a). This increasing presence is not only threatening the historical "White Native" demographic majority, but most importantly, is also threatening to transform the original "White Native" culture (Spiro, 2008).

Within this sociopolitical context, the early 1990s brought about a number of immigration reforms with a focus on internal enforcement (Hagan, Castro, & Rodriguez, 2010). The integrated policy analysis will examine only two of these reforms, The Antiterrorism and Effective Death Penalty Act (AEDPA) and the Illegal Immigration Reform and Immigration Responsibility Act of 1996 (IIRIRA). These two acts paved the way for the implementation of numerous programs that have since facilitated the identification, arrest and removal of the immigrant other once inside the United States (Hagan et al., 2010). Both, AEDPA and IIRIRA marked an immigration policy shift from border control to interior enforcement (Hagan et al., 2010), and substantially changed deportation guidelines, facilitating the removal of legal and "illegal" immigrants from the United States (Hagan et al., 2010), with serious consequences for mixed status families.

These two acts have caused the rupture and, sometimes permanent, separation of many mixed status families. They have also resulted in the extrication of American-born children from their birth country, the United States, due to changes in the deportation relief guidelines—in particular to guidelines pertaining to the hardship of dependent family members, such as American-born children (Chaudry et al., 2010). The redefinition of hardship standards regarding dependent family members has allowed for the deportation of many immigrants who, prior to 1996, would have qualified for deportation relief under previous hardship standards (Conference Report to accompany H. R. 2202, as cited in Fix & Zimmermann, 1999, "Dividing Families," para. 5; Hagan et al., 2010). In fact, "in 2013 ICE deported approximately 72,000 parents of U.S. citizen children (ICE, 2014a, 2014b), a decline from an estimated average of 90,000 deportations annually in 2011 and 2012 (Wessler, 2012a)" (Capps et al., 2015, p. 1). Given these figures, some questions begin to emerge: Why would a country enact immigration policies that result in the extrication of some of its citizens, thus leading to the internal fragmentation of its society? Are these American-born children less American, when compared to the children of "White Native" Americans?

These questions become even more complex when racial and ethnic deportation statistics are reviewed. An analysis of these statistics shows that Hispanic immigrants, whether legal or "illegal," have been disproportionally impacted and/or targeted for deportation since 1996 (Hagan et al., 2010).

In 2011, Kohli, Markowitz and Chavez reported that 93% of the individuals "identified for deportation" under ICE's Secure Communities Program[2] were Hispanic (p. 5); and most concerning is that "more than a third" of those arrested had an American citizen spouse or child (Kohli et al., 2011; Preston, 2011a, p. 2).

Given the racial/ethnic deportation statistics and the impact that some of the immigration policy reforms enacted since the 1990s, have had on American citizen children of immigrants, two American citizenships appear to exist associated with a binary and mutually exclusive conceptualization of culture: the first is the American citizenship of "White Natives" with its associated culture; and the second, the American citizenship of the other, the children born in United States territory to Hispanic immigrant parents (Rosaldo, 1997), who are identified as belonging to a non-white, inferior culture. The covert, hidden, exclusionary dynamics embedded within the American citizenship construct can be partially traced back to the racialized internal history of the United States; however, race does not fully explain the more complex historical exclusionary dynamics embedded within the American citizenship construct (Farina, 2013).

Furthermore, whereas "White Natives" seek to protect the white Anglo-Saxon race from its transformation, due to the increasing presence of the other, race alone fails to capture another element perceived by "White Natives" to be under attack due to the increasing presence of the foreign other, the original "White Native" culture. Culture, although intertwined with race, is individually and collectively performed through language and traditions, and intrapsychically constructed, influencing individual and collective identity (Ross, 2007). This analysis will first examine race within the context of the American citizenship construct, to explore its role as a "White Native" preservation mechanism.

## Race and American citizenship

With the independence of the United States from England, and the creation of the American Constitution (1787), the American citizenship came into existence and began to be conferred according to English common law tradition; that is, by place of birth "jus soli, or right of the soil," (Spiro, 2008, p. 11) but only to white, property-owning men. Women, children, non-land-owning white men, African Americans and the Indigenous peoples of this land were excluded from the original American citizenship construct. Although the American citizenship construct has changed and expanded over time to include some of the previously othered and marginalized groups, many of them continue to hold a "second class citizenship" (Rosaldo, 1997) that renders them vulnerable to dynamics of oppression, exclusion and subjugation. However, what social dynamics facilitated the creation of this second-class citizenship?

A brief sociopolitical historical overview and deconstruction of "American white nativism" and of the "White Native," and, their relationship to the American citizenship construct can shed clarity on the formation of the current two-tier American citizenship system, exposing its etiological racist ideology and social function. This brief overview will summarize, examine and question existing deconstructions informed by critical race theory (Brodkin, 1998; Crenshaw, Gotanda, Peller, & Thomas, 1995; Decker, 2013; Delgado & Stefancic, 2013; Harris, 1993; Lipsitz, 1998).

The rise of the scientific paradigm in the 1880s, prominently influenced by racial eugenics, provided "White Natives" with an othering, "scientific" mechanism by which to rationalize and legitimize the enslavement, subjugation and marginalization of the black, African American other. This subjugating mechanism has remained effective even after the inclusion of African Americans within the citizenship construct, as illustrated by historical landmark court cases such as Plessey vs. Ferguson (1892) and Brown vs. The Board of Education (1954). In fact, the legacy and continued existence of social policies embedded in a covert and/or overt racist ideology continues to have long-standing effects within the African American community. For example, Collins and Nieves (2016) reported that during the last 30 years, the average wealth disparity between African American and white households has grown from $288,000 in 1983 to $571,000 in 2013 (Collins & Nieves, 2016). These findings illustrate quite poignantly the gradual deterioration of the "slow racial advances" (Bell, 2013, p. 9) achieved in the 1960s and 1970s, as well as the ongoing persistence of systemic and structural historical racism.

However, as Ignatiev (1995) points out: "race explains nothing; it is something that must be explained" (p. 187) within the specific historical context of each racial group. Hence the need to interrogate not only subjugated racial constructions, but also whiteness and its associated subject, the "White Native," as these two constructs are often accepted as self-explanatory, stable, fixed and monolithic in nature. In addition, omitting a deconstruction of whiteness runs the risk of replicating and reifying subjugating racialized constructions about "the other," that allow whiteness to continue to operate in a hegemonic, unquestioned, normalizing, commonsense manner (Jacobson, 1998).

Whiteness has not been a fixed, racially stable categorical construct throughout American history, but rather a deeply, socio-politically contested, intergroup territory, instrumental in the creation of the "White Native" (Decker, 2013; Ferguson, 2007). In fact, race and national origin have been historically intertwined and implicated in the construction of the "American native" and of the American citizenship (Ngai, 1999, 2014; Shklar, 1991), as illustrated by Brodkin (1998) when quoting Kenneth Roberts in "When did Jews become White Folk?"

> The American nation was founded and developed by the Nordic race, but if a few more million members of the Alpine, Mediterranean, and

Semitic races are poured among us, the result must inevitably be a hybrid race of people as worthless and futile as the good-for-nothing mongrels of Central America and South-eastern Europe.

(p. 274)

Kenneth Roberts (1885–1957), a well-known American historical fiction novelist, wrote in the 1920s some of the "strongest anti-Southern and Eastern European immigrant pieces of any that appeared in the popular media" (Simon, 1997, p. 15). His writings clearly reflect the 1880s–1930s historical construction of whiteness and of being American (Decker, 2013). To be white meant to be of "Nordic racial" descent; a "race" identified as responsible for the establishment and development of the American nation-state, and defined as morally and intellectually superior to other "races" (Decker, 2013; Ngai, 1999, 2014; Simon, 1997). Kenneth Roberts' anti-immigrant rhetoric reflects the rise of eugenics in the scientific paradigm of the 1920s; its social constructionist function as a tool of oppression and subjugation; and, the "cultural anxiety and political unease about national identity, shifting racial and social hierarchies, and gender roles" of that historical period (Wray, 2006, p. 79). Yet, although Kenneth Roberts' writings implicitly allude toward the existence of an American native, the "Nordic race," he did not explicitly engage in this linguistic usage. Commons (1904) and Mayo-Smith (1890), among other social scientists and writers of that time period, however, did explicitly refer to the "Nordic race" as "native Americans" or "natives" (Decker, 2013). This linguistic usage of "native American," in lieu of "Nordic race" or of "Anglo-Saxon descent" is further explained by Decker (2013), who states

the authors cited here used the terms "native American" and "native" in the late nineteenth and early twentieth century to refer to people of Anglo-Saxon descent born in the territory of the United States while using the term "American Indian" for descendants of the original inhabitants of North America.

(p. 5)

Decker's explanation (2013) poignantly exposes how social scientists of the late nineteenth and early twentieth centuries used the eugenic "scientific" paradigm as a mechanism by which to socially construct, and linguistically birth/create the "native American." By linguistically converging native and American in written text as "native American," social scientists were able to provide politicians with a means by which to legitimatize sociopolitical platforms that asserted previous Nordic European immigrants (settlers and colonizers) and their "native born white descents" (Decker, 2013, p. 5) as the original natives and creators of the "American nation." These sociopolitical movements, through their discursive "native American" practices also created a "White Native" subject in need of protection from an impending transformation and collective, social destruction, giving way to a politic of fear and native protectionism (Wodak, 2015), "White Nativism."

Early examples of these sociopolitical, constructive, discursive ideological processes are well captured by Simon (1997) who wrote *In the Golden Land: A Century of Russian and Soviet Jewish Immigration in America*. In this book, Simon engaged in an analysis of written text, primarily using magazine and scholarly texts produced between the late nineteenth and early twentieth centuries. Among these multiple magazines, Simon examined written pieces produced by the Saturday Evening Post, where she found articles cautioning "that Italians, Jews, Poles, Russians, Greeks, and others would destroy U.S. society, [since] they had higher rates of insanity, crime, and other forms of deviance than people from other parts of Europe" (1997, p. 17). Similar sociopolitical discursive practices continue to pervade contemporary American sociopolitical debates, as exemplified by President Donald Trump's 2016 right-wing electoral campaign and current presidency. For example, when discussing immigration during the 2016 presidential debates, Donald Trump stated,

> When Mexico sends its people, they're not sending their best. They're not sending you. They're sending people that have lots of problems, and they're bringing those problems with us. They're bringing drugs. They're bringing crime. They're rapists. And some, I assume, are good people.
>
> ("Donald Trump Speech," 2016, para. 4)

President Trump's politic of fear and protectionism, propelled his electoral, presidential "victory" in 2016, and it has proven to be one of his most effective political tools. His rhetoric of fear was, and continues to be, very compelling for "White Native" working-class workers who, since the 1990s, have experienced an ongoing economic decline, that was further exacerbated by the most recent, 2007 economic recession. But most importantly, the 2016 American presidential election served to expose the "White Nativist" populous movement that had been growing since the early 1990s, due to the effects of globalization in the American labor market, the declining world economy, and the ongoing racial and ethnic demographic shift taking place in the country (Huntington, 2004a; Swain, 2002, 2007).

The similarities between Donald Trump's contemporary right wing political rhetoric, based on fear and group base protectionism, and that of the late nineteenth and early twentieth centuries, is stark, directly linking this country's past "native/nativist" political discourses to modern times. These similarities also blur contemporary conceptual differences established between White Supremacy and White Nativism (Huntington, 2004a, 2014b; Swain, 2002), fragmenting existing definitional borders that construct these two ideologies as distinct and exposing White Supremacy and White Nativism as one and the same, despite linguistic manipulation and concealment.

By historically contextualizing and deconstructing the discursive and sociopolitical origins of the "native" ideology, "nativism" emerges as a socially constructed ideology that came into "being" when the "native American" was linguistically and conceptually birthed. Since its inception, the "native" ideology has served to reinforce, reify and preserve the existence of the white "native American" as a legitimate, stable, real entity. Without the white "native" ideology, the ongoing existence of the "native American" ("White Native") could be susceptible to conceptual fragmentation, exposing its true nature: a historically constructed myth, necessary for the development of a shared, sociocognitive national identity that "White Natives" could claim, due to the real absence of a shared historical origin as a people (Loewenberg, 1995; Van Dijk, 1995, 2000; Volkan, 2013).

The creation of the "White Native" and "White Nativist" ideology, therefore, provided "White Natives" with a mechanism by which to sociocognitively construct and legitimize a needed, shared past and national identity. This "native/nativist" identity, in turn, served to legitimize their social dominance, providing "White Natives" with a "natural" claim to the Indigenous lands they had appropriated and colonized. This process of legitimation facilitated the legal creation of the American citizenship, which further reified their sense of nationhood. The "White Native" ideology was also instrumental in ascribing "White Natives" with the power to confer the American citizenship they now "possessed" (Harris, 1993) to other subjugated, "non-native" and "racially" distinct groups, including African Americans, Indigenous peoples of the United States/Native Americans, and new immigrant "others." However, the citizenship granted to this "racial, non-native other," was different and unequal to that of "White Natives."

In the case of African Americans, it wasn't until the passage of the Reconstruction Amendments, comprised by three amendments to the United States Constitution—the Thirteenth Amendment (1866), abolishing slavery; the Fourteenth Amendment (1868), providing citizenship to freed blacks; and, the Fifteenth Amendment (1870), forbidding voting race-based discrimination—that African Americans were "granted" American citizenship (Chambers, 2013). However, as argued by Chambers (2013), and as illustrated by Collins and Nieves (2016), laws cannot guarantee societal inclusion, being accepted as a member of, or as "belonging to" that society (Chambers, 2013). They can, however, provide a possible path to claiming those rights. For example, although the Fifteenth Amendment to the Constitution gave African American men voting rights in 1870, they were often prevented from voting until 1965, when the Voting Rights Act was passed (Chamber, 2013). This example, not only illustrates the differential, second-class citizenship status conferred to African Americans, but also the historical legal incongruence and contradictions of the policies developed/governing the American citizenship and, hence, the "legal logics" used by "White Natives" to continue to subjugate "the other" (Chamber, 2013; Kennedy, 2013; Olivas, 2013).

By both overtly granting and subsequently re-interpreting legal text to not grant American citizenship to African Americans, as originally constructed for "White Natives," it became possible to construct African Americans as citizens and yet, as different from the "White Native" American citizen, effectively relegating African Americans to an unequal, second-class citizenship. This legal, but incongruent, conceptual conundrum illustrates well the discrepancies that can exist between the explicit and implicit intent of any policy. In other words, although "White Natives" were explicitly designing policies that would grant citizenship to African Americans, they were also concurrently, partially overtly and "covertly," using those same legal policies to resist and hinder the integration of the African American "subjugated other" as a citizen of this nation. In Plessy vs. Ferguson, Homer Plessy "challenged the constitutionality" of racial segregation (Chambers, 2013, p. 507) based on the Fourteenth Amendment. This amendment states: "that all citizens [and thus Africans Americans at that time in history] would enjoy the same citizenship rights" (Chambers, 2013, p. 507). The court interpreted the Fourteenth Amendment to mean that separate was indeed equal, thus upholding segregation and a two-tier American citizenship model, by which a person could be both a citizen and yet not a citizen.

Not surprisingly, African American history and the history of the Indigenous peoples of this land is saturated with examples in which the "White Native" legal courts have refuted African Americans' and Indigenous peoples' claims of unequal treatment, opportunity and protection under the law (Bell, 2013; Gotanda, 2013; Rollings, 2004). Lawrence (2013) best speaks to this historical, societal collective process of conscious and unconscious incongruence and denial, or historical, "collective unconscious" (Layton, 2006), when examining the Equal Protection Clause, and race-based discrimination,

> Requiring proof of conscious or intentional motivation as a prerequisite to constitutional recognition that a decision is race dependent ignores much of what we understand about how the human mind works. It also disregards both the irrationality of racism and the profound effect that history of American race relations has exerted on the individual and collective unconscious.
>
> (p. 314)

The history of the Indigenous peoples of the United States and of their path to American citizenship is certainly similar and yet different from that of African Americans. It should be noted that the term Indigenous peoples is used in this analysis to recognize that the only group with a native claim to the United States' territory, are and were the Indigenous tribes that live/d in this land prior to its colonization. In fact, as Mahtowin Munro, member of the Lakota Nation and co-leader of United American Indians of

New England (UAINE), stated during a speech at the November 18, 2006 Boston Workers World Party,

> The U.S. has a short memory and is in denial of its historical facts. This government is descended from immigrants who came... and took our lands, and resources, either by force, coercion or dishonesty, and banned the religions, languages and cultures of the original Indigenous peoples of this continent.
>
> (Workers World, 2006, para. 5)

Mahtowin Munro's words speak directly to the history of appropriation and collective genocide perpetrated by the original European colonizers against the Indigenous peoples of this land. The creation of the "native American" in the late nineteenth and early twentieth centuries certainly served to demarcate the boundaries between previous Nordic European immigrant groups and Southern and Eastern European new immigrants. However, it also ascribed "native Americans" ("White Natives") as natural claimants of this land, erasing the existence of the Indigenous tribes as rightful Native Americans, as well as the genocide perpetrated against them (Decker, 2013; Dunbar-Ortiz, 2015; Ngai, 1999, 2014; Olivas, 2013; Workers World, 2006).

Although a systematic review of American policy, as related to the Indigenous peoples of this country, is beyond the scope of this book, a cursory historical policy review (Ngai, 1999; Rollings, 2004) reveals a history of land appropriation by war, treaties, genocide and cultural erasure through assimilation, in the path to American citizenship (Dunbar-Ortiz, 2015; Ngai, 1999). In fact, during the nineteenth century "Most Americans did not consider Indian people civilized or intelligent enough to become American citizens and opposed any efforts to make Indians citizens" (Rollings, 2004, p. 127). Treaties after battles provided "White Natives" with legal mechanisms to claim increasing ownership of Indigenous' land, at times offering American citizenship in exchange. This citizenship was contingent on evidence of full assimilation and cultural erasure, as Rollings' (2004) discussion of Indigenous peoples' American citizenship and suffrage explicitly states: "accompanying these grants of citizenship were demands that these Indian citizens abandon their tribal communities, move to separate individual land allotments, and begin to live 'civilized' lives " (p. 130). Many Indigenous tribes did not seek this American citizenship, resisting "White Native" assimilationist policies. Instead, Indigenous tribes continued to preserve their form of life, identity and culture, coming into direct opposition with the "White Native" socioeconomic expansionary policy that required increasing land for the American subject (Dunbar-Ortiz, 2015).

This Indigenous act of resistance led "White Natives" to enact the Indian Removal Act of 1830, forcibly removing and relocating "over 80,000" (Rollings, 2004, p. 130) Indigenous people west of Mississippi. This forced migration became known among the Cherokee people as "The Trail of Tears," since an estimated "four thousand Cherokees died" (Zinn, 2003, p. 148) in this "White Nativist" legal genocide (Dunbar-Ortiz, 2015). The Removal Act of 1830 created the "legal and lawful" mechanism for a subsequent "White Native" politic of land appropriation and tribal dissolutions. This politic, through various forms of "White Native" violence, ultimately led to the Indigenous peoples' forced assimilation and absorption into the American citizenship. The post-Civil War period of land allotment that began with the passage of the General Allotment Act of 1887, or the Dawes Act, illustrates well this "White Native" politic.

The Dawes Act, signed into law by Theodore Roosevelt in 1887, represented a compromise between the Eastern United States' assimilationist movement, which sought to "save the Indians" by advocating for their assimilation as American citizens on "humanitarian and civilizing" moral principles (Rollings, 2004, p. 131), and the Western movement, which sought to dismantle Indigenous tribes, through land appropriation, confinement and extermination (Dunbar-Ortiz, 2015; Rollings, 2004; Royster, 1995). The Dawes Act, therefore, had to accomplish two contradictory tasks. First, to advance the White Nativist extermination project through the dismantling of Indigenous tribes. Second, to confer American citizenship to the Indigenous people who had successfully proven their assimilation to the "White Native" economic and cultural structure by both becoming land property owners and farmers, and by relinquishing their tribal ties and collective way of life (Royster, 1995). To accomplish both goals, the Dawes Act had to contain language by which to allot land to Indigenous people, while preserving "White Nativist" economic interests consistent with the extermination of Indigenous cultural and tribal life, as well as language by which to incorporate Indigenous people into the American "White Native" way of life and citizenship—consistent with an assimilationist Indigenous extermination. It is within this apparent, legal, overt and covert incongruence of assimilation and extermination, that social policy re-emerges again, simultaneously conferring American citizenship, while systematically excluding and subjugating a people.

To accomplish its subjugating, assimilationist, and yet exterminating aim, the Dawes Act allotted each "Indian" a portion of their Indigenous reservation land; between 80 and 160 acres depending on single or head of household status, placing the allotted land in a 25-year trust (Rollings, 2004; Royster, 1995). At the end of the trust period, the land was to be permanently transferred to the individual, provided the individual had successfully "assimilate(d) to agriculture, to Christianity, and to citizenship" (Royster, 1995). Assimilationists opposed the 25-year Federal trust clause, on grounds that it interfered with the expedient assimilation and absorption of Indigenous people as American citizens. The Dawes Act, consistent with its "White Nativist" exterminating aim, also included legal provisions for the redistribution of "unclaimed" Indigenous reservation land among "White Natives," providing a second legal mechanism for the appropriation and dismantling of the Indigenous tribes.

The Dawes Act was amended and replaced by the Burke Act in 1906, to allow for the "early issuance of fee patents," (Royster, 1995, p. 10) to assuage assimilationists who had opposed the Dawes Act's 25-year trust requirement prior to the final individual adjudication of allotted lands. By the end of the allotment era, "White Natives" had successfully used policy to appropriate 90 million acres of previously held indigenous land, resulting in the effective dismantling of the Indigenous tribal structures and culture (Dunbar-Ortiz, 2015; Royster, 1995). While the allotment era proved successful in its tribal dismantling efforts, it failed to provide "assimilated" Indigenous people, who had "lived among the whites" (Royster, 2004, p. 132) with access to the American citizenship. Similarly to African Americans, "assimilated" Indigenous people were excluded by the Reconstruction Acts; and, thus relegated to a citizenship that was not equal to that of the "White Native." In fact, "in Mackay v. Campbell, ...and Elk v. Wilkins, the western courts ruled that Indians were not...citizens and that the Fourteenth and Fifteenth Amendments did not apply to them"[3] (Rollings, 2004, p. 132).

It wasn't until 1924, with the passage of the Indian Citizenship Act, that "non-citizen Indians born in the United States" (Rollings, 2004, p. 132) were granted citizenship. However, as with African Americans, their citizenship did not ensure their right to vote, relegating them to, and reifying, the two-tier citizenship system created by "White Natives" for the "racialized, subjugated other" (Ferguson-Bohnee, 2015; Rollings, 2004). For example, in 1928, the Arizona Supreme Court, in Porter v. Hall, upheld Pinal County's decision to deny "Indians'" the right to vote. The Arizona Supreme Court, in making this determination, stated that "Indian" tribes were dependent on the federal government and thus wards of the United States. By constructing "Indians" as wards, the Arizona Supreme Court used Section 2, article 7 of Arizona's State Constitution (Porter v. Hall, 1928, p. 13) to deprive Indigenous peoples in Arizona of their constitutional right to vote. This law stated: "No person under guardianship, non compos mentis, or insane, shall be qualified to vote at any election" (Porter v. Hall, 1928, p. 13). Arizona was not alone in depriving Indigenous peoples of their constitutional right to vote despite the 1924, Indian Citizenship Act. In fact, the Arizona Supreme Court, in arguing Porter v. Hall, 1928, cited the Cherokee Nation v. Georgia ruling, in which the Georgia Courts had successfully argued that "Indians were not capable of managing their own affairs" (Freguson-Bohnee, 2015, p. 1105), thus declaring them wards and stripping Indigenous peoples of their full American citizenship.

Yet, this citizenship had been imposed on them as part of the "White Native" assimilative and extermination project (Dunbar-Ortiz, 2015). In fact, the Indian Citizenship Act of 1924, unlike the Reconstruction Amendments of 1866, 1868 and 1870, rested in an assimilationist ideology. "White Natives" had intentionally sought to absorb the Indigenous "other" into the citizenship construct as a legal mechanism by which to further erase the existence of a people with a native claim to the land that "White Natives" occupied. By constructing the "Indigenous other," as foreign within their own native land, and thus in need of absorption into the American citizenship, "White Natives" further legitimized their own nation-state, sense of nationhood, and native identity (Ferguson-Bohnee, 2015), while the "other" and their "native civilization" were on a path toward near extinction (Dunbar-Ortiz, 2015).

The allotment era came to a close in 1934, with the Wheeler-Howard Act, also known as the Indian Reorganization Act, which stopped the assimilationist policy movement and the allotment of Indigenous land, while returning "unclaimed" land to existing Indigenous reservations (Royster, 1995). However, in the 1940s "White Natives" resumed previous assimilationist efforts, marking the beginning of the termination era. Tribal assets were sold and control over Indigenous reservations was transferred from the federal to the state level. The dismantling of Indigenous communities ended in 1968, with President Johnson, who initiated the "policy of 'self-help, self-development, and self-determination' for Indians" (Royster, 2004, p. 18) that continues to inform modern-time Federal "Indian" policy. Indigenous peoples were finally granted access to voting rights in 1965, through the Voting Rights Act. However, the effects of their historical exclusion, oppression and marginalization can still be felt.

Efforts to thwart Indigenous peoples' voting participation continue to take place (Ferguson-Bohnee, 2015), evidencing their ongoing second-class citizenship and a historical legacy of "disenfranchisement as a matter of law and practice" (Ferguson-Bohnee, 2015, p. 1099). Ongoing contestation over Indigenous land and land treaties violations continue to occur, such as the land dispute between the Standing Rock Sioux Tribe and the Dakota Access Pipeline. In 2014, the Dakota Access Pipeline (DAPL) corporation presented a plan to build an oil pipeline "that [would run] through North and South Dakota, Iowa, and Illinois" (Heim, 2016, line 3, para. 5). The proposed plan included running the oil pipeline through Indigenous sacred land, which had been appropriated by the federal government through a number of treaties over the last 150 years. Indigenous peoples contested this project, resisting its construction to defend their sacred land, as well as the Sioux Tribe's way of life since the pipeline could contaminate the water supply.

Initially, DAPL took possession of the land in the proposed pipeline's path through eminent domain. On October 31, 2016, Indigenous peoples occupied the privately held Indigenous land, through eminent domain, stating that this land belonged to the tribes under the treaty entered into with the federal government in 1851 (Wade & Scheyder, 2016). Despite support from the international community, including the U.N. Permanent Forum on Indigenous Issues, the conflict continued without resolution (Heim, 2016; Wade & Scheyder, 2016). In December 2016, the Obama Administration halted the construction of the pipeline; the U.S. Army Corps of Engineers "denied the Dakota access pipeline company a permit to drill underneath the Missouri river" (Goodman, 2016), stating that alternative routes needed to be explored. However, in January 2017, President Donald Trump issued an executive memorandum clearing the path for the construction of the Dakota Access Pipeline (Baker & Davenport, 2017).

As this analysis has shown, American citizenship and race are inextricably linked to each other. Through the construction of a "racialized, non-native other," "White Natives" were able to delineate a native identity, while constructing a shared past and sense of nationhood. Within this historical context, American citizenship policy became a legal mechanism by which to legitimize the ongoing exclusion of the "black, African American other," rationalizing their second-class citizenship status. In the case of the "Indigenous other," American citizenship policy became one of the legal mechanisms by which to dismantle, assimilate, and thus erase a people. As Dave Archambault, chairman of the Standing Rock Sioux Tribal Council, said during a recent interview, "How do you eliminate a people? That's what the government has been trying to do for 200 years. But we are still here. We have maintained our culture. We've maintained our way of life. We've maintained our dignity. We're still here" (Heim, 2016, para. 32).

## Race, economic systems and immigration

Citizenship and immigration policy share a common inclusionary and exclusionary purpose in regards to admission and participation within the mainstream of American society (Shklar, 1991). Yet, race in each of these policy areas plays a parallel, although different, function as "there is a vast difference between discriminatory immigration laws and the enslavement of a people" (Shklar, 1991, p. 4), or the colonization of Indigenous peoples, dismantling their structural and cultural life. Despite some dissimilarity, the function of race as an exclusionary or inclusionary mechanism in both, citizenship and immigration policy, has often been understood to be one and the same (Cohen, 2007; Shklar, 1991). Yet, does a purely racial exclusionary perspective effectively explain the complex dynamics of survival and preservation related to the historical identity of the American "White Native," and the fate of those constructed as racially and/or immigrant "other"? (Johnson, 2004).

In the case of the African American population, Wallerstein's (2003) conceptualization of racism can further contextualize the dynamics that propelled slavery. Wallerstein (2003) explains racism as a mechanism used by a dominant group within the capitalist world economy to justify the inherent socioeconomic inequities necessary for wealth acquisition and maximization. As discussed by Adam Goodheart during his NPR interview on *Fresh Air* (2011), slavery, given the plantation economy of the South, was necessary to maximize production at a minimum cost, while maximizing the economic gains of "White Native" plantation owners. In fact, slavery was not only a means of production but also a concrete source of capital, "the largest single investment of the Southern planter," a "liquid asset… worth 4 billion dollars by 1861." Goodheart's remarks (2011) illustrate well Wallerstein's conceptualization (2003) of racism as a mechanism of "White Native" socioeconomic preservation and supremacy, as it pertains to the experience of the African American population in the Unites States.

Wallerstein's (2003) conceptualization of racism can also explain the dismantling of Indigenous tribal life through land appropriation, necessary to support the "White Native" agricultural economy that eventually gave rise to the plantation economy. In other words, the historical breach of land treaties, facilitated by legal logics embedded in a white, "native American" racist ideology, legitimized the White Nativist politic of Indigenous land appropriation, leading to the successful economic exploitation of seized territory, propelling the birth of the plantation economy (Bell, 2013).

Wallerstein's (2003) socioeconomic explanation of racism, certainly complements and further complicates a purely sociocognitive conceptualization and deconstruction of racism, "White Nativism," and the necessary "subjugated racial other" (Derrida, 1984), as it pertains to African Americans and the Indigenous peoples of the United States. However, this more complex deconstruction of racism does not fully explain sociopolitical discourses pertaining to Southern and Eastern European immigration during the late nineteenth and early twentieth centuries, which were marked by fear and anxiety, despite the skin color of this new wave of immigrants. The immigration discourses of that era reflect concerns related to the preservation of the "White Native" identity and of its "White Native" culture; a culture "White Natives" experienced as threatened by a possible transformation brought about by the national origins of the "new immigrants" (Simon, 1997, p. 13). "White Natives" did not believe that these new immigrants had the capacity to assimilate into the "White Native" culture and its way of life, instead bringing about its inevitable gradual transformation and destruction unless they were prevented from entering American territory. Simon (1997) best illustrates this growing fear when she states,

> Nativist movements, among the earliest of which was the pre-Civil War Know Nothing party, expressed consternation, fear, and anxiety and hostility at the seeming endless stream of new immigrants who kept arriving at the U.S. door steps…[alleging that] they would lower the level of culture, [and] fragment American values and loyalties.
>
> (p. 13)

It is this experience of being under threat, whether real or imagined, and its accompanying anxiety, that is neither captured nor explained by a solely sociocognitive and economic conceptualization of the history of race, racism and immigration policy in the United States. How can this fear be explained?

In other words: what is the etiology of the individual and collective fear that emerges when a group is faced with the possible transformation, and therefore loss, of its original identity as historically constructed? Why does identity change and transformation evoke fear within any group, and in this case for the "White Native"? To answer these questions, the function of race within the history of both American immigration and economic policy needs to be examined.

As discussed by Johnson (2004) in *The Huddled Masses*: "A cursory review of history reveals [how] ... U.S. immigration laws and their enforcement have barred racial minorities, political dissidents, the poor, actual and alleged criminals, and homosexuals from our shores..." (p. 9). Johnson's (2004) remarks highlight the exclusionary function of American immigration policy (Hing, 2004; Shklar, 1991), but add a more complex dimension. That is, the historical exclusion of certain groups from U.S. territory has occurred due to various aspects of a person's identity, such as socioeconomic status, educational level, disabilities, sexual orientation and race, just to name a few; hence there are gaps and limitations to a solely racialized explanation.

Critical race theory certainly explicates the initial exclusion experienced by the non-Nordic and racial other, such as Chinese, Asian Indians and Japanese immigrants as illustrated by the Chinese Exclusion Act of 1882; the United States v. Bhagat Singh Thind (1923) Supreme Court case in which the court decided that "Indians, like Japanese, would no longer be considered white persons, and were therefore ineligible to become naturalized citizens" (Hing, 2004, p. 45); and, Korematsu v. United States (1944), where the Supreme Court legitimized as constitutional the detention and internment of Japanese immigrants and American-born Japanese-Americans under national security grounds (Johnson, 2004, p. 26).

However, Southern and Eastern Europeans, and the Irish, were also initially excluded and marginalized by "White Natives." These immigrant groups, in a similar fashion to many current Hispanic immigrants who "possess" white skin, were conceptualized as "non-white" upon entering the United States, and thus relegated to a "second-class citizenship" previously only held by the African American and Indigenous other (Ignatiev, 1995; Johnson, 2004). Racism, as explicated by Wallerstein (2003), does not fully account for the history of these previously excluded immigrant groups, as they eventually became part of the white construct. The question is, how did they become white given the prevailing eugenics racial "White Native" ideology (Hing, 2004; Ignatiev, 1995; Johnson, 2004)? The answer to this question is pertinent to contemporary Mexican immigration reform policy discourses, since many Hispanic immigrants share a similar color "ambiguity" to the one posed by these previously excluded immigrant groups (Ngai, 1999). It may be possible to uncover dynamics that, although obscured under purely racialized explanations of exclusion, continue to fuel the current marginalization of Hispanic immigrants and their American-born children by exploring the process that led to the inclusion of these earlier immigrant groups.

The race of the Irish, Southern and Eastern immigrants, their skin color, did not change but somehow the "White Native" did come to eventually view some of these groups as "white." This change, in turn, eliminated the previous threat these groups had posed to the collective "White Native" identity, also eliminating the fear they experienced (Loewenberg, 1995). Loewenberg best speaks to the collective "psychohistorical" "White Native" fear and anxiety when he states,

> the psychohistorical understanding of anxiety is that it is a response to a sense of powerlessness, a loss of mooring or centering. The experience of an epidemic, a lost war, and old order destroyed… are the social equivalents of the death of a parent.
>
> (1995, p. 220)

This analysis will illustrate how these foreign others did not constitute a threat to the collective "White Native" identity due to the color of their skin, but were instead "other" due to something different and more elusive, their own native cultures, which were tied to their national origins. Contemporary "White Nativist" ideology and discourse is certainly consistent with this hypothesis, as Huntington (2004a) illustrates in his discussion of White Nativism and cultural transformation, where "White Nativism" is defined as an ideology that advocates for cultural preservation, asserting that "culture is a product of race" (Huntington, 2004a, p. 41).

Southern and Eastern European immigrants were indeed other, albeit not racially, but other at a symbolic and intrapsychic cultural level. The cultural origins of these "new" immigrants were certainly different; previous immigrant groups had originated from, "Germany, Scandinavia, the Low Countries, and the British Isles" (Hing, 2004, p. 52) and had gradually united under a "White Native" collective identity and culture. This identity provided these diverse immigrant groups with a mechanism by which to construct a mythical, shared past necessary to maintain the created American nation-state (Volkan, 2013). Ngai's (1999) analysis and deconstruction of the Immigration Act of 1924, implemented to curtail the Southern and Eastern immigration influx, is consistent with this conceptual assertion, and highlights the importance of problematizing further existing deconstructions of the Immigrant Act of 1924 that are solely informed by the era's prevailing ideology of racial eugenics and social Darwinism. In other words, although a solely racial deconstruction tells "an important story… [it] does not adequately explain and may, in fact, obscure from view other ideas about race, citizenship, and the nation that [are] both encoded and generated" by this act (Ngai, 1999, p. 69).

With the Immigration Act of 1924, "White Natives" were able to legally establish a National Origins Quota System for immigration (Hing, 2004;

Johnson, 2004) by which to legally curtail Southern and Eastern immigration to defend and preserve their original critical mass representation and "White Native" identity (Huntington, 2004b). To accomplish this goal, the Immigration Act was developed, using the 1890 nationality census, which predated the influx of Southern and Eastern European immigrants (Hing, 2004; Johnson 2004). While this is the historically succinct description of the act, a closer analysis reveals a different history, one in which national origin and race were intertwined to reconstruct and racialize the national origins of the American population and the excluded immigrant "other," thereby re-affirming and maintaining "White Natives" as the primary group with a native identity and claim to this land. This constructivist process emerges clearly when the method by which the Quota System was established is examined (Ngai, 1999, 2014).

One of the central challenges faced by the Quota Board was the lack of complete census and immigration records necessary to determine the national origins of the existing and previous non-foreign and foreign-born population. Population immigration data was not recorded until 1820, and was only "classified according to origin" in 1899 (Ngai, 1999, p. 71) "when it was arranged… according to a taxonomy called 'races and people'" (Ngai, 1999, p. 71). When these taxonomies were developed, the Quota Board listed under country of origin "five 'colored races' (black, mulatto, Chinese, Japanese, and Indian)" (Ngai, 1999, p. 73) as well as 53 countries, designed to capture the national origins of primarily white identified individuals. The Quota Board also encountered a number of methodological and conceptual challenges when examining the 1890 census, since "the census did not differentiate the foreign born until 1850 and did not identify the places of birth of parents of native born until 1890" (Ngai, 1999, p. 73). To solve this problem, the 1790 census was used to retrace, presume and estimate the population's national origins in 1890. To retrace national origin, head of households' surnames were assigned to supposed, plausible, national origins (Ngai, 1999). This methodology attributed English national origin to "87 percent of the population," discounting possible attributional errors, and potential overestimation produced by the immigrant practice of surname Anglicization, which was not uncommon during that era. Despite dubious methodology, which was further revised, manipulated, and adjusted,[4] the Quota Board's findings were accepted as "factual" and enacted into law in 1929, without further scrutiny. The act accomplished its primary aim, successfully decreasing the influx of Southern and Eastern European immigrants, "and struck most deeply at Jews, Italians, Slavs, and Greeks" (Hing, 2004, p. 69), while also barring immigration from Asian countries under the ineligibility to citizenship clause, achieving full "Asiatic exclusion," which had began with the Chinese Exclusion Act of 1882 (Ngai, 1999, p. 81).

The 1924 Immigration Act illustrates well the social constructivist processes used by a people to legitimize and maintain their collective identity, as historically constructed, even if history needs to be altered to conform with existing sociocognitive identity schemas (Van Dijk, 2000, 2002). The Immigration Act emerges in this light as a "White Native" socioconstructivist, legal mechanism that legitimized the primacy of "White Natives" through "scientific" research and statistical methods based on the prevailing eugenics paradigm of the era, while also birthing the modern racial paradigm (Ngai, 1999). This new paradigm, while embedded within racial eugenics, incorporated nation-state constructions (Wallerstein, 2000, 2003), that is, national origin, to establish new codifying categories by which a person could be both white and yet, not white, due to national origin (Ngai, 1999). This new conceptual and linguistic construction provided a mechanism by which "the other" could be both white and unassimilable, just as the Indigenous or African American other, thus "effectively" circumventing racial eugenic categories that had proven conceptually inadequate due to the skin color of these new immigrants.

Mexicans, on the other hand, posed a codification dilemma for "White Natives" and the National Origins Quota System that requires a retracing of the nineteenth- and twentieth-centuries inter-nations history. During the early nineteenth century, specifically by 1821, Mexico had successfully expanded into north America, incorporating into its borders California, Texas, New Mexico, Arizona, and "part of Colorado, Utah, and Nevada" (Hing, 2004, p. 117); at the same time, the United States was seeking expansion toward the south, initially focusing on Texas. This quest culminated in the annexation of Texas in 1845, and the 1846 war between the United States and Mexico, with the subsequent American occupation and conquest of New Mexico and California, and eventual advance into Mexico's capital (Hing, 2004). The war ended with the Treaty of Guadalupe Hidalgo in 1848, which gave the United States possession over "California and New Mexico (including present-day Nevada, Utah, and Arizona) ... [amounting] to 55 percent of Mexico's territory" (Hing, 2004, p. 117). The treaty required Mexican citizens who remained in the occupied territories to declare their intention to maintain Mexican citizenship or seek American citizenship. Mexicans who did not declare their intention within a year were automatically considered American citizens (Hing, 2004; Ngai, 1999); the majority remained within the United States.

Despite national animosities and historical grievances between the United States and Mexico, the United States continued to look toward Mexico for cheap labor, encouraging Mexican migration, while concurrently rejecting and marginalizing Mexicans on the basis of "inferiority" (Hing, 2004, p. 199). In fact in 1911, "the Dillingham Commission... concluded that Mexicans were undesirable as citizens but needed as cheap labor for the expansion of industry and the exploitation of natural resources" (Hing, 2004, p. 122). The Immigrant Act of 1924 brought to the forefront the competing political discourses that had surrounded the "Mexican problem," as well as the incongruences of the White Nativist, eugenics legal logics. To begin with, Mexicans could not be prevented from entering the United States since Mexicans were already living in the American "conquered" territory, and had been absorbed as American citizens under the Guadalupe Hidalgo Treaty of 1848, unless otherwise stated by the individual; hence, separating Mexicans from other groups, such as "Asians" who had been excluded by the Immigration Act's citizenship clause, was legally impossible. Secondly, Mexicans were needed from an economic perspective to provide cheap labor for the American manufacturing economy. And, from a "White Nativist" eugenics political ideology, Mexicans had been determined "white" under the 1897 Rodriguez federal court case ruling, preventing their racial exclusion. In this federal case, Rodriguez, a Mexican man who had been residing in Texas, had requested and was denied American citizenship, based on the 1872 federal statute by which only Caucasians or Africans could become citizens. The court ruled in favor of Rodriguez, stating "that the Fourteenth Amendment granted citizenship to all people born or naturalized in the United States regardless of color or race; [concurrently upholding] the legal rights of Mexicans as 'white'" (Vargas, 2011, p. 152).

To reconcile the competing economic needs of the United States and the existing national origins–racial ideological paradigm of the Immigration Act, Congress needed to find a different legal avenue by which to "limit" the presence of the Mexican "other" in American territory, while meeting necessary labor supply demands (Hing, 2004; Ngai, 2014). To this aim, existing Mexican–American border enforcement laws, which had been previously largely disregarded, were now strictly enforced to control the entry of the Mexican other; secondly, existing deportation legislation was revived, lifting the statute of limitations in 1924 and facilitating the removal of the Mexican immigrant other (Hing, 2004; Ngai, 1999, 2014). In 1929, to further delineate the boundaries between existing Mexican Americans and foreign Mexican immigrants, Congress redefined "unlawful entry [as] a misdemeanor, punishable by one year of imprisonment or a $1,000 fine, or both, and made a second unlawful entry a felony" (Ngai, 2014, p. 60), giving birth to the current legal and illegal construction of the Mexican other. These legal mechanisms successfully curtailed the Mexican population in the United States, resulting in 8,438 Mexican deportations in 1930, and an additional 13,000 deportations under "voluntary" premises (Ngai, 1999, 2014). The creation of the illegal Mexican other, paved the way for the final deconstruction of Mexicans as "whites"; in 1930, the Census Bureau tied the Mexican national origin to a new racial category, the Mexican race, creating the national origin-racial means by which to racialize the previously "white" Mexican, alleging that they were "not definitely white, Negro, Indian, Chinese, or Japanese" (Ngai, 1999, p. 91). As a result of this recodification, "over 400,000 Mexicans (half of them children with United States citizenship) [were deported] during the Great Depression" (Ngai, 1999, p. 91).

The creation of the Mexican race allowed "White Natives" to legitimize the subjugation of the Mexican, "undesirable," racially ambiguous needed others, while also setting a historical precedent by which the American-born children of Mexican descent could be both citizens and yet other, deportable, thus allowing "White Natives" to control the critical mass representation of the Mexican other in the United States. In addition, this American-born, Mexican other had a native claim to the now American, Mexican-conquered land, and was therefore a symbol of the enemy and previous invader. Their presence constituted a reminder of lost battles, national wounds and an active threat for the "White Native" nation-state, unless their critical mass representation within the United States could be controlled and contained.

Southern and Eastern European immigrants did not share a history of land contestation, war, lost battles and conquest with White Natives. They were also European, unlike Mexicans, and they did not pose the racial ambiguity of the Mexican other, due to their skin hues. Although initially Southern and Eastern European immigrants were relegated to the exclusion experienced by Mexicans, as well as other native-born populations, they were able to work toward and achieve whiteness (Roedinger, 2006). Even though they had initially formed alliances with other "racially" subjugated groups within the labor market, their skin color set them apart, but was insufficient. It was only when Southern and Eastern European immigrants were able to prove their capacity for cultural assimilation into "White Native" whiteness that they were accepted as belonging to this group and identity (Jacobson, 1998; Roedinger, 2006), that is, when their cultural otherness gradually decreased giving way to a new identity performance, an identity tailored according to the "White Native" identity.

"White Native," Anglo-Saxon cultural identity markers replaced old traditions, native languages and other cultural symbols. The English language became their primary spoken language and, most importantly, they accepted their skin color as a form of social wage (Jacobson, 1998). Southern and Eastern immigrants became white by shading their previous cultural identities and by accepting whiteness as a tool for upward mobility, joining forces with "White Natives" in the oppression of the darker other; in other words, they accepted the cultural racialization of the "White Native," dominant sociopolitical discourse (Roedinger, 2006). This is well illustrated by Ignatiev (1995) in his remarks about the assimilation process of the Irish immigrant: "To become white they had to learn to subordinate county, religious, or national animosities, not to mention any natural sympathies they may have felt for their fellow creatures, to a new solidarity based on color" (p. 96). In other words, Southern and Eastern immigrants ceased to pose a threat to the "White Native" culture and way of life, when they gave up their cultural symbolic representations, evidencing their assimilation and Americanization (Roedinger, 2006); and when they accepted the "White Native" socioeconomic system of racial segregation and subjugation. Roedinger (2006) best speaks about this process when stating,

> The great liberal mobilization of the New Deal and industrial union-
> ism in the 1930s made space in which new immigrants could mobilize
> as whites and exclude others. As houses were constructed, so too was
> the idea—validated by popular campaigns for segregation of neighbor-
> hoods in the 1920s and then by New Deal housing policy—that African
> Americans were "antineighbors" and that all Europeans could unify
> around this realization.
>
> (p. 8)

Through this sociocognitive process of identity transformation and unifica-
tion, racialized national origin codifications that had previously separated
Northern European immigrants, and their descendants, from Southern and
Eastern European ones fell apart, giving birth to a new unifying identity, that
of White Europeans. This identity, instead of threatening the old "White
Native" social order (Loewenberg, 1995), reified it while concurrently increasing their critical mass representation, necessary to maintain the social power
by which to continue to subjugate those who had been historically racialized
as "other," that is, Indigenous peoples, African Americans, Mexicans and the
racially, unassimilable. By "working toward whiteness" (Roedinger, 2006) to
improve their social and economic location and escape "White Native" subjugation, Southern and Eastern immigrants eliminated the "White Native"
intrapsychic fear posed by the threat of the impending transformation of their
original identity (Ross, 2007). In fact, this "White Native" fear would have
intensified if Southern and Eastern immigrants had continued to join ranks
with the "racialized" subjugated other. This previous alliance could have
given this collective "other" enough of a critical mass to subvert and eventually dismantle the "White Native" system of dominance.

The new "White European" identity, which required the acceptance
of racism and the rejection of non-"White Native" cultural symbolic
representations, also provided "White Natives," Southern and Eastern
immigrants, and their descendants, with a mechanism by which to establish
a shared, large intrapsychic linkage, necessary to establish and maintain
synthetic nations that lack a historical collective national past. This process
is consistent with Loewenberg's (1991, 1995) and Volkan's (2013) discussions
of synthetic nations, and introduces affective, internal, individual and
collective processes that remain unexplained by a purely sociocognitive
and economic construction of individual and collective identity formation.
That is, individuals and groups think about their identity, reproduce it and
protect it, but they also develop affective ties to its symbolic cultural representations, as in the case of the Mexican other, who embodies for "White
Natives," affective associations connected to a shared past of war, loss and
conquest, for example.

Volkan (2013) defines a synthetic nation as one comprised of "people [who] came from different places with different experiences" (p. 94), who had to synthesize dissimilar influences to live together. Volkan (2013) suggests that the United States accomplished this synthesis by creating "an idealized white-national large-group identity, psychologically speaking... supported by racism" (p. 94) which facilitated the linking process despite the absence of a shared common heritage. Yet, it is precisely the absence of this shared history, that "increases [the] need to ...project unwanted ideas and feelings that cannot be integrated within the developing synthetic large group onto the Other" (Volkan, 2013, p. 94). When "this other" cannot give up aspects of the self that threaten the achieved, synthetic, idealized white-American–national large group identity, and cannot concurrently accept aspects consistent with this synthetic identity, he/she will likely serve as a suitable target of unintegrated, white-American ideas and feelings. Within this context of synthetic integration, the Mexican other emerges as an ideal suitable target of "White Native" externalization, since this other cannot claim a shared European past with "White Natives," overcome skin color ambiguities, or different cultural traditions. It is important to emphasize that ideas and feelings, which cannot be integrated into the idealized white-American identity, need to find an external outlet, as they will otherwise produce internal conflict, destabilizing and challenging the "coherence" of the synthesized, American nation-state. However, has the time arrived for the fragmentation of this idealized identity? What is the cost of perpetuating this idealized "White Native" synthetic identity? And, most importantly, can this idealized, "White Native" identity be maintained within the context of a capitalist system that requires the "immigrant other" to maximize production and wealth creation?

The psychological formulation presented in the next section will examine and explain the psychological, affective processes that are involved in and that complement the sociocognitive formation of the "White Native" collective synthetic identity. This next section will also discuss and explore the manifestations and implications of a thwarted collective mourning process for both "White Natives" and the Hispanic, immigrant other, paying special attention to the American-born children of Mexican immigrant parents.

## Notes

1 It is important to note that the term "Hispanic other" is being used in this discussion to capture the overt and covert complexity surrounding the term and its use within the current immigration sociopolitical discourse.
2 The Secure Communities Program was first implemented in 2008 by the Immigration and Customs Enforcement Agency (ICE). This program enabled state and local law enforcement officers in participating jurisdictions to collaborate with ICE in the screening of detainees' criminal records and immigration status (Kohli, Markowitz, & Chavez, 2011). In 2015, this program was replaced by the Priority Enforcement Program (PEP). PEP, although similar

to the Secure Communities Program, prioritized "the identification and arrest of immigrants convicted of a criminal offense and others who pose a danger to public safety" (ICE, 2014, para. 1).

3 In Mackay v. Campbell, "the court ruled that because [Mackay had] Indian blood, he had not been born subject to the jurisdiction of the United States" (Rolling, 2004, p. 132), effectively excluding Indigenous people from the American citizenship granted under the Fourteenth Amendment to the U.S. Constitution. In Elk. v. Wilkins, Elk was denied the right to vote, despite having lived and worked among "Whites" in "Omaha for several years" (Rollings, 2004, p. 132), on the basis of not being an American citizen under the Fourteenth Amendment of the U.S. Constitution (Rollings, 2004).

4 See Ngai (1999).

# Part II
# Psychological framework

# 3 Political psychology
## Individual and group identity[1]

## Introduction

The sociopolitical historical critical discourse analysis of White Nativism, American citizenship and immigration policy linked contemporary immigration discourses and reforms to their historical origins. The analysis revealed a complex sociocognitive process of identity formation, maintenance and partial transformation by which "White Natives" established a large collective idealized national synthetic identity. Within this context, immigration policy and deportation emerged as a historical, White Nativist, collective, conscious and unconscious legal mechanism that enabled "White Natives" to create and protect their original collective identity and culture, from an impending transformation. This legal mechanism also provided "White Natives" with the means by which to regulate the presence of the immigrant other, an "other" needed as a means of production, given the United States' capitalist economic system.

The sociopolitical critical historical analysis uncovered the sociocognitive processes involved in the creation of the "White Native" and White Nativist ideology. However, it was unable to explain the affective processes linked to this identity and the fear evoked by its possible transformation. This chapter will integrate a psychological conceptual framework by which to explore group, collective-affective linking processes related to the development of a synthetic national identity and its implications. The psychological conceptual framework will illustrate how these shared, linking, intrapsychic affective processes fueled and manifested in the creation of White Nativist, collective, sociocognitive schemas that reinforce and legitimize the "White Native" identity and the subjugation of the other. It will also reconceptualize immigration policy as an external manifestation of intrapsychic conscious and unconscious collective group efforts, aimed at preserving the "White Native" identity and culture from its inevitable transformation due to capitalist labor demands.

## Political psychology

Political psychology integrates and applies individual psychological theoretical frameworks to large, group collective processes to explain the conscious and unconscious nature of these processes, and their sociopolitical manifestations. A tenet of political psychology, therefore, is that group processes are influenced by the individual, collective journeys of the group's members. As Volkan discusses,

> There are echoes of individual psychology in large-group psychology shared by thousands or millions of persons, but large groups do not have one brain to think with or two eyes to cry. Thousands or millions in a large group share a psychological journey, such as going through a complicated mourning after major shared losses, or when they use the same psychological mechanism such as "externalization," making the Other a shared target. These journeys become social, cultural, political or ideological processes that are specific for the large group under study. Considering large-group psychology in its own right means making formulations as to a large groups' conscious and unconscious shared psychological experiences and motivations that initiate specific social, cultural, political or ideological processes that influence this large group's internal and external affairs.
>
> (V. Volkan, personal communication,
> February 22, 2014)

Consistent with political psychology, this section will present three conceptual theoretical frameworks that will facilitate the integrated psychological analysis of contemporary American immigration policies. The first, already introduced, is Volkan's large groups psychological theory. The second is Winnicott's object relations theory, which will explain the individual psychological processes involved in the formation of the self, and that, in combination with Volkan's large groups psychological theory, will link individual psychological identity formation processes to those of large, collective groups. These two theoretical frameworks will also contextualize and expose the obscured psychological dynamics fueling contemporary American immigration reform policies, with a focus on deportation reforms. The third theory, Freud's (1917) theory of mourning and melancholia, will link these individual psychological processes to collective, large group processes of identity preservation, protection and mourning.

## Contemporary immigration policy and deportation

Border enforcement and deportation policy, which began in the late 1920s, provided "White Natives" with a mechanism by which to reduce the presence of the Mexican other. By the early 1930s, over 400,000 Mexicans had been deported, of which 200,000 were American citizen children of Mexican parents. Unfortunately, history can and does repeat itself, linking contemporary immigration reform policies, with an emphasis on the deportation of the Mexican other, to a complicated historical past of "White Native" identity formation and preservation. Since the implementation of IIRIRA and AEDPA, many mixed status families have been permanently divided with significant long-term implications for the children living in these families (Capps et al., 2015; Passel, Cohn, & Gonzalez-Barrera, 2012).

Reports by the Urban Institute (Capps et al., 2015) indicate that upon parental deportation children often remain in the United States under the care of another parent or relative, some enter the foster-care system, and others join the parent/family in their country of origin. In fact, between 2005 and 2010 the number of U.S.-born children living in Mexico increased from 240,000 in 2000, to 500,000 in 2010 (Passel et al., 2012); although official statistics are not available, the findings suggest that "a potentially large share of these children moved there with or soon after a deported parent" (Passel et al., 2012, p. 12). It is important to note, that the U.S. Department of Homeland Security did not begin to collect statistical information on the number of parents of American citizen children being deported until 2012. Given the effects that contemporary immigration reform policies are having on mixed status families and their children, and since American citizen children are also departing from their home country, why are current immigration sociopolitical discourses advocating for a continuation of these policies?

Immigration reform efforts since 1996, as in the 1920s, have focused on keeping the immigrant other outside of the U.S., unless needed to meet the labor demands of the country. However, contemporary efforts have not accomplished their aim, as "the other" has continued to be within the United States, because they are "being birthed" and raised within the United States (American Hispanics, 2015), confirming "White Native" fears related to the gradual demographic transformation of the U.S. population. The fear and anxiety "White Natives" are experiencing due to this demographic change is clearly palpable in Donald Trump's, Anne Coulter's and Jason Richwine's political rhetoric. For example, when discussing immigration, Donald Trump stated: "they're taking our jobs. They're taking our manufacturing jobs. They're taking our money. They're killing us" (Kohn, 2016). Ann Coulter, social and political journalist, in a recently published book, *Adios America: The left's plan to turn our country into a hellhole*, went on to say: "we no longer ask anything of immigrants in terms of assimilation" (Kohn, 2016). Jason Richwine, Harvard Ph.D. graduate and research analyst for the Heritage Foundation, when discussing the "unassimilability" of Mexicans stated: "[E]ven early Mexican Americans... have been living in the country for a long time and have not assimilated to the cultural mainstream as typified by white Americans" (Kohn, 2016). As these quotes reveal, "White Natives" experience the foreign other, who is often described as belonging to a culture that is morally and intellectually inferior ("Donald Trump Speech," 2016; Huntington, 2004a), as an active threat to a cherished possession: the manifestation or symbolization of the "White Native," collective, cultural identity and way of life. This culture, as Volkan (1985) postulates, is one in which "White Natives" have invested significant individual and collective positive, loving emotions. In fact, when discussing ethnicity, nationality and culture, Volkan (1985) explains that these individual and large group identities are embedded in affective responses that "...function to provide psychological borders for the individual..." (p. 223), connected to the individual's definition of the self.

However, how does this sense of ethnic and national self emerge in the first place? Volkan (1985) uses Winnicott's (1965) conceptualization of the transitional object and the transitional phenomena as a stepping stone for a phenomenon he labels "suitable targets of externalization," (p. 235) which he postulates are used and shared by children, within a given group or nation, to project onto unintegrated good or bad aspects of the self. These collective suitable targets are not only invested with individual psychological meaning, embedded in an affective experience, but also have a collective shared meaning that influences group dynamics (Volkan, 1985, 2013). To fully understand how these affective group dynamics are central to the analysis of contemporary American immigration reform policies, the integrated analysis will first introduce and discuss Winnicott's (1965) and Volkan's (2013) psychological theories; to then, return to a discussion of sociopolitical implications.

## The development of the self, Winnicott and Volkan's symbolization of culture

Winnicott's Object Relations Theory (1965) is a theory of individual development, which partially informs Volkan's (1985, 1998, 2013) large groups theory, related to collective identity formation and contestation. Winnicott (1965) begins his conceptualization of the developing self by introducing us to the early experiences of infants within the context of the caregiving relationship. In his theory, Winnicott (1965) paid significant attention to the intrapsychic integration of part-object representations of the self and others into whole-object representations, which he considered essential for the formation of an integrated and cohesive self. Winnicott identified three developmental stages: the stage of absolute dependence; the stage of relative dependence; and, the last stage, toward independence. This analysis will explain and incorporate the first two stages of development.

During the first stage of development, the stage of absolute dependence, Winnicott (1965) presents an infant who is completely dependent on his/her caregiver and on the caregiver's ability to meet the infant's needs in a "good enough," consistent, nurturing and attuned manner, capable of protecting the infant from external "impingements" that "... the infant cannot manage or that cause the child to shut down or feel annihilated" (St. Clair, 2004, p. 75). The caregiver's ability to attune to the infant's needs and to protect the infant from external impingements, allows for the development of an early omnipotent sense of self; a self that believes that others are under his/her control. It is he or she who controls the caregiver's behavior; the caregiver is not yet experienced as a person with her or his own needs, wishes, or will.

As the infant grows, Winnicott (1965) begins to describe a different child and caregiver. In the second developmental stage, relative dependence, the caregiver begins to gradually expose the child to a different world, one that is not under the control of the child; the caregiver "adapts less and less perfectly, in synchrony with the infant's increased ability to deal with the [caregiver's] inevitable failures" (Applegate & Bonovitz, 2004, p. 2004). These calibrated gradual failures in caregiving, and the accompanying disillusionment experienced by the child, mark the beginning of a gradual separation process that begins to gently pierce the child's earlier omnipotent sense of self, while introducing him or her to a different world, one that is not under his or her control. It is at this point that the infant begins to experience the world, the self and others in a pleasurable or frustrating manner, in dichotomous terms, "all good" or "all bad." It is also this point, that Winnicott introduces the transitional object and transitional phenomena.

At the stage of relative dependence (Winnicott, 1965), the internal world of the child begins to be populated by unintegrated, partial representations of the self and others, for example, thoughts, feelings and images of being either all good or all bad. However, if the child is to achieve an integrated sense of self, he/she needs to find a way to integrate these internal, partial representations of the self and others, into a whole, single representation of the self, and others; for example, the child has to come to experience the self and the caregiver as being both pleasurable and frustrating rather than as only good or bad. When the child is able to integrate both "good and bad" aspects of the self and others, although some aspects always remain unintegrated, the child enters the last developmental stage, toward independence, moving to find his or her place within society.

Winnicott (1965) believed that children are able to initiate this gradual integration process through the use of transitional objects and the transitional space, placing the location of culture within this later one. The transitional object (Winnicott, 1965) is an object that is chosen by the child, that is both discovered and created by the child, part of the external environment that comes to be imbued with magical qualities. It "is not an internal or subjective object, and it is not merely an external object; it is the first not-me possession" (St. Clair, 2004, p. 73) that the child uses for self-regulation during moments of separation from the caregiver, or during moments in which the caregiver is experienced as a bad object; for example, the special teddy bear that a 2-year-old child carries everywhere, specially when leaving the house, not even allowing others to wash it due to its special smell; or a preferred small blanket, carried everywhere, which becomes essential if the 2-year old is to fall asleep alone in his/her room, while stroking it. As many caregivers have discovered, these treasured items can never be replaced by any "look alike," even if it is an identical replica, as the new blanket, for example, will never be the one originally chosen by the child and therefore, lacks the soothing powers the child had attributed to it. For Winnicott, it is the transitional object, discovered and created by the child, that allows the child "to maintain the illusion of the gratifying caregiver while [the child] build[s] up a capacity to tolerate and benefit from disillusionment" (Applegate & Bonovitz, 2004, p. 46).

Volkan (1985) builds on Winnicott's conceptualization of the transitional object and transitional phenomena, to explain the formation of collective suitable targets of externalization, and cultural amplifiers that, as suggested by Volkan (1988), serve to establish an external collective sense of "we-ness" (Volkan, 2013) and "otherness." This discussion will first define and explain the intrapsychic function of Volkan's, collective suitable targets of externalization, to examine the psychological dynamics involved in the construction of the "other." The definition of cultural amplifiers will then be presented, as well as their psychological function for the establishment and maintenance of in-groups, specifically focusing on the "White Native" in-group.

Volkan (2013) begins his explanation of suitable targets of externalization by describing a child who is relying less and less on his or her chosen transitional object for internal affect regulation, stating that,

> As the child develops, under normal conditions the magical qualities of the transitional object diminish and finally disappear ... [But] as he matures... he is engaged in bringing together his opposing images of himself and the world. He imposes some of his unintegrated aspects of himself and perceived others onto "suitable targets." In selecting these he is influenced by the views of those around him, attributing "badness" of his own to those his mother calls "those people (or things)," for example.
>
> (p. 234)

To fully understand how suitable targets of externalization are developed, as well as their relevance for the intrapsychic construction of the other, Volkan (1988, 2013) makes an essential distinction between protosymbolic processes and affects, and symbolic processes; attributing the initial affective construction of the other, to the pre-oedipal stage of development and to protosymbolic processes. The pre-oedipal stage of development, encompassing the first three years of life, is by and large a preverbal stage, characterized by raw, intense affective states, and it is within this context of raw affect that the child's transitional object first emerges. The intensity and early quality of these affects, which the child cannot yet verbally formulate, interferes with the child's capacity to symbolize. The child cannot differentiate without confusing the symbol from what it affectively represents, experiencing them as one and the same. These initial attempts at symbolization are thus best understood as protosymbolic (Volkan, 1988, 2013), where protosymbols "directly 'present' a meaning rather than 'represent' it" (Volkan, Ast, & Greer, 2002, p. 174; Werner & Kaplan, 1963, p. 16).

It is only later, when the child reaches the age of four, an age that marks the beginning of increasing cognitive development and verbal capacity (oedipal stage of development), that pre-oedipal protosymbols begin to be "transferred to symbols" (Volkan, 1988, p. 45). The child's increasing and expanding cognitive and verbal capacities allow the child to reflect on inner affective/emotional states, enabling him or her to understand, and hold, the difference between symbols and their affective meanings. For example, the child now can use a picture of her mother to comfort herself during the mother's absence, without confusing the picture with the actual affective experience of the mother. This process of collective, shared symbolization emerged clearly in the media coverage of Fidel Castro's death in November 2016.

After Castro's death was announced, Cuban Americans turned to the streets in Florida to gather in celebration. When people were interviewed on November 17, 2016, including ABC's anchor, Giovanni Benitez, he explained that he and others were not celebrating the death of a man, but rather the end of what he represented. His regime had tortured, oppressed and forced many into exile; his death represented the possibility of change, of a long-awaited, different Cuban sociopolitical future. Giovanni Benitez's remarks reflect the ability to differentiate the symbol from what it represented to millions of Cuban Americans, who were descendants of parents who had fled the brutality of Castro's regime. However, when the ability to separate the signifier (symbol) from the signified (meaning) is lost, or unavailable, a different narrative emerges, such as: we are celebrating and rejoicing the death of the man, Fidel Castro. In this later narrative, the person and what he represented have now become fused into one another, and the expression of joy is no longer related to the possibility of a better future, but rather joy over the actualization of murderous fantasies previously held about this Cuban dictator.

Cognition, within this context of symbol formation, emerges as the mediating mechanism by which children, and in the case of the United States, "White Native" children, learn to ascribe earlier, negative, distressing, non-verbal affective states to existing acceptable "White Native" symbols, such as the racialized, immigrant, or Mexican other. It is also through this cognitive ascription process that children, that is, "White Native" children, both affectively link, and learn and accept, their group's sociocognitive schemas about the other, thereby reifying the White Nativist social system in which they live, and its ideology. This cognitive process of affect and symbol ascription also explains how an ideology first operates out of awareness at an affective level. Before a child can comprehend and examine a particular ideology, he/she has already come to unconsciously and affectively accept it in an unquestioned, common sense, normalizing, non-ideological manner. In other words, the family's performance of the ideology, mediated by the caregiving process, serves to identify for the child the external symbols upon which negative, pre-cognitive, internal affects can be deposited.

It is important to emphasize here that racism, given this conceptual framework, emerges first as an affect-laden, pre-verbal experience, born out of consciousness, that helps American, "White Native" children to "avoid feeling object relations tension" (Volkan, 2013, p. 89), that is, tension a child would otherwise feel if he/she had to hold, without externalizing or attributing (projecting) to others, uncomfortable negative feelings about the self or a person he/she loves. Racism, in this context, functions as a mechanism by which "White Native" children can externalize their early, raw, unwanted affect onto caregivers' identified, acceptable, targets of externalization, namely, the racialized, brown, black "bad," immigrant, enemy other. This unconscious externalization process decreases the internal affective tension the child feels, and prevents feelings of internal fragmentation (annihilation of the self), that would otherwise be experienced given the raw affects of love and hate that pervade early psychological life. These intense loving and hateful feelings are well exemplified in toddlers, who intensely love their caregivers when they are being gratified by them, but quickly feel hate toward the same caregiver when she or he sets limits that thwart the toddler's wishes or wants, despite how illogical these wants may be.

Yet, just as the child externalizes negative unintegrated aspects of the self, the caregiver, and the caregiver-me relationship onto permanent, external, suitable reservoirs, he/she must also find permanent, external, suitable targets of externalization for unintegrated good aspects of the self and others (Volkan, 2013). Caregivers are again instrumental in this process, as they attribute and relate with positive affect to the language shared by the members of their group, as well as to the children's folktales, nursery songs, foods and religious traditions, all of which gradually come to be recognized by the children in that group as "'good targets of permanent externalization" (Volkan, 2013, p. 87). The pre-oedipal process of externalization, therefore, marks for the children of a common group both "the beginning of 'we-ness' and the beginning of Others in a concrete way" (Volkan, 2013, p. 88). In this manner, it establishes the initial foundation of what the child will come to conceptualize, during the oedipal stage of development, as their "ethnicity, nationality, or other large-group labels" (Vokan, 2013, p. 88). Consequently, these shared collective suitable targets of externalization link individual psychological processes to those of large groups (Volkan, 1998), and function as cultural amplifiers or cultural symbols.

In the case of "White Native" children, the traditional "White Native" foods and smells, the English language, etc., are shared, good, affect-laden, suitable targets of externalization, that function as cultural amplifiers. They are symbolic representations of the shared "White Native" cultural identity, rooted within the earlier, caregiving experience of childhood. These "good" external reservoirs form the intrapsychic and external representations of the "White Native" culture and are used by "White Natives" throughout life to establish and reify their culture and their sense of native belonging. As Volkan (1985, 2013) states,

> although [the suitable targets of externalization] are actually part of the environment rather than part of the child, the child will invest

something of himself in them accompanied by raw feelings of love and hate directed by early concepts of "mother-me."

(p. 235)

In this manner, the good, affect-laden, external reservoirs, shared by all children and adults of a certain group not only establish and maintain the intra-group's affective linking connection, but also link each member to the group's shared identity. Hence, individual group members are affectively, inextricably and personally, linked to their collective cultural symbols, as they bind each member to each other at an affective and sociocognitive level. Furthermore, since suitable targets of externalization

> contain parts of ourselves and are invested with certain emotions, for the rest of our lives (especially while in regressed states), we remain emotionally and intimately attached both to our own ethnic (or other identity) large-group and to our shared enemies.
>
> (Volkan, 1998, p. 2)

It is with Volkan's (1998) final conceptualization that the nature of what American "White Natives" experience as "being lost," threatened and under attack by the increasing presence of the immigrant other, clearly emerges: the "White Native," group-specific externalizations of unintegrated good aspects of the self and others that provide "White Natives" with comfort and ethnic reaffirmation. These cultural amplifiers tie them together as members of a shared, intrapsychic, collective experience and historical journey (Volkan, 2013). For example, the language spoken within the "White Native," caregiving relationship, the smells of the foods prepared and eaten, the religion practiced and its rituals, are all symbols, and function as amplifiers, of the "White Native" collective culture. But most importantly, these cultural amplifiers are symbols of the early unconscious loving emotions experienced by "White Native" children within the caregiver-me relationship.

The gradual transformation of the "White Native" external cultural symbols, due to the increasing presence of the immigrant other and of their American-born children, therefore, presents not only a concrete threat to the "White Native" culture, but also to the "White Native" individual and collective selves. Moreover, the slow "demise" of the "White Native" good, affect-laden permanent cultural symbols, also brings about the transformation of the internal, "White Native" individual and group borders, threatening to "contaminate its own large-group identity with the one belonging to the enemy..." (Volkan, 2009a). Within this context, the American child born to the Mexican, immigrant other, emerges now as a symbol of impending transformation and of increasingly diffused intrapsychic group boundaries, since the hybrid other is not always distinguishable from the "White Native," despite "White Native" claims of Hispanic otherness and unassimilability (see Chapters 8 and 9). This fear of being contaminated and perverted can be historically traced to the late nineteenth and early twentieth centuries, and continues to be articulated by contemporary academics, such as Huntington (2004b), right wing politicians, such as Donald Trump, and pervades current White Nativist sociopolitical immigration discourses.

Yet, the other, as discussed by Volkan (1998) is also intrapsychically needed by "White Natives," posing a paradox similar to, and yet different from, the one created by capitalism, which demands access to a cheap immigrant labor force. In other words, although "White Natives" experience "the other" as a threat to their culture and identity, they also need "this other" to maintain their collective, psychological stability and "White Native" identity due to the synthetic nature of this identity. The absence of a historical, shared collective past was first overcome through the development of the Nordic European identity, as illustrated in the sociopolitical historical analysis, eventually leading to the birthing of the native American identity and the American nation-state. The mythical quality of this historical native American identity (Volkan, 2013) emerged clearly in the sociopolitical historical critical analysis of the American citizenship and the Immigration Act of 1924. This mythical shared past, built on notions of "White Native" exceptionalism and manifest destiny (Guyatt, 2007) reflects the idealized nature of the American nation-state and of the "White Natives" who "built it." This idealization is best captured by congressman Charles Jared Ingersoll, in the 1830s–1840s, who when speaking about the future of the United States stated, "whenever I reflect on the destinies of this country, my mind is irresistibly carried forward from the past and the present, glorious and pleasant as they are, to the refulgent anticipations which illuminate the future" (as cited in Guyatt, 2007, p. 166).

This idealized, shared "White Native" identity is one in which "White Natives" have invested something important belonging to their individual and collective selves: "loving unintegrated affects related to the individual self, and to their early childhood. Yet, this "White Native," synthetic, idealized identity prevents "White Natives" from achieving a more realistic self representation, as it requires denying the existence of more complex aspects of their shared history, including the lack of a shared collective historical past and the legacy of slavery and genocide. For example, to maintain the idealized collective self, "White Natives" must deny the means by which they established their nation-state, and its implications for those subjugated by the White Nativist ideology. At the same time, the denial of this shared, collective, subjugating past leads to and supports the White Nativist ideology, which is an ideology consistent with what Volkan (2013) defines as entitlement ideologies.

Volkan (2013), when discussing entitlement ideologies and the mythical shared identities that support them, states that synthetic, collective groups, "deny difficulties and losses that had occurred during [their synthetic process], and imagine their large group as if it is composed of persons belonging to a superior species" (p. 184), such as in the case of "White Natives." The denial required to maintain this synthetic identity and its entitlement ideology, White Nativism, prevents the mourning of the unresolved, historical, collective, racial, ethnic and cultural trauma experienced, due to the means by which the American nation-state was built by "White Natives." This denied, collective racial, ethnic and cultural trauma continues to be intergenerationally transmitted, pervading the American sociopolitical life of the country, while remaining obscured by the idealization process required to maintain the "White Native" identity (Volkan, 2009b). At the same time, this process of collective self idealization, denial and thwarted mourning, maintains the ongoing devaluation and subjugation of those constructed as other, who are needed to function as external reservoirs of unintegrated, negative, individual and collective affects. If these unintegrated affective experiences were not externalized, they would lead to intra-group tension and to the eventual collective, psychological fragmentation of the "White Native" identity, exposing its mythical quality.

Given this conceptualization, the immigrant other is then a necessary "White Native" external reservoir of unintegrated "bad," negative aspects of the self, the caregiver, and the caregiving relationship. It is also one of the mechanisms by which "White Natives" have historically preserved their internal, collective homeostasis, and idealized synthetic identity, supported by the White Nativist, entitlement ideology. However, this individual and collective, "White Native" intrapsychic homeostasis cannot be maintained if the immigrant other's critical mass representation increases, threatening to transform the "White Native" culture; or, if the other begins to be less discernible from the "White Native," beginning to blur individual and group psychological boundaries and borders. This psychological analysis leads to a different conceptualization of immigration reform policy and an accompanying phenomenon, the birthing of American children that belong to the other. The hybrid "other" presents a problem. "White Native" "we-ness" and immigrant "otherness," as previously discussed, can no longer be clearly delineated at a psychological and cognitive level, since the American-born children of the immigrant, Mexican other have been born and raised in this country; and yet, they are other by nature of parentage which precludes them from being absorbed into the "White Native" group, unlike the descendants from earlier immigrant groups—Southern and Eastern European immigrants who shared a continental similarity.

## Collective mourning

By integrating Winnicott's and Volkan's conceptualization of the development of the self and the symbolization of culture into the sociopolitical historical critical analysis of immigration policy, it became possible to capture more clearly the nature of the fear experienced by "White Natives," as the demographic presence of the immigrant other continues to increase, albeit not due to immigration but due to natality (American Hispanics, 2015). It is not only the "White Native" culture that is being transformed and thus experienced as "dying" due to the increasing presence of the Hispanic other, but most poignantly it is the experience of the "White Native" self, as an integrated, continuous entity that feels threatened. The presence of the other, within this context, induces fear at an annihilatory level. News headings such as "Showdown over immigration: 'This is an invasion'" (Payne, Martinez, & Yan, 2014), or Bobby Jindel's remarks during the September, 2016 GOP immigration debate: "immigration without assimilation is invasion" (Salo, 2015), reflect the affective experience of "White Natives." They are being overtaken, which in turn evokes a need to defend and protect the self against the invader, the immigrant Mexican other, reawakening old historical traumas pertaining to the southern expansion of the United States into Mexican territory. In other words, the increasing presence of the Hispanic, Mexican, immigrant other and of the American citizen born to Mexican parents, seems to inevitably awaken intrapsychic fear, embedded within a historical context of aggression, war and annexation. This leaves the individual and collective "White Native" self vulnerable to experiences of psychological fragmentation and disintegration, causing an individual and collective psychological regression. This regression in turn propels a return to earlier individual and collective developmental stages that interfere with the symbolization process. This assertion is supported by Volkan's (2013) discussion of collective traumas and entitlement ideologies, where he states that the

> [r]eactivation of a large group's chosen trauma and an entitlement ideology linked to it leads to "time collapse." Feelings, thoughts, wishes, and fears stimulated by the shared reactivation of the chosen trauma and the entitlement ideology collapse into perceptions and effects about a current... conflict and magnif[y] danger.
>
> (p. 187)

In this regressive psychological state, the immigrant Mexican other is no longer a symbol of a previous enemy, but has become the enemy that during the 1830s had advanced into the north, eventually losing this territory in 1848 to the United States. In this protosymbolic state, the other, is "all bad," while the "White Native" individual and collective self is only "good," that is, hard-working, resilient, omnipotent, highly developed and cultured. This experience of psychological fragmentation, induced by the increasing presence of the immigrant other, and of their American-born children, is also augmented by the possible disappearance of the "White Native" external, good, affect-laden reservoirs and cultural amplifiers, never to be accessed again as originally remembered and unconsciously stored.

It is at this point that integrating individual psychological processes related to mourning and melancholia (Freud, 1917) could further complement the integrated analysis of immigration policy and White Nativism. Freud (1917), in discussing mourning, postulated that when an individual experiences the death of a loved object, he/she is confronted with the need to divest the loved object from the libido it had invested in it; however, he also stated that there is internal opposition/conflict experienced within the person, and "This opposition can be so intense that a turning away from reality takes place and a clinging to the object through the medium of a hallucinatory wishful psychosis [emerges]" (p. 244). How can Freud's conceptualization of libidinal forces and loss apply to "White Nativism" and to contemporary immigration policy debates in the United States?

Volkan (2009b) describes the mourning process as one in which the individual "[reviews] and psychologically [deals] with the mental representations of a lost person or thing" (p. 91). Yet, for an individual to mourn, he/she must first recognize that the loved person or thing has been lost. Unless the individual, through the reality-testing principle, is able to recognize this loss, he/she will be unable to begin to divest the loved object from the libidinal energy it had originally invested in it. However, do "White Natives" recognize their cultural identifications as something that has already changed and thus been lost as originally conceived or not? The answer to this question is essential in order to uncover and understand the complex forces fueling contemporary immigration debates.

"White Nativists," as described by Huntington (2004b) and Swain (2002) do not appear to think about their cultural identity as something that has already changed. Instead, they want to believe that their culture has remained untouched despite the impact of capitalism. They do, however, foresee a looming cultural demise; this demise seems to be attributed to the shifting demographic composition of the United States and the increasing presence of the other. Since "nothing" has thus far died, "White Natives" are not yet preoccupied with grieving and mourning their cultural loss and originally conceived idealized synthetic identity. It is important to note that such a process would also require "White Natives" to acknowledge, confront and mourn the implications of their role as perpetrators of violence against a number of historically, racialized groups, such as the Indigenous peoples of what is now the United States, African Americans and certain immigrant others. Embarking therefore in a mourning of the idealized, mythical "White Native" identity would lead "White Natives" to have to recognize the collective historical trauma upon which their American nation-state was built.

This collective, unprocessed trauma continues to reverberate within the social fabric of this nation, emerging into collective consciousness during moments of racial unrest precipitated, for example, by encounters between law enforcement officers and communities of color. These reverberations, that often times shatter the collective denial of the historical, American racial trauma, reflect the American societal inability to process the affective implications of the trauma. This trauma has remained largely un-mourned (Volkan, 2009a, 2009b), despite legislative policies that have sought to sociocognitively address the social inequalities produced by this legacy of racial, ethnic and cultural aggression and subjugation. In fact, Volkan (2013) when discussing large group, complicated mourning processes and entitlement ideologies states, "Affective aspects of some chosen traumas may remain dormant...[but] those that become connected with... 'entitlement ideologies' are prone to reactivation by emotions, and play a significant role in large-group social, political and military affairs" (p. 186).

It is not surprising that "White Natives" are continuing to perseverate in the denial of this more complex aspect of their historical identity, wanting to maintain their idealized synthetic identity, rather than engaging in a collective mourning process that would dismantle the sociocognitive schemas upon which their "White Native" identity and nation-state was built. Mourning the real, non-mythical nature of their identity would also evoke significant shared feelings of guilt, as well as complicated shared feelings of humiliation, within the subjugated others (Volkan, 2013). "White Natives," therefore, continue to invest group and individual libido into their nativist culture. A culture, that is a symbol and a reservoir of "White Native" group identifications and earlier affect-laden "caregiver-me" experiences that provide "White Natives" with individual and collective intrapsychic stability and sense of existential continuity.

On the other hand, this "love object/culture" that "White Natives" continue to cling to, appears to be facing a possible annihilation due to the increasing presence of the other. Hence, from the perspective of the "White Native," their culture will indeed "die," unless the other can be stopped in time. Immigration policy and, in particular, deportation reforms, provide "White Natives" with the necessary legal mechanism by which to stop the immigrant other, while concurrently, and covertly, forcing American-born children of Mexican parents to leave their own country. These dynamics will be explored in the analysis of IIRIRA and the AEDPA in Chapter 5.

## Integrated sociopolitical and psychological hypothesis: Implications for immigration reform

This review has uncovered a complex, unconscious, intrapsychic, "White Native" individual and group process of externalization, manifesting in historical sociocognitive schemas, related to identity formation and integration. That is, the externalization of affect-laden good and bad "mother-me" unintegrated aspects of the individual self onto acceptable, collective "suitable targets of externalization," (Volkan, 1985, 2013) provides "White Natives" with an unconscious mechanism by which to maintain their intrapsychic, individual and group identity (Volkan, 2013). This "White Native" externalization process also serves to legitimize affect driven behavior, as it supports and reifies sociocognitive schemas of "White Native" superiority, as well as native claims to the nation-state. This process also mediates the affective and sociocognitive integration of individual and collective identities, creating external, symbolic affective ties that bind White first-class citizens to each other, while legitimizing the White Nativist ideology of entitlement (Volkan, 2013). These affective ties, in turn, provide a sense of "shared affective experience" that supports the group's internal cohesion and identity. However, this internal cohesion can only be maintained if the unwanted and unintegrated aspects of the large group identity can be projected, deposited and thus externalized onto an other, in this case the Hispanic other. The presence of the Hispanic other, therefore, facilitates the integration of the "White Native," large group identity, while also providing an external reservoir of displaced "White Native," unintegrated aggression that would otherwise find expression within the "White Native" group. If not externalized, this aggression would challenge the existing, "White Native," mythical shared identity, as well as the affective and sociocognitive schemas that support this synthetic identity (Volkan, 2013), ultimately challenging their native claim to the United States.

Through the integrated sociopolitical and psychological analysis, immigration policy emerged as the sociocognitive, legal mechanism used by the United States to control its labor supply, as well as the legal mechanism used by "White Nativists" to avert mourning. Immigration policy, therefore, is best understood as a sociocognitive process, embedded in and informed by an intricate, unconscious "White Native" intrapsychic defense system that aims to protect the "White Native" individual and group psyche from a frightening realization. A cultural identity or "love object" has indeed died. Furthermore, the policy efforts that attempt to avert the collective mourning of the "White Native" identity will ultimately destroy the self of the "White Native." In other words, the collective denial of the synthetic original "White Native" identity prevents "White Natives" from integrating all aspects of their individual and collective selves, locking them into a position of forced narcissistic idealization and sociocognitive devaluation of those constructed as other. This collective denial also thwarts their ability to engage in and complete a normal mourning process by which the racial, ethnic and cultural collective trauma of the nation could be processed, stopping its intergenerational transmission. The failure to mourn, also precludes "White Natives" from achieving a different, more adaptive and integrated intrapsychic and sociocognitive individual and group "American self," a self that does not require the idealization of one group and subjugation of another. This new "American self" would free "White Natives," and the racialized other, from perennial social, large group, racial enactments in which members of each group have to adopt the position of perpetrator, victim or helpless bystander, with the associated feelings of fear, shame, humiliation and guilt that each of these positions may evoke (Volkan, 2009, 2013).

This new "White Native" identity would in turn reflect a reality-based affective and sociocognitive construction of the individual and large collective self, that is, a self devoid of the annihilatory fears and anxiety that currently fuel "White Native" efforts to preserve an identity that never existed, other than as affectively imagined, and sociocognitively constructed. However, efforts to preserve the existing "White Native" identity, only perpetuate existing annihilatory fears and anxieties, and can eventually lead to the gradual collapse of the American nation-state. Efforts to avert mourning and protect the "White Native" identity are resulting in the covert, forced expulsion of American citizen children of Mexican parentage, often rupturing families permanently. These efforts are also marginalizing the caregivers and children that remain in the United States, with lasting emotional and financial consequences for the families and for society at large.

Yet, how is this White Nativist, American immigration, sociopolitical context impacting the ethnic identification, acculturation and sense of national belonging of American-born children of Hispanic immigrant parents? And most importantly, is the current White Nativist, immigration, sociopolitical discourse indeed producing what it fears? That is, American-born children, of Hispanic heritage, who, despite living in the United States, are not "assimilating" into the larger American society, as they are struggling to conceptualize their individual selves as belonging to the larger American society. Furthermore, given White Nativist assimilationist discourses that posit that adherence to ethnic particularisms prevents the societal integration of the Hispanic other, does an ethnic identification preclude American-born children of Mexican immigrant parents from developing a sense of national belonging?

Ross's (1997) conceptualization of ethnic conflict and cultural contestation can provide a bridge by which to begin to examine the dynamics related to perceived collective and individual self-continuity and belonging (Sani, Bowe, & Herrera, 2008)—especially as it pertains to the "White Native" identity, the Hispanic, Mexican, immigrant other and their American-born children, who are the recipients of the White Nativist aggression manifest in the current immigration sociopolitical context of the United States. Ross (1997), as well as Volkan (1985, 2009a, 2009b, 2013), believes that "[c]ultural identities, such as ethnicity, connect individuals through perceived common past experiences and expectations of shared future ones" (p. 22). The experience of a shared future is what feels threatened when an aspect of a group's culture, or in this case two groups, "White Natives" and the Hispanic other, appear to be in conflict with each other, and thus under attack and in need of protection. The annihilatory fear evoked in each group (Davies, Steele, & Markus, 2008) can, in turn, propel a process of cultural contestation designed to defend their threatened collective identities and collective selves (Abdelal, Herrera, Johnston, & McDermott, 2009; Ross, 1997). This process of ethnic preservation and contestation is well captured and explained by Cordell and Wolf (2010), who state that,

> ethnic groups perceive threats and opportunities. The more deeply felt are these perceptions, the more they will be linked to the very survival of the group… This links the issue of ethnicity to the notion of political

power... [and it] has important political consequences in that any ethnic group that is conscious of its uniqueness... strives to acquire the amount of power it deems necessary in order to preserve its identity as a distinct ethnic group—that is, to defeat the threats and seize the opportunities it faces.

(p. 84)

In the next section, the integrated analysis of immigration policy will discuss various conceptualizations of ethnicity, acculturation and national belonging, examining dynamics of power and cultural contestation, and their implications for the individual and collective self of the American-born children of the Hispanic, immigrant other.

## Note

1 This chapter, as well as some subsequent ones, includes content from a previously published article: Farina (2013).

# Part III

# Integrated sociopolitical and psychological framework

Ethnic identity, acculturation and sense of national belonging

# 4 Conceptualization of ethnic identity, acculturation and sense of national belonging of Hispanic youth

Until now the integrative analysis has examined the historical etiological, affective and sociocognitive processes leading to the formation of the "White Native" identity and its entitlement ideology, White Nativism. However, how does the immigrant other conceptualize their individual and collective self? And, how does the White Nativist sociopolitical context of the United States, in which contemporary immigration policy reforms are embedded, affect the identity, acculturation and national sense of belonging of the Hispanic immigrant other and their American-born children? This chapter will explain how dynamics of power and subjugation may affect the identity development of the ethnic other, and its relevance to the analysis of contemporary immigration policy reforms and White Nativism. The integrated sociopolitical and psychological analysis will also discuss how the current immigration sociopolitical context affects the acculturation processes of the American-born Hispanic youth and their sense of national belonging.

## Conceptualization of ethnic identity

### Social identity

Stern (1995) and Ross (1997), similar to Volkan's (1988, 2013) views on collective identities and affective linking processes, conceptualize social identity development as an affective and sociocognitive process that links individuals to a large group. Ross (1997) writes: "Social identity, including attachment to a group, begins to develop at the earliest stages of the lifecycle and its intensity is crucial to explaining why people are willing to make great personal sacrifices in its name" (p. 22). These sacrifices that manifest as cultural enactments during ethnic conflict reflect "collective psychological and social processes" (Ross, 1997, p. 12), that link a group's collective, affective experience to that of their large group, social identities. Social identity has been defined in a variety of ways. Tajfel (1982) defines social identity,

> as that part of the individual's self-concept which derives from their knowledge of their membership of a social group (or groups) together

with the value and emotional significance attached to that membership....Some of these memberships are more salient than others; and some vary in salience in time and as a function of a variety of social situations.

(pp. 2–3)

Tajfel's definition (1982) refers to aspects of an individual self-concept that become most prominent depending on the context surrounding the person and/or group (Ashmore, Deaux, & McLaughlin-Volpe, 2004; Miller & Garragan, 2008; Stryke & Serpe, 1982). The current American sociopolitical immigration context, as the integrated policy analysis showed, is one marked by "White Native" political claims and legal statutes that seek to control the Hispanic other, to prevent the contestation of the "White Native" social identity and culture. Yet, Tajfel's (1982) definition does not fully capture the dynamics of power that pervade the sociopolitical, national environments in which group and individual identities develop, and are contested to ensure the survival of those identities (Cordell & Wolf, 2010; Ross, 1997; Simon, Aufderheide & Kampmeier, 2004; Tajfel, 1982).

Power dynamics are central to a discussion of individual and collective self-identities and American immigration policy. Existing "White Native" identity constructions render the identity of the American-born Hispanic other as inherently incompatible with the "White Native" identity, due to parental ethnic, racial and cultural heritage (Deschamps, 1982; Ross, 1995). The Hispanic other, regardless of birthing origin, is considered "too different" to assimilate within the "White Native" identity construct (Citrin & Sears, 2009; Huntington, 2004). This perceived failure to assimilate leads to othering constructions, that prime the Hispanic other as an ideal suitable target of externalization, where unintegrated, "White Native," negative affect can be placed (Crocker & Quinn, 2004; Volkan, 1985). These "White Native" feelings and externalizations manifest sociopolitically as behaviors, political claims and legal statutes that devalue, and can damage, the sense of self of the "Hispanic other," fostering a sense of marginalization and alienation (Crocker & Quinn, 2004; Miller & Garragan, 2008). This dominant devaluation and hostility frequently manifests through the social "assignment of evil" to the other (Scheibe, 1995, p. 200), and in this case the Hispanic Mexican other, referred to as a criminal, rapist or as intellectually inferior. In fact, Nolan and Branscombe (2008), when discussing the human self and moral exclusions, elaborate on this process of vilification, highlighting its historical implications "...history is replete with examples of dehumanizing conceptions of the other such that only members of one's own subgroup are equated with what it means to be human" (p. 205). Nolan and Branscombe's (2008) conceptualization makes explicit and links negative group ascriptions to dangerous historical processes, where the dehumanization of the subjugated other led to the legitimization of their mass genocide.

## The self-concept and social identity

Tajfel's (1982) social identity conceptualization links individual, self-concept constructions to group membership (Markus & Kurf, 1987; Tajfel, 1982). However, why is the individual self-concept pertinent to a discussion of immigration policy, deportation, White nativism and the sense of national belonging of the American-born Hispanic other? And, how is the self-concept defined?

There are multiple definitions of the self-concept, and the construct itself is often vague and difficult to research. Markus and Kurf (1987) define the self-concept as "dynamic… and capable of change…" (p. 299), explaining that, "it interprets and organizes self-relevant actions and experiences" (p. 299). Scheibe (1995) and Oyserman (2004) define it as that part of the identity that helps us describe who we are individually and as part of a collective group. Oyserman (2004) expands this definition, explaining that "Self-concepts differ in complexity (Linville, 1987), organization of positive and negative self-relevant information (Showers, Abramson, & Hogan, 1998), and the extent that they promote persistent striving versus disengagement, sense of general contentment or incipient despair" (p. 5). Oyserman's definition (2004) is particularly relevant, as it highlights the disengagement and despair that individuals may experience in certain devaluing and subjugating contexts, such as the one in which American-born children of Mexican immigrant parents are growing up in.

Erikson (1968) further contextualizes the self-concept as historically determined, stating that "the historical era in which [a child] lives offers only a limited number of socially meaningful models for workable combinations of identity fragments" (pp. 53–4). Erikson's (1968) conceptualization emphasizes the inability to separate individual growth from societal/collective change, suggesting that it is impossible to "…separate the identity crisis in individual life and contemporary crises in historical development because the two help to define each other" (p. 28). Contemporary research efforts, recognizing the importance of the social context in determining aspects of the individual and collective self-concept/identity, have focused on exploring how certain social contexts, such as a subjugating one, influence "…self-concept development, content, and structure, [as well as] the behavioral, motivational, and affective consequences of self-concept[s]" (Oyserman, 2004, p. 12).

Social contexts, however, are not static. It is this tension of continuity and change that creates the paradox embedded within any individual and collective identity (Chandler & Proulx, 2008; Ethier & Deaux, 1994; Sarbin, 2000), and that is relevant to a discussion of identity preservation and contestation; that is, the individual self-concept and its associated collective identity function in two opposite ways. A lack of individual and collective self-continuity threatens the survival of the person and group; however, this continuity is challenged by the temporal nature of the self-concept, which is shaped by the historical context in which the individual and groups exist (Diehl & Hay, 2007; Markus & Kurf, 1987). Contexts are fluid and influenced by many forces, such as socioeconomic forces related to the global and American capitalist system, that require the exchange of transnational manpower as a means of production. Within this capitalist socioeconomic context, the presence of the immigrant other in the United States is necessary and welcomed, as long as this immigrant other can be controlled and is clearly identifiable as an immigrant and as other. However, American-born children of the Mexican other are not immigrants, nor are they clearly identifiable as other, symbolizing a social context marked by change and transformation, which in turn challenges existing American, "White Native," self-conceptualizations.

## Self-concept and devalued social identity research

When a social context fosters the dominance of a particular group, it promotes the development of a collective, self-concept that is often marked by claims of exceptionalism and superiority (Volkan, 2013; Wodak, 2015; Wodak, Cillia, Reisigl, & Liebhart, 2009). At the same time, a dominant group's collective self-concept also shapes, reifies and reproduces the social structures and policies of the context that fostered the group's dominant self-concept, in what becomes a circular and hermeneutic process (Van Djik, 2000; Woodak, 2015). This psychological, sociopolitical, legal process produces, and reproduces in turn, social inequality and supports the construction of a necessary devalued and subjugated other (Derrida, 1984). Oyserman (2004) makes explicit these contextual dynamics of power, dominance, subjugation and marginalization when she states that "social contexts enable, elicit, and scaffold certain selves while disenabling, suppressing, and dismantling others even in the face of what might appear to be objective evidence of these self-dimensions" (p. 13).

Self-concept research has often examined the influence that devalued social identity markers such as race, ethnicity, gender, etc., have on the development of individual self-concepts (Crocker & Quinn, 2004). This research has primarily sought to understand the consequences of the devaluation without considering the contextual aspects of the individual (Ashmore et al., 2004; Ethier & Deaux, 1994). This de-contextualization has led to assertions pertaining to internalizations of negative projections or externalizations (Volkan, 1988; Winnicott, 1965), in a static and non-context-dependent manner (Yip, 2005), rather than as temporary, context dependent "psychological states" (Crocker & Quinn, 2004, p. 131). The research on stigma has also focused on the internalization of the devaluation, failing to recognize the complexity of "...the social context and features of the immediate situation in which the stigmatized find themselves" (Croker & Quinn, 2004, p. 125), paying significantly more attention to the devaluation and its effects on the self-esteem of the devalued other (Bodkin-Andrews, O'Rourke & Graven, 2010; Cohen & Garcia, 2005; Crocker & Quinn, 2004).

This research emphasis can be partially understood as stemming from a number of accepted social psychology theories in which prejudice is believed to invariably "damage the self-esteem of its target" (Branscombe, Schmitt, & Harvey, 1999, p. 135). However, Ashmore et al. (2004) present a more complex conceptualization that considers the intersectionality of the context with the specific individual self-concept held by the person. This conceptualization recognizes the existing protective factors that devalued groups and individuals can use to preserve their positive self-regard. Ashmore et al. (2004) suggest that the effects of the devaluation are contingent on the social context of the person and on the importance the devalued identity marker has for the person's individual self-concept. Hence, Ashmore et al. (2004) suggest that two levels should be considered when assessing self-concept importance: "explicit importance" and "implicit importance" (p. 87). Explicit importance refers to "...the individual's subjective appraisal of the degree to which collective identity is important to her or his overall sense of self" (p. 87); and, implicit importance refers to "the placement from low to high, of a particular group membership in the person's hierarchically organized self-system" (p. 87).

Ashmore et al.'s findings (2004) are not new to the field of self-psychology; Crocker and Major (1989) after reviewing research conducted over 20 years in the area of stigma and self-esteem concluded that, "...prejudice against members of stigmatized or oppressed groups generally does not result in lowered self-esteem for members of the stigmatized group" (p. 611). It is important to emphasize that this finding does not imply that prejudice and discrimination do not negatively affect those who are devalued and subjugated, but is rather understood as capturing complex processes that also recognize contextual and individual variables that can mitigate or resist the effects of subjugation and devaluation. Crocker and Major's (1989) findings support Ashmore et al.'s (2004) theory of devaluation and also complement it, by exploring how attributional processes may function as protective defense mechanisms. Croker and Major (1989) found that stigmatized groups can use the presence of prejudice to attribute to it negative feedback, rather than internalizing it as an accurate appraisal of the self. Likewise, identifying with a group can also help maintain positive individual self-appraisals, as "People experience increases in self-esteem when fellow group members succeed" (Cohen & Garcia, 2005, p. 566).

McCoy and Major (2003), however, found some limitations to the protective effects of attributional processes (Ashmore et al., 2004; Crocker & Major, 1989). In their quantitative study of group identification and "self-evaluative emotions" (depression and self-esteem) (McCoy & Major, 2003, p. 1005) McCoy and Major showed that attributional processes only preserved a positive self-concept when the person's identification with the devalued group was low, that is, "...for highly group identified individuals, prejudice against the in-group is a threat against the self" (p. 1005). However, in the case of the Hispanic other, the disowned "White Native" aggression pervading current immigration sociopolitical discourses does not appear to have the effects predicted by McCoy and Major (2003). This contradiction is clearly illustrated by the Hispanic paradox and acculturation research.

## The Hispanic Paradox: Implications of de-contextualizing research

Epidemiological studies conducted to evaluate the physical and mental health of immigrant children show "...a health advantage... among first-generation young immigrants compared to U.S.-born Anglo-American adolescents, including both better mental health and less risk behavior, [however, this health advantage] seems to vanish over the generations" (Oppedal, Roysamb, & Heyerdahl, 2005, p. 646). This health paradox (Oppedal et al., 2005) has also been found in epidemiological studies about the Hispanic population, resulting in what has been called the Hispanic Paradox (Castro et al., 2007).

In 1998, The National Research Council Institute of Medicine, after conducting a review of the research compiled on the health of children of immigrants, concluded that the health advantage present in first generation young Hispanic immigrants, who exhibited better mental health and less risk behaviors than their US-born, Anglo-American counterparts, disappeared by the third generation (Oppedal et al., 2005). Multiple studies have tried to explain the health advantage of Hispanic, first generation immigrants and children (National Research Council and Institute of Medicine, 1998, 1999), controlling for various factors, such as assimilation, acculturation, cultural risk and protective factors, as well as ethnic identity, among others. Castro et al. (2007), in their quantitative study of cultural protective factors, where 23 father–son pairs were sampled, found a positive correlation between higher acculturation levels; higher prevalence of health problems in Hispanic youth; and, increasing identity formation conflicts among Hispanic children with higher acculturation levels, consistent with Szapocznik and Kurtines' research (1989).

Similarly, Coatsworth, Maldonando-Molina, Pantin and Szapocznik (2005) when studying the connection between acculturation strategies in Hispanic immigrant youth and health, using a sample of 315 Hispanic youth, identified high assimilation levels as predictive of a higher incidence of behavioral problems. Wadsworth and Kubrin (2007) and Rogler, Cortes and Malgady (1991) also reported an analogous positive relationship between assimilation and increasing mental health problems. In fact, Wadsworth and Kubrin (2007) citing Sorenson and Jacqueline (1988) stated that "Mexican-Americans born in Mexico displayed significantly lower suicide levels than Mexican Americans born in the United States, with the lowest levels documented among those least assimilated into the U.S. culture" (p. 1854). It is also important to note that both Wadsworth and Kubrin (2007) and Sorenson and Jaqueline (1988) found that overall, Hispanics, even when controlling for nativity, exhibited a lower suicide risk than non-Hispanic whites "arguably the most assimilated group" (Wadsworth & Kubrin, 2007, p. 1854).

This brief overview of the Hispanic Paradox and research seems to challenge traditional notions of acculturation, that have suggested that higher acculturation levels, and ultimately assimilation, lead to better immigrant mental health outcomes. These traditional notions presumed that increasing familiarity with the country of reception, and its dominant culture, would gradually decrease the stress associated with having to navigate the new environment and culture (Phinney, 1992; Rogers-Sirin, Ryce, & Sirin, 2014). What contemporary research seems to suggest, instead, is that higher acculturation levels place children of immigrants at higher risk for physical and mental health problems, suggesting that increasing American-ness poses a health risk to children of immigrants (Rogers-Sirin et al., 2014). These contemporary findings create an inherent conflict, as "White Natives" argue for assimilation as proof of Americanization, and Americanization seems to be associated to increasing health risks among children of immigrants.

## Conceptualization of acculturation

Current research efforts pertaining to the Hispanic Paradox have begun to identify methodological problems related to the operational definition of acculturation. Initial research on acculturation followed a linear, unidimensional model which presumed that an individual's gradual abandonment of his/her original immigrant culture, coupled with the gradual incorporation of the host country's culture, culminated in the individual's final assimilation to the host culture and nation (Abraido-Lanza, Armbrister, Florez, & Aguirre 2006; Berry, 2005; Castro et al., 2007; Coatsworth et al., 2005). This definition privileged assimilation over other possible acculturation strategies, such as biculturalism, and measured acculturation against the white dominant culture, excluding dynamics pertaining to segmented assimilation theory (Abraido-Lanza et al., 2006; Berry, 2005; Coatsworth et al., 2005).

More recent research on acculturation has been conducted from a multidimensional model perspective, although unidimensional research still predominates (Abraido-Lanza et al., 2006; Berry, 2003; Coatsworth et al., 2005). As discussed by Zane and Mak (2003) and Coatsworth et al. (2005) multidimensional models vary significantly in the psychological functional domains they emphasize, and contain "specific assumptions about how a person can change" (p. 42); that is, many models presume "…a bipolar adaptation in which individual ties and psychological involvement with their culture of origin weakens as they acculturate to the majority culture" (Zane & Mak, 2003, p. 42).

## Berry's acculturation model

Berry's acculturation model (2001, 2003), however, recognizes that it is possible for a person to acculturate to the dominant culture without decreasing his/her individual and psychological ties to his/her ethnic group culture, developing instead what Berry (2002, 2003) refers to as acculturation strategies. Berry (2003) identified four strategies individuals can employ to adapt to their immigration context: assimilation, integration, separation and marginalization. Each of these strategies evolves along two different dimensions; the first dimension pertains to "the degree of actual contact and the resulting participation of each group with the other" (Berry, 2001, p. 617); and, the second is concerned with "the degree of cultural maintenance manifested by each group" (Berry, 2001, p. 617).

Within this dimensional model, assimilation strategies are understood as reflecting the individual's desire to adhere to the host country's dominant group's culture, while seeking ongoing interaction within the societal mainstream of the host country. Integration strategies reflect the person's desire to maintain their own cultural values and beliefs, while seeking ongoing interaction within the dominant mainstream society. Separation strategies, conversely, indicate a person's desire to adhere to their cultural heritage, while avoiding interaction with other societal groups. Lastly, marginalization strategies reflect a rejection of both the person's original cultural heritage and the dominant group's culture, as well as a lack of desire to interact as part of the dominant societal mainstream, often "for reasons of exclusion or discrimination" (Berry, 2001, p. 619). Berry's (2003) multidimensional and multilinear model highlights the influence of the social and ecological context on the individual, and the relational and reciprocal nature of acculturation processes (Abraido-Lanza et al., 2006). The model examines the degree to which each group seeks contact and participates with each other, as well as the level of cultural adherence within each group, which allows for varying degrees of intra-group permeability, that is, from complete impermeability to full permeability and assimilation. The varying degrees of intra-group permeability are contextual, and depend on the nature of the systemic societal structures in which the groups exist (Berry, 2001, 2003).

This multidimensional conceptualization adds further measuring complexity to the acculturation construct (Coatsworth et al., 2005); and, highlights the transactional quality of acculturation also proposed by Abraido-Lanza et al. (2006) and Coatsworth et al. (2005). All of these conceptualizations emphasize that an individual's ability to integrate him/herself within a certain community is not only contingent on the individual and his/her own individual characteristics, but is also subject to the host country's historical and sociopolitical context in relation to the individual's ethnic group (Abraido-Lanza et al., 2006; Berry, 2003).

As posited by Berry (2003), cultural integration cannot be attained unless there is "…a mutual accommodation…, involving the acceptance by both groups of the right of all groups to live as culturally different peoples within the civic framework of the larger society" (p. 24). This conceptualization also suggests that a sociopolitical contextualization of acculturation research is essential. In fact, acculturation research that fails to account for the historical and ecological context of the immigrant other, and that "Simplif[ies] culture into 'ethnic, 'assimilated,' or other 'risk' categories... can inadvertently fuel weak explanations of health disparities by focusing attention on culture rather than on structural constraints..." (Abraido-Lanza et al., 2006, p. 1344). Given the current Immigrant Health and Hispanic Paradox, it follows to question whether some elements reflect not paradoxes, but rather a failure to expand research efforts from a micro, culturally based focus to a relational, cultural and structural, person in environment model, as postulated by Coatsworth et al. (2005) and Berry (2003).

Abraido-Lanza et al. (2006), consistent with Berry's (2003) acculturation model, highlight the importance of examining how national policies inhibit or foster specific individual acculturation strategies. Abraido-Lanza et al. (2006), who examined health disparities influencing immigrant groups by comparing the health outcomes of the Cuban population in the U.S. to that of other Hispanic immigrant groups, illustrate well the importance of considering structural elements. In their study, Abraido-Lanza et al. (2006) questioned whether the health advantage displayed by the Cuban population living in the U.S. was not a paradox per se, but rather a byproduct of immigration policies. Their discussion contextualized the findings, contrasting the American immigration policies enacted to support the integration of Cuban immigrants fleeing from the Castro regime between 1960 and 1970, to the less hospitable immigration policies encountered by Salvadorans and Mariel Cubans immigrants. Their discussion ended with a question analogous to the one explored in this chapter: "What is the impact (if any) of ... historical and political factors on acculturation processes and health outcomes, and how might they contribute to different patterns among the various Latino groups in the United States?" (p. 1345). To answer this question, it is important to explore further what is understood as acculturation, and how it interacts with existing conceptualizations of what it means to be an American.

## Acculturation and American national identity

American, "White Native" concern over multicultural discourses has been growing, recently pervading sociopolitical, immigration discourses. Donald Trump's right wing platform spoke directly to "White Native" fears (Wodak, 2015), polarizing White Nativists against Mexicans through a fear-based, assimilationist ideology. "White Native" assimilationists reject multicultural, societal conceptions, stating that a multicultural ideology (Berry, 2001) encourages the adherence and preservation of ethnic, foreign, cultural values and traditions, discouraging the assimilation efforts of the immigrant other. Within this context, a multicultural national construction of the United States is understood as inherently antithetical to the "White Native" assimilationist ideology, increasing "White Native" fears pertaining to the potential erosion of "a national American Identity" (Renshon, 2000, p. 259; Glazer, 1993). However, Renshon (2000) problematizes the use of national American Identity as a self-explanatory construct that does not require further explanation (Van Dijk, 2001, 2002), asking for further conceptual clarity, stating, "Just what is the nature of the culture to which we want immigrants to assimilate?" (p. 295). As Abraido-Lanza et al. (2006) discuss, acculturation research has often measured acculturation in terms of the acquisition of "…a standardized set of values, primarily those associated with 'White American culture' (p. 1344); such a measure implicitly equates "White Native" cultural norms as "…markers for American-ness" (p. 1344). The acceptance of this measure as an indicator of successful Americanization excludes other existing American cultural markers, such as those belonging to African Americans, Indigenous peoples, and other "non-white" American ethnic groups. This methodological and conceptual acceptance concurrently supports the White Nativist ideology, as it reproduces through academia, standards that normalize the enthronement of White Europeans as the only natural, native Americans to this land.

## Segmented assimilation theory

Segmented assimilation, on the other hand, recognizes the complexity of the acculturation process (Abraido-Lanza et al., 2006; Gratton, Gutmann, & Skop 2007; Portes, Fernandez-Kelly, & Haller, 2005; Portes & Rumbaut, 2006). This conceptualization postulates that the assimilation process of immigrant groups is not only determined by the immigrant other, and his/ her willingness to assimilate, but is also determined by: (1) the particular characteristics of the host country; (2) the country's dominant sociopolitical discourse; (3) the country's structural policies; and (4) the dominant views of the ethnic group to which the immigrant other belongs. Under this view, "The process of 'growing up American'" (Portes & Zhou, 1993) can lead to two different outcomes, with important consequences for the American-born children of immigrant parents. Depending on the characteristics of the child, the immigrant parents' ethnic group and the country's sociopolitical context influencing their development (Portes & Zhou, 1993), American-born children of immigrant parents can either engage in upward or downward assimilation. In upward assimilation, immigrant children identify with "…the socioeconomic status, family structure, fertility and marital features common to the [White] majority of native-born persons in the U.S." (Gratton et al., 2007, p. 2). In downward assimilation, the children identify with the "…socio-economic status and family structure among native-born groups marginalized by racial or ethnic prejudice" (Gratton et al., 2007, p. 2).

Overall, existing research suggests that American-born children of immigrant parents have assimilated, and will continue to do so in regards to language acquisition, English and knowledge of mainstream dominant cultural norms (Alba & Nee, 2003; Gratton et al., 2007; Portes et al., 2005).

Nonetheless, these assimilation markers have proven insufficient, since White Nativists' concern over the "Americanization" of American-born children of immigrants has continued to grow. This concern has been further augmented by the findings of epidemiological studies involving the Immigrant and Hispanic Paradox, and by the observed downward assimilation path of "a sizable minority" of these children (Portes et al., 2005, p. 1032), albeit, not the primary assimilation path for the majority of American-born children of immigrants. Nonetheless, scholars such as Gratton et al. (2007) and Portes et al. (2005) have been calling attention to the risks posed by downward assimilation, as well as to the danger of ignoring the social forces that fuel such an outcome, since American-born children of immigrants account for an increasingly larger percentage of the American birth rate (Portes et al., 2005; Urban Institute, 2010). The implications of segregating and marginalizing an increasingly larger segment of American society are significant and can have lasting effects not only for the Hispanic other, but also for society at large. To address the consequences of these social inequities, Gratton et al. (2007) and Portes et al. (2005) advocate for a policy context that fosters social programs designed to facilitate "selective acculturation... [providing] compensatory resources to deal with poverty and outside discrimination" (Portes et al., 2005, p. 1033).

While the majority of American-born children of immigrant families do not follow a downward assimilation path, as predicted by segmented assimilation theory, not all ethnic groups face the same barriers when trying to integrate into the mainstream of American society. Existing research indicates that American-born children of Mexican immigrant parents are at greater risk than other groups for downward assimilation (Gratton et al., 2007; Portes & Rumbaut, 2001; Portes & Zhou, 1994) due to their parents' low human capital; and the "...negative [American] context of reception" (Gratton et al., 2007, p. 277), due to the anti-Mexican rhetoric that has characterized the nation's immigration and sociopolitical discourse for "over 100 years" (Gratton et al., 2007; Portes & Rumbaut, 2001).

The higher risk toward down assimilation for the children of Hispanic immigrants is certainly cause for concern. Equally troubling is how White Nativists use this increased risk, within contemporary, White Nativist, sociopolitical immigration discourses (Huntington, 2004b), interpreting it as evidence of the Hispanic other's reluctance to assimilate. In fact, this higher risk allows "White Natives" to locate the problem within the Hispanic immigrant and his/her children, preventing the examination of both the social context in which the Hispanic other finds him/herself, and the structural forces exerting pressure on the nature of their assimilation path (Citrin & Sears, 2009; Gratton et al., 2007). This contextual neglect, allows "White Natives" to continue to actively legitimize their dominant societal position under an ideology of superiority and entitlement (Van Dijk, 2000; Volkan, 2013; Wodak 2015), while blaming the Hispanic other for the effects of the White Nativist, subjugating sociopolitical context. "White Natives" also use the greater risk toward downward assimilation to reify, support and maintain "White Native," decontextualized, negative, sociocognitive and affective schemas about the Mexican other. These sociocognitive and affective constructions produce and become social, self-fulfilling prophecies (Aleinikoff & Rumbaut, 1998) that allow "White Natives" to construct the Hispanic other as an assimilative challenge and identity threat. Thus, the presence of the Hispanic other symbolizes a possible American cultural demise, and "...the replacement of white culture by black or brown cultures that are intellectually and morally inferior" (Huntington, 2004a, p. 41).

Within this White Nativist sociopolitical context of identity contestation and survival, "White Natives" (Huntington, 2004a; Swain, 2002) seem to compare the assimilation pattern of the "Hispanic other" against the assimilation pattern of Southern and Eastern European immigrants, during the 1890s and 1920s. This era and immigration wave, often referred to as the 'classic case,' is held as the assimilation standard against which all subsequent immigrant groups are compared, when evaluating their assimilation success or failure, and thus their successful "Americanization" (Citrin & Sears, 2009; Gratton et al., 2007; Sidanius, Feshback, Levin, & Partto, 1997). However, the Americanization process by which this 'classic case' became first White, and then American, is omitted from these analyses. This omission maintains the White Nativist ideological hegemony, and re-focuses the gaze of the observer (Jacobson, 1998) away from White Nativist dynamics of subjugation and marginalization, and toward the subjugated other, who is now "failing to become American." The effects of the White Nativist, devaluing ideology are thus obscured, and the other becomes the subject of sociopolitical discourse. This discourse about identity, culture and acculturation, is aided by unidimensional conceptualizations of acculturation that privilege assimilation. These conceptualizations also juxtapose assimilation, and thus Americanization, to ethnic cultural pluralism, defining the latter as inherently erosive and undermining to a cohesive, American national identity.

The increasing concern over the "Hispanic assimilation problem" (Huntington, 2004a) and its "White Native" feared byproduct, "...the disuniting of America..." (Sidanius et al., 1997, p. 102), has raised questions about "...whether it is possible to foster loyalty to and identification with one's own ethnic particularism, while at the same time, maintaining shared national values and a sense of common national identification" (Sidanius et al., 1997, p. 103). This notion of a common national identification is relevant to the current conflict surrounding immigration and immigration reform. It leads to question whether or not American children of Mexican immigrant parents can experience themselves as belonging to the collective self of the United States, when the immigration sociopolitical context reflected in policies enacted since 1996 treats them as "other" due to their parents' ethnicity and immigration status. At the same time, and most importantly, can these children experience themselves as belonging to the collective self of the United States, when their ethnic heritage defines and constructs them as a threat to the "White Native" individual and collective identity? These are the questions that will subsequently be explored.

## National belonging, ethnic pluralism and patriotism

Until this point, identity has been discussed as related to the individual and collective self-concept of a group, leading to an exploration of ethnic and cultural pluralism and assimilation. These are all aspects of a complex, conscious and unconscious, "White Native," identity contestation process that is taking place through contemporary immigration policy. Both ethnicity and acculturation are thought to influence the American sense of national belonging of the immigrant other. Yet, national belonging is a construct that can be defined in multiple ways, and that often appears linked to discussions about patriotism and nationalism. However, does patriotism measure an individual's sense of national belonging? And, is there a difference between patriotism and nationalism? Kosterman and Feshbach (1989) provide construct and operational clarity when examining the relationship between individuals and their nation-state, defining patriotism and nationalism as two separate constructs with different implications. Kosterman and Feshbach (1989) defined patriotism as a measure of "...the affective component of one's feelings toward one's country" (p. 271); and, nationalism as "...reflect[ing] a perception of national superiority and an orientation toward national dominance" (p. 271).

Garza, Falcon and Garcia (1996), Sidanius et al. (1997) and Citrin and Sears (2009) examined national belonging as a function of patriotism. Two of these studies used data collected before or in 1996, providing an opportunity to examine how the White Nativist, anti-immigrant context may have affected the sense of national belonging of the Hispanic other.

Garza et al. (1996) studied patriotism as part of the ethnic civic incorporation of Mexican-Americans in the United States, using data collected through the 1989–1990 Latino National Political Survey (LNPS). The data sample preceded the immigration policy shift toward interior enforcement, and the deportation reforms enacted since 1996. In their study, Garza et al. (1996) concluded that Mexican-Americans, independent of acculturation level, were "...no less likely and often more likely to endorse values of individualism and patriotism than Anglos" (p. 335). These findings directly challenge "White Native" claims, articulated by academics such as Huntington (2004b), where Hispanics' ethnic identifications were understood as interfering with their assimilation process and therefore, with the development of a sense of national belonging, as manifested in patriotism.

Nonetheless, Garza et al. (1996) emphasize the importance of distinguishing between cultural assimilation and structural integration, stating that assimilation does not inherently produce integration. In fact, Garza et al. (1996), found that, despite evidence of patriotism among Mexican Americans, as they became more familiar with the "American culture," they were more able to recognize the structural racial barriers preventing their upward mobility, leading to resentment. Portes and Zhou's (1994) research, which focused on the experience of Mexican-American youth in the United States, also reported similar findings, linking systemic, White Nativism to the downward assimilation path followed by some American children of Hispanic parents. Their study showed that American-born children of Mexican parents "…seeing their parents and grandparents confined to menial jobs and increasingly aware of discrimination by the white mainstream… [joined] reactive subcultures as a means of protecting their sense of self-worth…" (pp. 27–8), complicating their access to upward mobility.

Sidanius et al. (1997), using two data sets; one based on data collected in 1993 from 823 UCLA undergraduate students; and, the second based on a national probability sample "collected as part of the 1992 National Election Study (NES)" (p. 113), also found no evidence to support White Nativist claims pertaining to ethnic identifications and national belonging as reflected in patriotism. Sidanious et al. (1997) found "…no evidence in either the student sample or national probability sample that Latinos were any less patriotic than whites" (p. 129), consistent with Garza et al.'s study (1996). However, Sidanious et al. (1997) did find "…asymmetry in the relationship between patriotism and measures of ethnic group attachment in the UCLA student sample" (p. 129) suggesting, and consistent with White Nativist assimilationist ideology, that individual attachments to an ethnic identity do diminish patriotism. This finding, which was specific to the 1993, UCLA sample, is best understood as contextually produced, given the increasingly White Nativist nature of the anti-immigrant, sociopolitical context in California, at the time of the study (Ashmore et al., 2001). Proposition 187 was at the center of California's immigration sociopolitical debates during that time. This law, which was never enacted due to Federal intervention, was designed to bar undocumented immigrants, predominantly Hispanic, from accessing public services, such as schools and medical care. The UCLA study's findings, therefore, provide evidence of, and support, the reactive subculture phenomenon described by Portes and Zhou (1994). In fact, Sidanious et al. (1997) when contextualizing their findings, link Latinos' lower patriotism to the "…intense anti-immigrant feeling in [California]… [that] largely focused [on]… 'Latinos' in general, and Mexicans in particular" (p. 129).

Citrin and Sears (2009) explored the relationship between national identity, conceptualized as American, hyphenated American, or ethnic and patriotism. The data samples were obtained through the 1992 and 2002, American National Election Studies (ANES); the 1994 and 1996 General Social Survey (GSS); and the LACSS survey, 1994–2000. Citrin and Sears' (2009) research study captured a more complex sociopolitical immigration context, as it covered three different sociopolitical contexts and time periods: pre-immigration reforms, 1992–1995; enactment of immigration reforms, 1996; and post-immigration reforms and enforcement, 1997–2002. Although Citrin and Sears (2009) did not consider the implications of these three different, structural immigration policy contexts, their research findings will be presented integrating this needed sociopolitical contextualization.

Citrin and Sears (2009), when examining respondents' self-identifications in the 1994 GSS national sample, found that only 7% identified in ethnic terms, while 90%, comprised of both white and "minority respondents," including native-born and immigrant Hispanics, identified solely as American. The findings differed slightly when the LACSS 1994, 1995 and 1997 survey samples were used, showing a decrease in the percentage of respondents identifying solely as American, from 90% to 80%. The LACSS sample was larger than the GSS national sample, and also more diverse, capturing a larger percentage of minority respondents. However, when the two samples were examined together, most of the minority respondents identified solely as American, including 79% of the Hispanic respondents in the 1994 GSS sample.

A subsequent analysis of the 1995, 1999, and 2000 LACSS survey samples, where respondents could self identify solely as American, ethnic, or as both American and ethnic, found that a third of the Hispanic respondents iden-tified only in ethnic terms, and 7% solely as American. Overall, the findings showed that immigrants and their children were more likely to identify "in primarily ethnic terms... consistent with Huntington's concern" (pp. 161–2); yet, over time and with increasing participation in the mainstream of American society, the tendency toward an ethnic identification seemed to decrease (Citrin & Sears, 2009). However, since the LACSS samples in-cluded data collected in 1999 and 2000, 3 and 4 years after the implementa-tion of the deportation immigration reform policies, the tendency toward a primary ethnic identification could have been influenced by both the anti-immigrant, sociopolitical context, as well as by the option to identify as American and ethnic. This latter option, as mentioned by Citrin and Sears (2009), had not been provided in the 1994 GSS survey or in the dichotomous analysis of the 1994 and 1995 LACSS samples.

In regards to patriotism and identity, Citrin and Sears (2009) obtained similar findings when analyzing the 2002 American National Election sample; the 1994 and 1997 LACSS samples; and, the 1996 GSS samples, despite changes within the immigration sociopolitical context of the na-tion. Citrin and Sears' (2009) 2002 American National Election sample analysis revealed that Latinos showed "just as much patriotism as whites... [replicating] the findings of the National Latino Election Study conducted in 1989" (p. 162). The LACSS 1994 and 1997 analyses yielded similar results, indicating that both, native-born Hispanics and naturalized Hispanics were as patriotic as white respondents. The 1996 GSS analysis confirmed again previous findings, indicating a "high level of patriotism among Hispanics" (Citrin & Sears, 2009, p. 164). Citrin and Sears (2009) concluded that "only ethnic minorities who categorized themselves solely in ethnic terms [had shown] diminished patriotism... [and] the only substantial numbers that categorize[d] themselves in ethnic terms [had been] new immigrant Latinos"

(p. 171). Their research findings, consistent with Garza et al. (1996) and Sidanious et al. (1997), did not find evidence to support White Nativist claims that suggest that individual ethnic conceptualizations of the self and cultural pluralism, undermine the American national identity or the sense of national belonging, that is, patriotism, of Hispanic immigrants and their children.

## National belonging and civic engagement

Although national belonging has been discussed thus far in ethnic, cultural and patriotic terms, it can also be defined in civic commitment terms. This conceptualization is often considered to be more inclusive (Wakefield et al., 2011, p. 1) and "...supports a more voluntaristic definition in which membership is handed out as a reward for loyalty and not on the basis of un-chosen criteria such as race" (Wakefield et al., 2011, p. 2). Beltrandy y Rudquist (2012) concurs with Wakefield et al. (2011) stating that "...states have moved toward the rewriting [of national] identity in civic terms" (p. 1), while also holding on to previous ethnic and cultural definitions of national belonging. Ethnic and cultural constructions of national belonging lead to the development and implementation of "stricter immigration and asylum laws, [and] introduce citizenship tests which check for the compatibility of the culture of the newcomers" (Beltrandy y Rudquist, 2012, p. 1). Civic constructions emphasize the need to develop "common values, shared interests and a set of common institutions, as the ties that bind members together" (Beltrandy y Rudquist, 2012, p. 1), leading to social policies designed to foster a national sense of belonging through citizenship participation and social engagement. However, there is a lack of consensus as to what is meant by civic participation and civic engagement (Adler & Goggin, 2005; Gibson, 2000).

Adler and Goggin (2005) suggest that the definition of civic engagement appears to be contingent on who needs to define the construct and on the motivation for doing so. Keeter, Zukin, Andolina and Jenkins (2002) identify three different dimensions of engagement: (1) "Electoral Action: things people do around campaigns and elections;" (2) "Civic Action: things people do to help in their communities or ways in which they contribute to charities;" and (3) "Political Voices: Things people do to give expression to their political and social viewpoints" (pp. 9–10); as well as nineteen activities/indicators by which to measure individual levels of electoral, civic or political action/voice. Civic indicators include: "community problem solving; regular volunteering for a nonelectoral organization; [and] active membership in a group or association" (Adler & Goggin, 2005, p. 242). Electoral indicators include: "regular voting; persuading others; ... and, volunteering for candidate or political organizations" (Adler & Goggin, 2005, p. 242). Political voice indicators include: "contacting officials; ... contacting the broadcast media; protesting; e-mail petitions; written petitions" (Adler & Goggin, 2005, p. 242).

Putnam's (1995) definition of civic engagement is more inclusive than Keeter et al.'s (2002) and rests on the principle of social capital, which Putnam (1995) describes as "...features of social organization such as networks, norms, and social trust that facilitate coordination and cooperation for mutual benefit" (p. 2), thereby considering any activity that "builds social capital" (Adler & Goggin, 2005) as a measure of civic engagement. For example, in his analysis "...of organizational membership among Americans..." (p. 4) based on data from the General Social Survey, Putnam (1995) identified religious affiliation as one of the most common organizational memberships in the United States, and consequently as a measure of civic engagement. Crowley (n.d.), on the other hand, defines civic engagement along a continuum, from informal/private individual action to formal/public collective actions; and, as Keeter et al. (2002), Crowley (n.d.) grouped activities/indicators of engagement into two clusters: (1) community activities; and (2) political activities. Community activities include: "helping neighbors; contributing to charity; membership in a religious, fraternal or community group" (Adler & Goggin, 2005, p. 240). While political activities include: "voting; advocating for a policy; active participation in a party or interest group; and running for office" (Adler & Goggin, 2005, p. 240). Diller (2001), presents yet another conceptualization, defining civic engagement as, "...the means by which an individual, through collective action, influences the larger civic society" (p. 6).

Adler and Goggin's (2002) definition of civic engagement, in conjunction with Putnam's conceptualization (1995), appears to be most pertinent when examining belonging in relation to the American-born children of Mexican immigrants. For Adler and Goggin (2005), "Civic engagement describes how an active citizen participates in the life of a community in order to improve conditions for others or to help shape the community's future" (p. 241). Putnam (1995, 2000) and Carpini (2000) add another dimension, that of opportunity to become involved, which reconceptualizes civic engagement as a bidirectional process, that is, people can only become engaged if, in addition to motivation, they have the opportunity to do so. Putnam (1995, 2000) and Carpini (2000) suggest that these opportunities are shaped "by the civic infrastructure: from the structure and processes of election to the number and type of civic and political associations" (p. 344). Given that an individual's level of civic engagement is partially influenced by the dominant societal infrastructure, exploring societal aspects that promote or thwart active citizenship participation seems necessary at this point.

Although electoral participation is discussed as an important indicator of active citizenship, Putnam (1995), Adler and Goggin (2002), Carpini (2000) and Crowley (n.d.) emphasize community participation as a measure of active citizenship, national belonging and integration. Moreover, Putnam (2000) and Crowley (n.d.) identify religious participation as a leading indicator of community participation, consistent with research pertaining to segmented assimilation, religion and mode of incorporation, as related to the upward or downward assimilation of first and second generation immigrants (Portes & Rumbaut, 2006). Putnam (2000) states that "Churches provide an important incubator for civic skills, civic norms, community interests, and civic recruitment," (p. 66) emphasizing that "...Religiosity rivals education as a powerful correlate of most forms of civic engagement" (p. 67). In fact, Putnam (2005) and Warner (2007) identify churches as primary contributors to the development of social capital in immigrant communities and communities of color, such as the African American community, and view "...religious involvement [as] a crucial dimension of civic engagement" (Putnam, 2000).

Putnam's (1995, 2000) and Warner's (2007) assertions are further supported by Portes and Rumbaut's (2006) longitudinal study of second generation immigrant children in the United States, conducted between 1991 and 2003. In the Children of Immigrants Longitudinal Study, (CILS), Portes and Rumbaut (2006) identify religion and religious affiliation as a mediating factor for the upward assimilation of second-generation immigrant children. Portes and Rumbaut (2006) and Hirschman (2003) explain that, "The centrality of religion to immigrant communities can be summarized as the search for refuge, respectability, and resources" (p. 27), where refuge refers to the immigrant's need for protection due to pre-migration and migration trauma, as well as the instability resulting from the relocation/migration process; respectability refers to "...opportunities for status recognition and social mobility [provided within the church structure] that [are often] denied in the broader society" (Hirschman, 2003, p. 28) due to "othering" dynamics fueling oppression and marginalization; and, resources speaks to the immigrant populations' housing and employment needs, among others, and the churches' referral and educational function within this context.

Portes and Rumbaut (2006), Warner (2007) and Hirschman (2003) also highlight the "role of religion in the development of ethnic communities and the reassertion of national cultures and language" (Portes & Rumbaut, 2006, p. 304). Hirschman (2003) expands this conceptualization, explaining how "immigrants became Americans by joining a church and participating in its religious and community life" (p. 5). Portes and Rumbaut (2006) found empirical support to Hirschman's (2003) assertions through the CILS 2001–2003 survey, reporting that religious institutions: "collaborate with authorities in promoting incorporation, while protecting immigrants from exclusionary policies; ... support selective acculturation and transnational ties; and, ... support parents' efforts toward overcoming discrimination and other barriers to successful adaptation of their offspring" (p. 305).

However, it is the "adaptation of their offspring" that White Nativists question, while concurrently interpreting the "creation of ethnic communities and the reenactment of elements of the immigrants' culture... [as undermining] the unity of the nation and ... its cultural identity" (Huntington, 2004, p. 304). This White Nativist perception contradicts historical evidence, as European immigrants were successful in their assimilation and integration efforts, because they were "allowed... to develop their own social and cultural institutions, including their parishes, schools, hospitals, temples, and synagogues" (Portes & Rumbaut, 2006, p. 305) rather than prevented from doing so. Despite this historical precedent, White Nativists believe it is the "foreign other," and particularly the Mexican "other," who poses a threat to their cultural symbols and collective affective ties; thus, "continu[ing] to rally against the 'foreign element' and its activities" (Portes & Rumbaut, 2006, p. 306).

Feshbach (1991), who explored the attachment processes influencing political ideology, suggests that there is a relationship between affective experiences, needs originating within the child–caregiver relationship, and the relationship that emerges between individuals and the nation. In other words,

> the nation-terrain, government, customs, with its connotation of father as protector and mother as source of nurturance, offers a socially acceptable context in which early attachment needs can be expressed and analogous reinforcements obtained. In many ways, the nation provides adult individuals with feelings of security and vicarious feelings of approval and related rewards through identifications that were directly experienced in the early childhood situation.
>
> (Feshbach, 1991, p. 211)

Feshbach's conceptualization is germane to this discussion, since "White Natives" experience the Hispanic other as a threat to their individual and collective identity, and to their associated suitable targets of externalization. However, "White Native" efforts to protect their external reservoirs of individual and collective shared affect, are thwarting the efforts of American-born children of immigrants to engage in the civic life of the United States. These efforts are also interfering with the children's ability to attach to the United States, increasing civic infrastructural barriers to their full participation as citizens of the nation (Carpini, 2000; Portes & Rumbaut, 2006; Putnam, 1995, 2000).

## Conclusion

As the integrative sociopolitical and psychological analysis of immigration policy has shown, immigration policy has been historically used by "White Natives" as a conscious and unconscious, legal, sociocognitive mechanism by which to construct, contest, reify and maintain the "White Native" identity and Nativist ideology. Within a context of gradual demographic change, American immigration policy has also emerged as a tool by which to avert the loss of the original, idealized, "White Native," affect-laden identity. This sociocognitive and psychodynamic hypothesis will now be applied to two contemporary immigration reform policies, IIRIRA and AEDPA. These two policies have provided the basis for subsequent immigration policy reforms that have facilitated the deportation of the immigrant other, with harmful effects for mixed status families, and specifically for Hispanic mixed status families, and their American-born children. These children, by nature of their parentage, have been constructed as second-class citizens, and thus as "other" than American, "White Native" children.

# Part IV

# Integrated sociopolitical and psychological model

Application to American
immigration policy reforms
and American-born children
of Mexican immigrant parents

# 5  Immigration policy and interior enforcement

## Hispanics: The Mexican border

Although contemporary sociopolitical debates about immigration as previously discussed, speak about the Hispanic other, this term implicitly refers to the Mexican other (Huntington, 2004b). Why is this group singled out in American immigration sociopolitical debates?

Mexico is the only Latin American country that shares its borders with the United States and the only Latin American country that "has asserted or could assert a historical claim to U.S. territory" (Huntington, 2004a, p. 36). The Mexican–American border, as discussed in Chapter 2, has a long history of fluidity, contestation, and eventual enforcement, dating back to the early nineteenth century, when Mexico expanded toward the north in 1821. These territorial gains, were eventually lost after the 1846, Mexican–American war, that ended in 1848 with the Treaty of Guadalupe Hidalgo. As a result of the war, Mexico lost 55% of its northern territory, changing permanently the territorial borders between Mexico and the United States (Massey, Durand, & Malone, 2002). This inter-nations border, therefore, encapsulates a long history of conflict, war, occupation and loss.

The Mexican–American border is also an important commercial route, linking Central and South America to North America, providing a path for the exchange of capital, goods, and resources, especially necessary transnational manpower. Mexico serves as a port of entry into the United States for Mexican citizens, as well as for many other Hispanic and non-Hispanic immigrants. It is not surprising, given Mexico's geographical position, and its central role as a transnational resource of manpower in the North American capitalist system, that American "White Nativists" turned their attention toward the Mexican border to control the entrance of the Hispanic other, and to avert the transformation of the "White Native" culture.

## American immigration policy: Historical overview

This section presents a historical review of the most significant immigration policies enacted since 1882, guided by their overt inclusionary or exclusionary goals (Hing, 2004; Johnson, 2004; Ngai, 2014; Shklar, 1991). The review will examine how the United States controlled the influx of transnational manpower through immigration policy. It will illustrate how the United States covertly created and facilitated a Mexican "illegal" labor force to maximize production and wealth acquisition (Wallerstein, 2003), while overtly advocating for racial equality and border control. The review will also expose the White Nativist legal statutes and logics that successfully cast the Mexican other, as an illegal, unwanted, immigration problem that threatened the welfare of the nation state.

The immigration policy period between 1882 and 1940 was a highly exclusionary period (Hagan, Castro, & Rodriguez, 2010; Massey & Pren, 2012), best known for the inception of the National Origins Quota System in 1924; that is, the Immigration Act of 1924. The National Origins Quota System, as discussed in Chapter 2, provided "White Natives" with the legal mechanism by which to establish and assert their native claim to the United States, while creating the current racialized, national, origins-based, exclusionary paradigm (Hing, 2004; Johnson, 2004; Massey & Pren, 2012; Ngai, 2014). This new racial paradigm gave birth to the Mexican race and provided the mechanism by which Mexican immigrants could be constructed as illegal immigrants (see Chapter 2). By 1930, the resulting immigration policy changes, coupled with the economic effects of the Great Depression, which fueled anti-Mexican sentiment, led to the deportation of undocumented Mexican immigrants, as well as of legal immigrants and Mexican American citizens (Hing, 2004; Massey et al., 2002). In fact, in 1930, 400,000 Mexicans, half of whom were children and American citizens, were deported (Ngai, 1999, 2014), and many more were "encouraged" to return to Mexico through repatriation initiatives (Hing, 2004; Johnson, 2004). The effects of these deportation and repatriation efforts, coupled with the strong anti-Mexican sociopolitical context of the nation, were deeply felt within the Mexican community, as Hing (2004) illustrates,

> Threats of physical violence induced many Mexicans to abandon jobs and long-established domiciles throughout the country. Trains, cars, trucks, and buses streamed southward from Los Angeles, Phoenix, El Paso, Denver, Kansas City, Chicago, Detroit, Pittsburgh, [etc.] During a five-month period in 1931, 50,000 Mexican nationals and their children were repatriated from Los Angeles alone. The U.S. Labor department reported that two million returned to Mexico over a fifteen-month period.
> (p. 126)

This forced mass exodus, which significantly affected the available American labor force market, coupled with the United States gradual economic recovery and impending involvement in World War II, resulted in an increasing agricultural labor shortage. The United States, despite its previous en mass deportation and repatriation of the Mexican other, looked again toward Mexico to meet its cheap labor needs. By 1942, the United States federal government, in conjunction with the Mexican government, and in collaboration with agricultural employers, implemented the Bracero Program (Hing, 2004; Massey et al., 2002; Ngai, 2014). This program allowed Mexican nationals to enter the United States under temporary contracts to work in agriculture (Hing, 2004), while ensuring their labor conditions and wages. The Bracero Program, however, failed to adequately protect the rights of Mexican workers once inside the country, leading to numerous human rights violations.[1]

With the end of World War II, the need for Mexican labor started to decrease, leading to job competition between returning American servicemen and Mexican immigrants. This inter-group job competition renewed the anti-Mexican sociopolitical rhetoric that had permeated the American sociopolitical discourse between the late 1920s and early 1930s. By this point in time, the Bracero Program had also failed to prevent the displacement of American native workers by the immigrant Mexican other, in part, because program mandates related to the bracero workers' equal compensation had been systematically violated. Thus in reality, the Bracero Program, due to the federal government's poor implementation and oversight, allowed agricultural employers to access a cheap labor force, that was often contracted at sub-part wages. As Ngai (2014) states, for example, "over a ten year period, the wages… in California dropped 40 percent, during which time the proportion of braceros hired… rose by 90 percent" (pp. 142–3). Although braceros could file legal complaints for contract violations, many were unable to protect their rights, because they had not understood the terms of their contracts; were sometimes unable to read; and/or feared the possible consequences (Hernandez, 2010; Hing, 2004; Massey et al., 2002; Ngai, 2014).

Despite human rights violations, as the Mexican economy declined, the promise of higher wages in the United States ensured a supply of workers willing to cross over, further compounding the problems of the Bracero Program. The surplus of transnational Mexican labor exceeded the work permits available through the Bracero Program, propelling Mexican workers to cross the border as "wetbacks" (Hing, 2004; Johnson, 2004; Ngai, 2014). Border enforcement patrols on the other hand, did not enforce border policy, allowing migrants to cross, whom agricultural employers quickly hired at sub-part wages. In some instances, INS subsequently legalized the status of these illegal workers, reinforcing agricultural, illegal hiring practices (Ngai, 2014). All in all, the Bracero Program, instead of providing "…a solution to illegal immigration, [compounded the problem] by generating more illegal immigration" (Ngai, 2014, p. 147) Eventually, "White Natives" came to experience the presence of the Mexican immigrant other as an invasion; a word linked to discourses of war and occupation, and therefore evocative of a not so distant invasion and armed contestation, the Mexican–American war (Massey & Pren, 2012; Ngai, 2014). This sentiment is well illustrated by General Swing's remarks "[this] 'alarming, ever-increasing flood tide'…[represents] 'an actual invasion of the United States'" (Ngai, 2014, p. 155). The anti-Mexican sociopolitical rhetoric eventually fueled an increasing number of violent acts perpetrated against the Mexican others (Hing, 2004) and culminated in the implementation of Operation Wetback in 1954.

Operation Wetback, which evolved into a militarized operation (Ngai, 2014; Peralta, 2015), was designed to forcibly remove Mexican illegal immigrants from the United States, while disincentivizing illegal crossing, and forcing agricultural employers to access Mexican labor through the Bracero Program (Hing, 2004; Ngai, 2014). Operation Wetback was successful in its removal efforts, deporting immigrant workers, along with their families and children, regardless of their citizenship status (Hernandez, 2010). Records indicate, "INS apprehended 801,069 Mexican immigrants from 1953 through 1955, more than twice the number of apprehensions made from 1947 through 1949" (Ngai, 2014, p. 156). Operation Wetback also succeeded in rerouting transnational labor and employers to the Bracero program. During the enforcement of Operation Wetback, the number of workers admitted through the Bracero program increased "… from 148,449 in 1954 to 215,162 in 1955 [and] to 298,012 in 1956" (Ngai, 2014, p. 156). Nonetheless, the Bracero Program ended in 1964, due to mounting criticism over its effect on wages; ongoing White Nativist, anti-Mexican immigrant sentiment (Johnson, 2004; Hing, 2004); and, the pervasive exploitation of bracero workers (Hernandez, 2010; Massey & Pren, 2012).

The end of the Bracero Program in 1964, in conjunction with the 1965 Immigration and Naturalization Act, marked the beginning of an almost "exclusively undocumented" (Hing, 2004, p. 131) transnational manual labor era and the beginning of a sociopolitical context characterized by efforts to "preserv[e] immunity for those employing undocumented workers," (Hing, 2004, p. 131). Any legislation that sought to regulate employer-hiring practices was hindered and opposed (Hing, 2004). This permissive shift, that enabled employers to benefit from the exploitation of undocumented workers, lasted until 1986 (Hing, 2004), when the Immigration Reform and Control Act (IRCA) was enacted. However, before discussing IRCA, it is important to examine the 1965 Immigration and Naturalization Act and its contribution to the creation of a largely undocumented Mexican labor force.

By the early1960s, the sociopolitical context of the United States had significantly changed as a result of the Civil Rights movement, leading to substantial social and immigration policy changes (Johnson, 2004). In 1965, the Immigration and Nationality Act replaced the Immigration Act of 1924, abolishing the national origins quota system (Chin & Villazor, 2015; Hagan et al., 2010; Hing, 2004; Johnson, 2004; Massey & Pren, 2012; Ngai, 2014). As Massey and Pren (2012) explain: "As the Civil Rights movement gathered force, discriminatory quotas against certain Europeans, [Southern and Eastern Europeans] and prohibitions on African and Asian immigration came to be seen as intolerably racist" (p. 2). However, the Immigration and Naturalization Act of 1965, despite being sociopolitically conceptualized as a landmark, race neutral policy, failed to uphold its inclusionary aim by further marginalizing Mexican immigrants (Massey & Pren, 2012; Ngai, 2014). The implications of this policy, which are sometimes described as intended by scholars such as Ngai (2014), and as unintended by others, such as Massey and Pren (2012), are best explained by Chin and Villazor (2015), "while the 1965 Immigration Act was in some sense a civil rights law, it was one of its era that perpetuated discrimination in certain ways" (introduction, "The End of the Race Line" section, para. 2).

The 1965 Immigration Act did abolish the 1924 national origins quota system that had previously restricted Southern and Eastern European immigration, and that had barred immigration from Asia and Africa, replacing it with a new "race neutral" system (Chin & Villazor, 2015; Massey & Pren 2012; Ngai, 2014). This new system initially assigned a 120,000 immigration, annual quota cap to the Western Hemisphere, and a 170,000 quota cap to the Eastern Hemisphere, as well as a 20,000 country-specific quota. The quota cap instituted for the Western Hemisphere effectively curtailed the hemisphere's immigration by 40%, adversely affecting Mexican immigrants, who had been able to enter the United States under the Bracero Program in significantly larger numbers (Massey et al., 2002). That is,

> Mexico went from an annual access to around 450,000 guest worker visas [Bracero Program] and a theoretically unlimited number of resident visas in the United States [averaging 50,000 per year] to a new situation in which there were no worker visas and just 20,000 resident visas [in 1976].
> (Massey & Pren, 2012, p. 3)

In 1976, as referenced by Massey and Pren (2012), the Immigration and Naturalization Act was amended to introduce a 20,000, Western Hemisphere, country-specific quota cap, which was also applied to Mexico and its transnational workers. The termination of the Bracero Program, in conjunction with the 1965 Immigration Act's failure to provide Mexican workers with a viable transition path from the Bracero to the 1965 H-2 guest worker program,[2] effectively recast "...Mexican immigration as illegal" (Ngai, 2014, p. 261). As deportation statics clearly show, after the 1965 Act's implementation "...the number of deportations of undocumented Mexicans increased by 40 percent in 1968, to 151,000... [and] in 1976, when the 20,000 per country quota was imposed, the INS expelled 781,000 Mexicans from the United States" (Ngai, 2014, p. 261). In 1978, the Immigration Act was further amended to establish a 290,000 annual, global, immigration quota cap and subsequently decreased to 270,000 in 1980 (Massey et al., 2002).

It is important to highlight that the 1965 quota system excluded from its stipulated immigration quotas, family members of American citizens, migrating to the United States under the family reunification guidelines that applied to parents, children and spouses (Chin & Villazor, 2015; Massey & Pren, 2012; Ngai, 2014). Legal permanent residents could also petition their immediate relatives under a limited number of country assigned immigration quotas. The family reunification provisions were included as part of the 1965 Act, to address the long-standing effects of the 1924 Immigration Act. This policy had caused many multi-generational, transnational separations due to the restrictive and exclusionary nature of the national origins quota system.

The family reunification provisions also facilitated the sociopolitical acceptance of the 1965 Immigration Act, assuaging "White Native" fears over a possible, substantial "racial," demographic population change that had been averted up until now by the 1924 Immigration Act (Massey & Pren, 2012; Ngai, 2014). In fact, due to the demographic composition of the United States as of 1965, it was expected that most of the family-driven migration would stem from Western European countries, ensuring the maintenance of the "White Native" paradigm. However, the demographic migration paradigm that emerged as a direct result of the 1965 Act, and specifically due to the family reunification laws, was far different from the one anticipated by "White Natives." For example, American citizens of Mexican descent, as well as legal permanent residents, and other Latin American and Asian groups unable to migrate due to country-specific quota caps, used the 1965 family reunification provisions to meet their own group specific needs (Ngai, 2014).

The Immigration and Naturalization Act of 1965 changed the demographic landscape of the United States in a lasting manner, breaking down previously erected barriers that had prevented the migration of Southern, and Eastern European immigrants, as well as immigrants from Asia and Africa. However, in failing to provide, while having terminated, a legal avenue for the hiring of necessary agricultural Mexican manual labor, the 1965 Act also redefined Mexican labor as primarily illegal in nature, fueling a largely undocumented labor pool that continued to meet the American agricultural employers' need for cheap labor (Massey et al., 2002). Agricultural employers, on the other hand, unable to persuade the federal government to substantially change the 1965 H-2 legislation (Hing, 2004; Massey & Pren, 2012), and able to continue hiring undocumented workers at sub-part wages without employer sanctions, continued to profit from the exploitation of the Mexican other (Hing, 2004; Johnson, 2004).

By the 1980s, concern over the presence of the illegal immigrant other, and in particular over the Mexican other, resurfaced within the sociopolitical context of the nation. Actual estimates of the number of illegal immigrants present in the United States varied widely, creating societal confusion, fear and uncertainty about the federal government's ability to both control and regulate the Mexican–American border. This increasing fear and preoccupation are well captured by Golfand and Bialik-Gilad (1989):

> What is most troublesome is the seeming inability of the U.S. government to control the current immigration flow, or even to accurately gauge its size. Illegal immigration predominates in the United States.

The number of illegal immigrants is estimated to be between 2 and 6 millions, but some estimates range as high as 20 million.

(p. 23)

Massey et al. (2002), who studied the migration history and patterns of Mexican immigrants, estimate that between 1965 and 1986, there were 5.7 million Mexican immigrants in the United States, of which 81% were undocumented. The sharp increase in undocumented Mexican immigration provides evidence of, and exposes, the "de facto guest worker program" (p. 941) that had operated since the inception of the 1965 Immigration and Naturalization Act. In fact, between the late 1970s and early 1980s, immigrants trying to cross the Mexican border faced a small risk of apprehension, 33% (Massey et al., 2002); and if apprehended, in 97% of the cases, Mexican immigrants agreed to a voluntary deportation to try to cross again (Massey et al., 2002). This revolving door, or cyclical crossing-return-crossing pattern, was well understood by Mexican immigrants, the border patrol and by agricultural employers, who were all too willing to hire immigrants upon their successful crossing, without facing any real sanctions (Hing, 2004; Massey et al., 2002). By the early 1980s, the presence of the Mexican other had become quite visible within certain areas of the United States, which, together with the prevailing socioeconomic uncertainty of the time, set the stage for renewed efforts to address the Mexican illegal immigration "problem" (Hing 2004; Massey & Pren, 2012; Massey et al., 2002). On January 1, 1987, President Reagan signed into law the 1986 Immigration Reform and Control Act, IRCA; this act was both inclusionary and restrictive in nature.

IRCA had two main goals: first, to control immigration through renewed border patrol efforts and employer sanctions; and, secondly, to provide a path for the legalization of illegal immigrants. To accomplish its first goal, IRCA increased funding for border patrol enforcement, while enacting for the first time, civil and criminal employer sanctions for knowingly hiring illegal immigrants, with "fines ranging from $250 to $10,000 per unauthorized worker" (Hing, 2004, p. 180). To accomplish its second goal, IRCA provided "amnesty" to long-term illegal immigrant residents (LTR), who had entered the United States prior to January 1, 1982; and, to special agricultural workers (SAW), who had resided in the United States for 90 days, during the 12-month period ending in May 1, 1986 (Enchautegui, 2013; Hing, 2004; Massey et al., 2002). Immigrants seeking to regularize their status under the LTR program were also required to demonstrate knowledge of the English language and American history and government, which created legalization problems for some applicants due to their age or level of literacy in their own native language. Immigrants seeking to regularize under the SAW program were exempt from this requirement (Hing, 2004; Massey et al., 2002).

Overall, IRCA led to the legalization of 3 million immigrants, of which 2.3 million where from Mexico—1.3 million attained legal status through the LTR program, and 1 million through the SAW program. IRCA also established a H-2 guest worker program that agricultural and low-skilled immigrants could use. Employers on the other hand, found the program costly, difficult to navigate and inadequate, as it did not provide them with a mechanism by which to flexibly respond to the increasing and fluctuating labor needs of the country. Due to these obstacles, agricultural employers continued to look toward the de facto undocumented labor program to access necessary labor with ease and flexibility (American Immigration Council, 2013; Chishti, Meissner, & Bergeron, 2011). At the same time, the United States ongoing agricultural labor needs, and the prospect of receiving better wages in the United States, continued to motivate Mexican workers to cross the border. By the mid-to-late 1980s, politicians, including President Reagan, began to refer to the ongoing Mexican immigration influx as a crisis and a threat to national security (Massey et al., 2012). In 1990, IRCA was amended in response to these ongoing White Nativist sociopolitical concerns.

The Immigration Reform and Control Act of 1990 had a more restrictive and exclusionary aim than its original version. The 1990 amendments sought to funnel increasing resources toward border enforcement; reinforce existing employer sanctions; facilitate deportation procedures; institute an annual, family migration quota cap of 480,000 visas; and facilitate the migration of professional/skilled workers by expanding the H-1B program (Hing, 2004). To address increasing White Nativist concern over the national origins of the existing immigrant population — predominantly Asian and Latin American by 1990—as well as concern over a gradual, racial, demographic population shift, IRCA restricted family migration from these two regions by instituting a 480,000 annual visa cap. It also created a new diversity visa category, capped at 55,000 visas, designed to increase the number of immigrants from nations that had been "adversely affected" by the 1965 Immigration Act (Massey et al., 2000, pp. 1697–8). This new visa category created a preferential White, "affirmative action" (Johnson, 2004, p. 32) admission path to preserve the "white" racial composition of the United States. Overall, the 1990 IRCA reflects a White Nativist effort to rectify and reverse some of the "unforeseen" consequences of the 1965 Immigration Act (Johnson, 2004; Massey & Pren, 2012; Massey et al., 2002; Ngai, 2014). The reforms also reveal the United States historical ambivalence toward the Mexican other, that is, a racialized, immigrant other, that is needed as a means of production, and yet not wanted, subjugated and ultimately constructed as an illegal invader.

This brief historical analysis of the 1965, 1986 and 1990 Immigration Acts has both summarized and exposed the overt and covert White Nativist, legal logics used to construct the Mexican other as "illegal" and unwanted, while concurrently creating and facilitating a "wanted" de facto, "illegal" Mexican labor force. Overtly, the 1965 Act changed, in an unforeseen and permanent manner, the racial demographic landscape of the

United States. Yet, this same act also created a largely illegal Mexican labor force that, although publicly condemned by the government, was covertly facilitated through the de facto guest worker program that operated outside public view. 1986 brought about an overt potential path toward legalization for the illegal, Mexican other; and, with amnesty and legalization Mexicans were given access to legal, family migration paths established in 1965 (Ngai, 2014). However, the path toward family reunification was lengthy and marked by long delays that disproportionately affected Mexican applicants. These delays, sometimes of up to 10 years, made family reunification very difficult to achieve through legal means, and as Chishti et al. (2011) state "the longer waits... may have [also] spurred increased illegal immigration" (The Legalization Problem section, para. 5).

By 1990, the increasingly White Nativist sociopolitical context, fueled by fears of an impending demographic change, led to the restriction of immigration from Latin America and Asia, and to the inception of the diversity visa category. However, this new visa category, as previously discussed, was a largely, linguistically codified covert effort to rebalance the demographic composition of the United States without using language reminiscent of the 1924 national origins quota system, which had been publicly recognized as racist. The diversity visa category and the concealed de facto guest worker program are two examples of a legacy of contradictory and incongruent legal logics that can be traced back to the creation of the second-class citizenship. In fact, the United States was successful in meeting the country's cheap labor demands, because of the 1965, 1980 and 1990 overt, explicit policy goals of racial neutrality and border control. These explicit goals allowed the United States government to hide and deny their active participation in the creation of the "Mexican immigrant problem," successfully constructing the Mexican other as an illegal invader within the sociopolitical discourse. Hence, the "other" was the one violating the boundaries of the American nation-state in an unwanted manner. As Massey et al. (2002) state, "If there is a one constant in U.S. border policy, it is hypocrisy. Through the twentieth century the United States has arranged to import Mexican workers while pretending not to" (p. 1885).

In 1994, in response to increasing anti-immigrant, White Nativist, sociopolitical pressures that demanded a solution to the Hispanic immigration problem, Bill Clinton adopted a new approach, "control through deterrence" (Hing, 2004; Massey et al., 2002). Control through deterrence aimed to dissuade Mexican immigrants from "illegally" entering the United States by increasing border patrol enforcement efforts and blocking traditional migration paths. These efforts resulted in the development of four regional border patrol initiatives: (1) Operation Blockade, 1993, El Paso, Texas; (2) Operation Gatekeeper, 1994, San Diego, California; (3) Operation Safeguard, 1994, San Diego, California; and, (4) Operation Rio Grande, 1997, Brownsville, Texas. These initiatives were designed to thwart crossing efforts, by forcing immigrants attempting to cross into significantly more dangerous and visible terrain, thereby increasing the likelihood of detection and arrest by the border patrols (Hing, 2004).

These new border patrol efforts did not prevent immigrants from entering the United States, but they did succeed in rerouting border crossings to more remote and less populated areas, hiding the "problem" out of public view (Hing, 2004; Massey et al., 2002). However, in crossing through more difficult terrain, the number of deaths during border crossings increased significantly. Operation Gatekeeper alone resulted in a 600 times increase of migrant deaths between 1994 and 2000 (Hing, 2004, p. 205). Recent studies continue to document the death toll directly linked to the control through deterrence policy; for example, data provided by the American Civil Liberties Union (ACLU) indicates that between 1994 and 1997 the number of known immigrant deaths were 80 per year, climbing to "481 per year in 1998–2008" (Argueta, 2016, p. 28). This increase is even more concerning than the numbers alone reflect, since border crossing attempts had decreased in that same period, suggesting "...border crossings have become more hazardous since the 'prevention through deterrence' policy went into effect in the 1990s" (Argueta, 2016, p. 28).

The failure to prevent the overt entry of the Hispanic other through border patrol efforts led to further reforms in 1996, culminating in the implementation of the Illegal Immigration Reform and Immigrant Responsibility Act (IIRIRA),[3] and the Anti-Terrorism and Effective Death Penalty Act (AEDPA).[4] These two acts, which will be discussed in greater detail, no longer sought to prevent the entry of the immigrant other into the United States, but instead focused on facilitating the arrest, detention and removal of the immigrant, often Mexican other, through deportation (Hagan et al., 2010). As a result of these two acts, the number of deportations between 1995 and 2008 increased "from 50,924 to 358,886, a six hundred percent increase in just thirteen years" (Hagan et al., 2010, p. 1808) and, of the 358,886 individuals deported in 2008, 68.8% were of Mexican origin (Hagan et al., 2010, p. 1809).

The immigration interior enforcement approach (Hagan et al., 2010; Hing, 2004; Massey et al., 2002), that began in 1996, in response to the critical mass representation achieved by the Hispanic, Mexican other (Huntington, 2004b), has continued to influence subsequent policy development. Since 1996, the federal government expanded the 287(g)[5] program enacted as part of IIRIRA, and the Secure Communities Program implemented in 2008. While the 287(g) program was developed to "train state and local police to identify and turn over to ICE any suspected criminal immigrants..." (Hagan et al., 2010, p. 1807), the Secure Communities Program was developed to facilitate electronic data-sharing between local, state police and ICE, that would permit cross referencing of criminal and immigration records of any individual arrested by state police (Kohli, Markowitz, & Chavez, 2011). In 2015, the Priority Enforcement Program (PEP) replaced the Secure Communities Program.

PEP, although similar to the Secure Communities Program, had a narrower focus. Whereas the Secure Communities Program sought to identify and arrest immigrants who had entered the country "unlawfully" and/or who were suspected of having committed a crime (American Immigration Council, 2011), PEP sought to prioritize the identification and arrest of immigrants "convicted of a criminal offense and others who pose a danger to public safety" (ICE, 2014, para. 4). Social justice advocates, state and local lawmakers, and police officials had significantly criticized the Secure Communities Program, in part due to the use of detainers in violation of the Fourth Amendment (ACLU, 2014; National Immigration Law Center, 2015). As ACLU (2014) explains,

> an ICE detainer asks a federal, state or local law enforcement agency (LEA) to "maintain custody" of a person for an additional 48 hours, plus weekend and holidays, "beyond the time when the subject would have otherwise been released from LEA's custody."
>
> (p. 1)

thereby effectively, detaining immigrants without having established probable cause as mandated by the Fourth Amendment. In fact, recent Supreme Court rulings, such as in the Arizona versus United States (2012) court ruling, have concluded,

> it is not a crime for a removable alien to remain present in the United States. See *INS* v. *Lopez-Mendoza*, 468 U. S. 1032, 1038 (1984). If the police stops someone based on nothing more than possible removability, the usual predicate for an arrest is absent.
>
> (IV C Section 6, para. 2)

Secure Communities had also been heavily criticized for expediting deportations without giving immigrants the opportunity to have their case heard by an immigration judge, or to access legal counsel (Kholi et al., 2011). Kholi et al. (2011), reporting on their study of the Secure Communities Program, based on a national sample of 375 individuals detained under this program in 2008, stated "only 24% of individuals arrested through Secure Communities and who had immigration hearings, had an attorney compared to 41% of all immigration court respondents who have counsel" (p. 2). A review of immigration court cases "involving 'adults with children'" (TRAC, 2016, para. 1) between July 2014 and September 2016, is consistent with Kholi et al.'s findings (2011). Of the 38,601 family cases decided by immigration judges during those 2 years, "27,015 of [them], or 70 percent" (TRAC, 2016, para. 1) lacked legal representation; of these cases, 43.4% were processed within 24 days, resulting in deportation orders. In contrast, only 4.4% of family cases with legal representation were processed as quickly (TRAC, 2016).

These findings underscore the implications of programs such as Secure Communities, which hinder immigrants' ability to access legal representation and immigration courts, thereby facilitating and expediting their deportation. Lastly, the racial and national origins composition of the immigrants arrested through Secure Communities had also raised racial profiling concerns (Rosenblum, 2015). Studies show "93% of the people identified for deportation through Secure Communities [were] from Latin American countries" (Kholi et al., 2011, p. 5), supporting allegations that Secure Communities had unfairly targeted immigrants of a particular group, Hispanics—a group that is one of the largest, minority groups within the United States, accounting for 18% of the total U.S. population (Kaiser Family Foundation, 2015).

IIRIRA and AEDPA have not only given way to more aggressive policies aimed at the arrest and deportation of the Mexican immigrant other, but "have been highly criticized for the devastation they have brought to immigrant families" (Hagan et al., 2010, p. 1800). In fact, IIRIRA and AEDPA and their direct effects, en masse deportations that will be subsequently discussed, share significant similarities with other highly exclusionary, White Nativist sociopolitical time periods and policies, such as the late 1920s and early 1930s, characterized by the Immigration Act of 1924 and Operation Wetback that resulted in the mass deportation of Mexican immigrants, as well as American citizens of Mexican descent, including American-born children. While some argue that this devastation has been "unintended" (Hagan et al., 2010, p. 1801), the subsequent integrative analysis of IIRIRA and AEDPA will illustrate the intentionality of this "unintended devastation."

## The Antiterrorism and Effective Death Penalty Act, and the Illegal Immigration Reform and Immigration Responsibility Act of 1996: Mixed status families

American-born children of one or two immigrant, Hispanic parents are not directly governed by immigration policy, but are part of a family unit that often falls under the direct purview of immigration policy. This family, which is often a mixed status family, is integral to the survival of the child (Chaudry et al., 2010; Dreby, 2012, 2015; Fix & Zimmermann, 1999). Accordingly, these American, Hispanic children are vulnerable to the effects of immigration policy due to the possible deportation of their family members. Some of these family members, such as parents, may be undocumented or legal residents and subject to removal, which renders these children vulnerable to "voluntary removal" in order to continue to grow up with their parent(s). At the same time, it is important to note that American-born, Mexican children, despite being protected from deportation by citizenship laws, have nonetheless been deported from the United States. As the historical analysis of immigration policy showed, these American children were indeed deported, along with Mexican immigrants, in the early 1930s and again during Operation Wetback (Hernandez, 2010). Given these two historical precedents, the integrative analysis will first examine how immigration and birthing rates have contributed to the changing demographic composition of the United States. This demographic contextualization will guide the analysis of IIRIRA's and AEDPA's overt and covert goals, concluding with a discussion of the policies' effects on mixed status families, and specifically, on American citizen children of Mexican parents.

According to the 2015 population census, 18% of the United States population, 56,872,700 people, are of Hispanic origin (Kaiser Family Foundation, 2015); a slight increase from 2014, at 17.3% (Stepler & Brown, 2016). Hispanics of Mexican origin are the largest Hispanic group, comprising 64% of the total Hispanic population (Stepler & Brown, 2016). However, whereas in the 1980s and 1990s, immigration seemed to be the primary factor fueling the Hispanic population growth, by the year 2000, birthing rates began to be the primary cause (Stepler & Brown, 2016). Although in the 1990s the Hispanic population grew by 8.1 million due to immigration, and by 7 million due to birthing, in the 2000s birthing replaced immigration as the leading factor fueling the growth. Between 2000 and 2010, there were 9.6 million births within the Hispanic population, and 6.5 million new Hispanic immigrants, reflecting not only an increase in birthing rates, but also a significant decrease in immigration, which has since continued. When examining the Hispanic population growth between 2010 and 2014, birthing, not immigration, was again the primary growth factor—3.9 million new Hispanic births and 1. 4 million new Hispanic immigrants. These most recent statistics also reflect a sharp decline in immigration that began in the early 2000s (Passel et al., 2010; Sterpel & Brown, 2016). Given the increasing number of Hispanic children born in the United States, how many of them live in immigrant and/or mixed status families? And, is the number of American citizen children born in immigrant families growing overall?

In 1990, prior to the implementation of IIRIRA and AEDPA, 13.4% of the children living in the United States had at least one immigrant parent; 77% of these children were American-born (Migration Policy Institute, 2016). By 2000, the number of children living with immigrant parent(s) had increased to 19.1%, of which 79.5% were American-born (Migration Policy Institute, 2016). By 2008, the number of children living with immigrant parents had reached 20%; 52.7% were children of a Hispanic, non-native born parent (or parents), who by and large was of Mexican origin—in 86.19% of the cases (The Urban Institute, 2010).

Current statistics continue to show increasing immigrant birthing rates among all groups. In 2014, 25% of the children living in the United States were born to immigrant families (Migration Policy Institute, 2016); and, the vast majority are American citizens, 88%, unlike their parents (Zong & Batalova, 2016). When parental immigration status and children's native origin are accounted for, statistics indicate that there are currently an "estimated 5.5 million [children living] with unauthorized immigrant parents, [and] about three-quarters [of these children] are U.S. born citizens" (Chaudry et al., 2010, p. viii). What is of additional significance is that of these 5.5 million children, 3.5 million are children of an unauthorized, immigrant Mexican parent (Dreby, 2012, p. 5). Additional reports indicate that, overall, the number of American-born children living with undocumented parents increased to 4.1 million in 2013 (Capps, Fix, & Zong, 2016; Menjivar & Gomez Cervantes, 2016).

Overall, the statistics clearly show that the number of children born in immigrant families, particularly within Hispanic, Mexican families, had started to increase by 1996, when IIRIRA and AEDPA were enacted. These two acts introduced a number of restrictive and exclusionary reforms aimed at facilitating and expediting deportation, while also changing some of the grounds for the cancellation of removal; these changes have had devastating consequences for an increasing number of mixed status families and their American-born children. Overall, IIRIRA and AEDPA:

- Mandate the deportation of legal permanent residents and illegal immigrants for relatively minor crimes, withdrawing [existing judiciary] discretion to consider the resulting hardship on family members.
- Limit judicial review available to immigrants facing deportation.
- Raise the "hardship" standards non-citizens have to meet to avoid deportation... extending from 7 to 10 years the required length of U.S. residence and by introducing a new annual cap of 4,000 where no previous limit existed (Fix & Zimmermann, 1999; "The Antiterrorism and Effective Death Penalty Act," para. 2).

At first glance, these two acts appear to be primarily designed to facilitate the removal of the Hispanic undocumented "illegal," or "criminal" legal, other from the United States. Both, AEDPA and IIRIRA, appear to be overtly informed by ideological principles rooted in national security and social welfare. This ideology of national protectionism is clearly reflected in the language of the policies' mandates, providing "White Natives" with the legal justification necessary to legitimize the deportation of the other. This nationalist, protectionist ideology emerges clearly in AEDPA, due to its focus on antiterrorism and criminality. AEDPA expanded the types of crimes that could constitute an aggravated felony and included crimes of moral turpitude as criminal grounds for deportation. IIRIRA, in turn, complemented AEDPA's national security focus, including specific provisions by which "criminal" immigrants, legal or "illegal," could be subject to expedited deportation proceedings due to their "criminality." The concurrent changes introduced by the two acts effectively established the legal logics by which deportation could be constructed as necessary and essential to the survival of the nation-state and its citizens. But most importantly, they also successfully constructed the Hispanic immigrant other as a threat to national security and, therefore, as a criminal. As Wolchok (1997) states when discussing the criminalization process of the immigrant other:

> Even one conviction for a crime of moral turpitude, such as shoplifting, is a deportable offense if the offense was committed within five years of entry... [Concurrently] The list of offenses considered to be "aggravated felonies" has been expanded to include most crimes of theft, violence and drugs. [Under] IIRIRA sect 321 "Aggravated felons" also face abbreviated deportation processes... [and] "cancelation of removal" is no longer available to long-term permanent residents with these convictions.
>
> (para. 13)

However, IIRIRA also introduced another significant reform. Whereas prior to 1996 an alien could petition the cancellation of removal due to the hardship that dependent family members could experience as a result of the person's deportation, IIRIRA narrowed this hardship clause. Under IIRIRA, the hardship standard was reinterpreted and explained in this manner: "the alien must provide evidence of harm to his spouse, parent or child substantially beyond that which ordinarily would be expected to result from the alien's deportation"(Conference Report to accompany H. R. 2202, as cited in Fix & Zimmermann, 1999, "Dividing Families," para. 5).

The effects of IIRIRA and AEDPA are very palpable and have certainly been felt by many mixed status families and American-born children. Reports by the Department of Homeland Security (2009), indicate that between 1998 and 2007, 2,199,138 immigrants were deported, of which 108,434 were parents of American-born children; 22.2% had no existing criminal convictions, while "77.8 percent had one or more convictions" (p. 10). A review of the criminal convictions revealed that in 34% of the cases, or 57,803 parents, had been deported due to "dangerous drugs," and 56.8% were deported due to aggravated felonies. Under the description of criminal offenses, some of the offenses that constituted grounds for deportation were immigration offenses (14.3%) and traffic offenses (7.4%), among other charges.

In 2008, after the inception of Secure Communities, the number of deportations increased, as well as the number of parental deportations. Between 2009 and 2012, 400,000 immigrants were deported yearly; this number decreased to 369,000, in 2013, and 316,000 in 2014 (Capps et al., 2015). With the cancellation of the Secure Communities Program in 2015, and the inception of the Priority Enforcement Program, deportations declined again to 235,413 in 2015 (Gonzalez-Barrera & Krogstad, 2016). However, in January 2017, President Trump cancelled the Priority Enforcement Program, reinstating the Secure Communities Program (see Chapter 8 for further discussion).

Parental deportation trends followed a similar path. After 2008, the number of parental deportations increased substantially, beginning to decline in 2013, consistent with the general deportation trends of 2013 and

2014 (DHS, 2014a, 2014b). Between July 2010 and September 2012, 205,000 immigrant parents of citizen children were deported, indicating an estimated yearly deportation of 90,000 parents, before beginning to decrease in 2013 to 72,000 (Capps et al., 2015; DHS, 2014a, 2014b).

As the statistics well illustrate, the changes introduced by IIRIRA to the hardship clause, which had previously allowed parents with dependent children to request the cancellation of their removal, led to the deportation of many parents who would have otherwise been able to stay in the United States. In addition, IIRIRA also introduced harsher penalties for immigrants who had violated immigration laws, such as entering without authorization. In such situations, IIRIRA barred the readmission of the deported individual for up to 10 years; thus effectively separating and alienating parents from children, unless the child and/or family decided to leave the United States to preserve their family unit.

IIRIRA and AEDPA have now been in effect for 20 years. Although initially the effects of these reforms could have been construed as "unintentional," there is now substantial data that clearly documents the effects of these two acts on mixed status families, and specifically on the children who are part of these families. Therefore, why are these provisions still enforced? And most importantly, why did IIRIRA change the hardship clause that enabled parents to petition the cancellation of removal, due to its impact on their children and other dependents? These questions are even more relevant, when considering that it wasn't until 2009, due to mounting criticism from advocacy groups, that the Department of Homeland Security began to track the number of parents of American citizen children who were being deported (DHS, 2009). Furthermore, the Department of Homeland Security still does not compile any official statistics on the number of American citizen children who may have left the country following parental deportation (Passel, Cohn, & Gonzalez-Barrera, 2012).

To understand the overt and covert policy goals and reforms introduced by IIRIRA and AEDPA, and specifically the changes made to the hardship provision, it is important to return to the demographic analysis of the United States at the time of their inception. By 1996, the Hispanic other had achieved a critical mass representation within the United States. This critical mass was not only due to immigration, but also due to child birthing rates; in fact, although immigrant child birthing rates were beginning to rise, "White Native" birthing rates had started, and continue, to decrease (Stepler & Brown, 2016). When demographic population growth and deportation statistics are examined concurrently, a correlation begins to emerge between immigration reforms that began in 1996 and the increasing presence of the Mexican other.

Overtly, the deportation reforms implemented in and since 1996 did seem to facilitate and expedite the removal of the Mexican-born other, "illegal" or "criminal" legal other, as previously stated. However, when the changes to the hardship clause are examined with the timing of their inception, a different understanding begins to emerge. IIRIA and the new hardship clause were created at a time when efforts to prevent the other from entering the United States had failed, while the number of American children born to the Hispanic other was increasing, especially in bordering states with Mexico. Within this historical, demographic and sociopolitical context, IIRIRA and AEDPA, and thus deportation, are exposed not as an unintentional, but rather as an intentional, covert, legal mechanism that sought to repatriate and remove American-born children of the Hispanic other from their home country. Recent reports are consistent with, and seem to support this hypothesis.

For example, Passel et al. (2012), found that the number of American-born children living in Mexico had increased from 240,000 to 500,000, between 2005 and 2010; Homeland Security News Wire (2016) also reported an ongoing increase, placing most current estimates at 550,000. The increase in the number of American citizen children living in Mexico is directly related to parental deportations and voluntary repatriations, as 1.4 million Mexicans have been deported from the United States since 2010 (Homeland Security News Wire, 2016). The challenges these children face, together with their families, are many—adjusting to a new environment, a new life and a different educational system, to name a few. Bureaucratic obstacles compound these problems, since the Mexican government does not recognize many of these children as Mexican.

Although these children can claim Mexican citizenship, they can only do so, if they have been registered at a Mexican Consulate in the United States, prior to arriving in Mexico; however, many children arrive without this required consular registration. As a result, they are caught in a lengthy and complicated process of citizenship determination (Homeland Security News Wire, 2016) and, until their citizenship is established, they are unable to access governmental "services and benefits [in Mexico] such as schools, scholarships, social programs and basic health services, such as vaccines" (Homeland Security News Wire, 2016, para. 5).

These children also incurre a number of losses through their "removal" from the United States, such as the loss of their home, familiar environment, culture and English language, friends, and other family members, who may have remained in the United States. Although leaving the United States allows American citizen children to stay with their parents, the emotional and psychological toll is significant; however, staying in the United States also jeopardizes their well-being.

## Effects of parental deportation: Children in mixed status families

Research studies show that after the arrest, detainment and eventual deportation of one or two parents, many mixed status families and American-born children experience significant financial difficulty, including housing instability and "food hardship" (Capps, Castaneda, Chaudry, & Santos, 2007; Chaudry et al., 2010, pp. viii–ix; Dreby, 2012). This economic hardship is certainly a predictable byproduct of deportation, since males are deported at higher rates than females, and they are more likely to be the primary provider. In other instances, it becomes very difficult for the parent who remains in the United States to support the entire family with one income, while also needing to adjust to suddenly becoming a single parent (Capps et al., 2015; Dreby 2012, 2015; Menjivar, & Gomez Cervantes, 2016).

Although as previously mentioned, American citizen children of Mexican parents do indeed leave the United States to join the deported parent(s) in Mexico (Chaudry et al., 2010; Dreby, 2012) in many instances, some family members remain in the United States. In these cases, families are often permanently divided, with children and parents living on both sides of the border (Chaudry et al., 2010, p. 24). In other instances, children who had been previously living with their parents found themselves in the foster care system following parental deportation (Capps et al., 2015; Wessler, 2011). As Capps et al. (2015) explain: "Once in foster care, the child's reunification with the immigrant parent may be interrupted because parents in prolonged immigration detention often cannot attend child custody hearings, and those who are deported cannot easily return to the United States" (p. vii).

These obstacles sometimes result in the termination of parental rights, and the subsequent adoption of these children, who, prior to parental deportation, were members of intact family units. In August 2013, in response to advocacy efforts and mounting criticism, ICE implemented a new directive, "Facilitating Parental Interests in the Course of Civil Immigration Enforcement Activities" (ICE, 2013). This directive is designed to protect the rights of detained and/or deported parents, facilitating their participation "in child welfare proceedings either in person or by video/phone conferencing" (Pinsky, 2014, para. 7). The directive also allows ICE to exercise prosecutorial discretion in regards to the detention and deportation of immigrant parents (ICE, 2013); however, as Pinsky (2014) explains: "Despite authority to use prosecutorial discretion, this privilege is seldom granted for parents" ("What Policy Does Not Address," para. 5).

Separation, economic hardship and being uprooted from their family and country of origin are not the only challenges faced by American-born Hispanic children and their families; death is also an unfortunate byproduct of parental desperation. In some instances, Chaudry et al. (2010) found that the deported parent, unable to enter the United States through legal means due to the AEDPA and IIRIRA regulations barring deported individuals from entering the United States for 3–10 years (Fix & Zimmermann, 1999), attempted to reunify with his/her child through illegal border crossing. The crossing sometimes ended in the tragic death of the parent—parents, who in their desperation, endured conditions that few could survive, as illustrated by the increasing death toll of the Hispanic immigrant other after the inception of border enforcement programs, such as Operation Gatekeeper

(Chaudry et al., 2010; Hing, 2004). Reports by the Department of Homeland Security, indicate that in 2013, 26,967 parents of American citizen children were arrested at the border while attempting to re-enter the United States to reunite with their children (DHS, 2014a, 2014b).

The human toll of parental deportation does not end here, however. American-born children also experience significant short- and long-term behavioral and emotional changes as a result of parental deportation and/ or separation (Capps et al., 2007, 2015; Chaudry et al., 2010; Debry, 2012; Menjivar & Gomez Cervantes, 2016). A number of studies have identified short-term behavioral problems in children after parental deportation, including loss of appetite, sleeping difficulty, frequent crying, fear and anxiety. Although these symptoms seemed to decrease after six months (Chaudry et al., 2010; Koball et al., 2015), other behavioral problems such as clinging and withdrawing behaviors, as well as anger, depression and aggression appeared to increase over time (Capps et al., 2015; Chaudry et al., 2010). In addition, many children of immigrant parents also report fear and anxiety, even when parental deportation has not occurred. The fear of losing a parent to deportation is often related to having lost other family members to deportation, as well as to the transmission of worry and anxiety within the family (Yoshikawa, 2011). As Zayas, Aguilar-Gaxiola, Yoon and Rey (2015) explain: "[I]mmigrant parents' own state of worry and anxiety about the vulnerable legal status they occupy is transmitted to their own children through words and deeds" (p. 3).

Given the significant financial and emotional hardships experienced by the American citizen children of immigrant Hispanic, Mexican parents due to parental deportation, is it possible for these children to experience a sense of belonging to this country? Or to experience themselves as "American citizens" when their families are being often permanently disrupted? Or, will they instead experience themselves as "second class" marginalized citizen others? (Fix & Zimmermann, 1999). Because they are American-born, Hispanic/Mexican children are American citizens; yet, parental deportation renders them other, second class citizens (Fix & Zimmermann, 1999), whose rights under the United States Constitution appear to be different from those of "White Native" children. "White Native" children, by virtue of their parentage, can never be vulnerable to parental deportation and to its emotional implications. Their right to be raised within an intact family will never be threatened by the United States Constitution; and, they will never fear a possible expatriation or removal from their birth country due to parental deportation, unlike the American-born children of Hispanic, predominantly Mexican, immigrant parents.

## Conclusion

The historical review of immigration policy, and the demographic con-textualization of IIRIRA and AEDPA revealed five specific policy conse-quences consistent with a formulation of identity contestation, preservation and annihilatory aggression. As the analysis showed: (1) American-born, Hispanic and primarily Mexican children do indeed leave the United States after parental deportation to be reunified with their parent(s); (2) those who do not leave the United States, endure long and sometimes permanent separations from the parent(s), which deprive them of growing up within their family environment; (3) these children and their mixed status families often experience significant poverty as a result of parental deportation, such as inadequate access to food, housing and other basic needs; (4) parental deportation exposes children to emotional deprivation, resulting in short- and long-term emotional/behavioral changes that interfere with their normal emotional and educational development and growth; and, (5) one of the most frequent, long-term behavioral symptoms experienced by children ages 6–17 after parental arrest, separation and/or deportation is anger and aggressiveness (Chaudry et al., 2010), behavior congruent with an experience of intrapsychic annihilation.

As the integrative analysis of IIRIRA and AEDPA has shown, immigration reforms implemented in and since 1996 have indeed resulted in the covert, legal extrication of American-born, Hispanic children from their birth country; an extrication hidden and legitimized by the criminalization of their parents under a White Nativist ideology of entitlement and national protectionism (Volkan, 2013). Under the guise of national security, "White Natives" successfully constructed the Hispanic, Mexican other as a threat, that is, as an illegal, criminal invader, thereby opening group, historical unconscious and conscious affective wounds related to war, expansion and territorial contestation. At the same time, this Hispanic, Mexican other had been covertly allowed in for decades to meet the United States' cheap labor demands, necessary for the nation's economic wealth maximization (Hernandez, 2010; Wallerstein, 2003). However, as the integrative analysis of immigration policy showed, and specifically the demographic contextualization of IIRIRA and AEDPA, these two acts, in a similar manner to the Immigration Act of 1924, had a different unstated aim: to decrease the presence of the American-born children of Mexican immigrants, covertly and outside public view, at a time when Hispanic population growth was increasing due to birthing rates rather than migration.

Unlike IIRIRA and AEDPA, previous historical deportation efforts had been explicit and public, forcing thousands of families and American children to leave the United States. These mass deportations, such as Operation Wetback, were also militarized in nature, and this militarization could not disguise the inherent White Nativist aggression tied to the legal measures. IIRIRA and AEDPA however, are different from previous family, mass deportations in that they aim to overtly deport the illegal, criminal, adult Mexican other, not the families or children. However, the White Nativist aggression tied to dynamics of identity contestation and preservation hidden in IIRIRA and AEDPA can still be detected, albeit in a subtler and thus more insidious manner; and it is certainly being felt by the American citizen children of the Hispanic, Mexican, immigrant other. As the analysis showed, parental deportations have been inflicting considerable emotional damage on the "American hybrid children" who remain in the country. The financial hardship these children must endure and the emotional pain resulting from permanent parental separation inflicts considerable, intrapsychic emotional damage, leaving these children feeling attacked, and fearful of a possible annihilation. This conclusion is well supported by a number of studies that have examined the effects of parental deportation, which have clearly illustrated that after parental deportation and permanent separation, children struggled with anxiety, depression, anger and/or behavioral aggression (Capps et al., 2015; Dreby, 2012, 2015).

The financial and emotional hardship experienced by these children further supports the theoretical argument presented and illustrated through the integrative analysis of immigration policy, and specifically IIRIRA and AEDPA. The other, who is now being born in this country and who has become part of the American self, is being destroyed due to long-term financial and emotional hardship. As argued in the integrative analysis, "White Nativist" efforts to protect the transformation of their group and individual, affect laden, suitable targets of intrapsychic externalization, are indeed resulting in the marginalization of American-born Hispanic children. This marginalization has also been shown to interfere with their emotional and educational development. While White Nativist, identity contestation and preservation efforts may have thus far proven partially successful, they have done so at a cost to the social foundation of the United States.

Furthermore, not only are these children being marginalized and hurt by the current immigration policies, they are also being constructed by "White Natives" as unassimilable within the sociopolitical discourse of the nation (Hunting, 2004b). While this construction, as Chapters 6 and 7 will illustrate, is unfounded, one has to also question whether it is possible for these children to assimilate into a society that is breaking up and subjugating them and their families. In other words, are these children failing and refusing to assimilate, or is the White Nativist ideology that pervades the American mainstream of society interfering with their assimilation and acculturation process? And, are "White Natives" ultimately blaming American citizen children of Hispanic, Mexican immigrants for the effects of their White Nativist, anti-immigrant, othering, sociopolitical discourse? (Huntington, 2004b). In fact, Aleinikoff and Rumbaut (1998) in their discussion of models of membership as self-fulfilling prophecies suggest that,

> concerns about assimilation—based...on race and national origin—may contribute to a shift to a less inclusionary membership model...[that may] produce behavior that... complicates the integration of newcomers... [Thus]... the formulation of public policy... helps to produce the conditions that affirm the public policies.

(p. 21)

"White Natives" claim that the Hispanic other is failing and refusing to assimilate into the "American society" and way of life. This claim also legitimizes the exclusion, subjugation and marginalization of the Hispanic other and his/her children. However, is this claim accurate? Chapter 6 will present and discuss the findings of a secondary data analysis of the Children of Immigrants Longitudinal Study (CILS). The chapter will integrate research findings to explore and examine whether or not American citizen children of Mexican immigrant parents did indeed perceive and detect the increasingly White Nativist sociopolitical context that began in 1996. Chapters 6 and 7 will also explore how an increasingly White Nativist sociopolitical context may affect the children's ethnic identity development, acculturation and sense of national belonging.

These two chapters will attempt to answer one central question: is the current White Nativist, immigration, sociopolitical discourse indeed producing what it fears? That is, American-born children of Hispanic heritage who, despite acculturation into the larger American society, struggle to conceptualize their individual selves as belonging to this larger American society.

## Notes

1 For further information about the Bracero program and its impact on Mexican workers, see Hing (2004).
2 For further information on the 1965, H-2 and H-1 guest worker programs, and their effects, see Chin and Villazor (2015).
3 See Pub. L. No. 104–208, 110 Stat. 3009-546 (1996) Retrieved from htt://frwebgate. access.gpo.gov/cgi-bin/getdoc.cgi?dbname=104_cong_public_laws&docid=f: publ208.104.pdf.
4 See Pub. L. No 104-132110 Stat. 1214 (1996). Retrieved from www.gpo.gov/fdsys/ pkg/BILLS-104s735enr/pdf/BILLS-104s735enr.pdf.
5 See Capps et al. (2011).

# 6 Secondary study of the children of immigrants longitudinal study

## White Nativism, ethnic identity development and acculturation

### Introduction

The integrative analysis of contemporary immigration policy reforms, with a focus on deportation reforms, uncovered a White Nativist process of identity contestation and preservation. This process has had devastating consequences for many American- and non-American-born children of Mexican immigrants, and has also damaged American society as a whole. Increasing numbers of American-born Hispanic children are growing up having felt directly or indirectly the effects of the White Nativist immigration policy reforms introduced in 1996 by IIRIRA and AEDPA. These two acts have led to mass deportations, and often times, to the permanent separation of American-born children of immigrant parents from one or both parents. Hispanic mixed status families have been affected in disproportionate numbers by the immigration reforms introduced by IIRIRA and AEDPA, and as parents are deported, American-born children are also leaving with them. Where as in 2005, there were 240,000 American citizen children living in Mexico, there are now 550,000 children; although official statistics are not available, "a potentially large share of these children moved [to Mexico] with or soon after a deported parent" (Passel, Cohn, & Gonzalez-Barrera, 2012, p. 12).

However, American citizen children of Mexican immigrant parents, as discussed in Chapter 5, often do stay in the United States with the remaining caregiver, or under the care of another family member (Capps et al., 2015; Dreby, 2012; Zayas et al., 2015). The effects of parental deportation on the children's emotional and educational development have been well documented. However, what is less understood is how these children are conceptualizing themselves in this country. Can they conceptualize themselves as American, or as belonging to this country, in an increasingly White Nativist sociopolitical context, marked by the deportation of the Mexican other, and the division of many Hispanic mixed status families?

As discussed in Chapters 2, 4 and 5, the Hispanic, Mexican other, has been constructed by "White Natives" not only as illegal and unwanted, but also as an assimilation problem. For the "White Native," this other is unwilling, or failing, to assimilate into the dominant mainstream of society (Huntington, 2004a, 2004b), holding onto their Spanish language, traditions and values, while concurrently rejecting "White Native," Anglo-Saxon cultural symbols. President Donald Trump's right-wing, nationalist, platform spoke directly to "White Native" fears related to the erosion of the American national identity and their nation-state. His politic of fear (Wodak, 2015) attributes this "American" national erosion to existing cultural pluralist discourses, embedded in a multicultural ideology (Renshon, 2000). "White Natives" attribute this multicultural ideology to the increasing presence of the "immigrant and refugee" other (Wodak, 2015), as well as to their perceived failure to assimilate into the "White Native" culture of the United States. President Trump's politic of fear has indeed succeeded in further polarizing "White Natives" against the Mexican immigrant other. The nationalist rhetoric that characterized his campaign, informed by an entitlement ideology of "White Native" superiority (Volkan, 2013), successfully problematized the Mexican other, through a discourse of criminality. This sociopolitical discourse, further constructed the Mexican other as responsible for the moral erosion and decay of the United States. Overall, President Trump's politic of fear and nationalism strengthened White Nativist, anti-immigrant sentiment, promoting, reifying and further legitimizing current deportation-based immigration policies.

As the integrative sociopolitical and psychological analysis of contemporary immigration policy has illustrated, assimilation is not a unidirectional process. Research on segmented assimilation has shown that the integration, assimilation and adjustment process of any immigrant group is not only contingent on the group's "willingness" to integrate themselves within the host country, but is also deeply influenced by the context of reception in which the immigrant group finds itself. However, despite the increasingly White Nativist, sociopolitical context of the United States, little is known about how such a context may be influencing the social identity of American-born children of Mexican immigrant parents. How does an increasingly White Nativist context affect the ethnic identity and acculturation style of these children? And ultimately how does such a context affect their ability to establish a sense of national belonging, necessary for their structural integration within the collective self of the United States?

To answer these questions, this chapter, along with Chapter 7, will discuss the findings of a secondary analysis of the Children of Immigrants Longitudinal Study, CILS[1] (Farina, 2015). This secondary study was designed with two purposes. The study first sought to test the White Nativism hypothesis that had emerged through the integrative analysis of contemporary immigration policy reforms. The integrative analysis linked the increasingly White Nativist sociopolitical context of the United States to the inception of more restrictive and exclusionary immigration policies, which culminated in the implementation of IIRIRA and AEDPA. To test this theoretical hypothesis of White Nativism, the study first sought to determine whether or not American-born children of Mexican parents indeed perceived the sociopolitical context of the United States as an increasingly White Nativist context, since 1992.

The study also sought to explore the evolution of the children's ethnic identity, acculturation style and sense of national belonging between 1992 and 2003. The findings, which will be presented in this chapter, as well as in Chapter 7, were contextualized within the White Nativist sociopolitical environment identified by the children, as well as within the corresponding, specific immigration policy context of each data collection time period (see Figure 6.1).

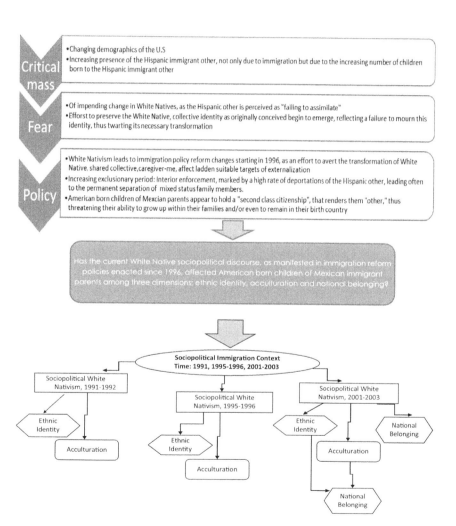

*Figure 6.1* Concept map.

## The CILS study

The CILS is the largest, longitudinal study of the adaptation process of second-generation[2] immigrant children to date (Portes & Rumbaut, 2005). The study began in 1992 and ended in 2006, collecting information on the adaptation process of immigrant children at three different time periods: 1991–1992, 1995–1996 and 2001–2003. The CILS was used for the secondary study because of its common focus on the adaptation process of second generation immigrant children, and because the data collection time periods overlapped with the integrated analysis' immigration contexts, that is, 1991–1992, prior to IIRIRA and AEDPA; 1995–1996, during the inception of the two acts; and 2001–2003, 7 years after their inception.

Students who participated in the CILS study were between 13 and 17 years old; and attended 8th or 9th grade, at one of the 49 public and private schools in Miami/Ft. Lauderdale, Florida and in San Diego, California, that participated in the study. The students also needed to be "U.S. born, or to have lived in the United States for at least five years and to have at least one foreign-born parent" (Portes & Rumbaut, 2005, p. 987). It is important to note, as discussed by Portes and Rumbaut (2005) that Miami and San Diego were located in "two of the [areas]... most heavily affected by the new immigration laws" (p. 988).

Initially, 5,262 children took part in the CILS study in 1992, with an average age of 14. The first follow-up survey was conducted 3 years later, between 1995 and 1996; followed by a second, and final, follow-up survey between 2001 and 2003, when the original study participants had reached an average age of 24 (Center for Migration and Development).

## Secondary research study

The secondary study presented here only examined the adaptation process of the American-born children of immigrant Mexican parents who participated in the CILS. This study included all children who had at least one Mexican immigrant parent and who had lived in the United States for no less than 5 years. Given these criteria, the total number of children included in the secondary study in 1991 was 446, followed by 364 in 1995, and 271[3] in 2001. The large majority of children in the secondary study lived in California, 95.29% in 1991 and 95.50% in 1995, although by 2001 some had left California. Most of the children were between the ages of 13 and 15 (93.52%) and except for a small percentage who had lived in the United States less than 10 years (13% in 1991 and 8% in 1995), most of them had lived in the United States all their life.

In terms of parental origin, in 1991, 77.58% of the children's fathers and 85.43% of the mothers were Mexican born, while 13.23% of fathers and 12.56% of mothers were American born. Parents often did not disclose their citizenship status (46.19% of fathers and 28.70% of mothers). However,

*Table 6.1* Parental demographic information, 1991: education

| Highest level of education[a] | Father | | Mother | |
|---|---|---|---|---|
| | N | % | N | % |
| **1991** | | | | |
| Elementary school or less | 82 | 18.39 | 106 | 23.77 |
| Middle school or less | 52 | 11.66 | 68 | 15.25 |
| Some high school | 52 | 11.66 | 64 | 14.35 |
| High school graduate | 92 | 20.63 | 86 | 19.28 |
| Some college or university | 54 | 12.11 | 37 | 8.30 |
| College graduate or more | 32 | 7.17 | 24 | 5.38 |
| Missing | 82 | 18.39 | 61 | 13.68 |
| **1995** | | | | |
| Elementary school or less | 79 | 21.79 | 92 | 25.27 |
| Middle school or less | 47 | 12.91 | 48 | 13.19 |
| Some high school | 52 | 14.29 | 59 | 16.21 |
| High school graduate | 62 | 17.03 | 91 | 25.00 |
| Some college or university | 60 | 16.48 | 39 | 10.71 |
| College graduate or more | 17 | 4.67 | 18 | 4.95 |
| Other | 0 | 0 | 2 | 0.55 |
| Missing | 82 | 18.39 | 61 | 13.68 |

a   Education: Question 36 (Father); Question 41 (Mother).

about 54% of the parents who did disclose this information reported being American citizens (52.91% of fathers and 56.26% of mothers), suggesting that a large percentage were either permanent documented or undocumented immigrants.

Overall, parental educational achievement reflected a low educational, human capital. In 1991, as illustrated in Table 6.1, only about 20% of the parents reported having graduated from high school, and less than 10% in either 1991 or 1995 reported having graduated from college. The home ownership profile was consistent with the parents' educational level and associated socioeconomic status. In 1991, 54.48% of the children who participated in the study lived in rented apartments, while 43.95% lived in homes owned by their parents.

## Measures and conceptual definitions

The measures used in the study relied on the structured questionnaires designed for the first, second and third data collection periods of the CILS study, 1991–1992, 1995–1996, and 2001–2003 (see Appendix A to access questionnaires; see Appendix C for operationalization of measures). This section will present each of the secondary study's conceptual measures, and will link them to the theories presented and applied in the integrative analysis of contemporary immigration policy. However, it is important to understand that the measures are a best approximation and attempt to capture the complex theoretical formulation of the constructs presented in the analysis. Likewise, the study's findings do not prove causality, but rather show a correlation between the different measures that form the basis of the integrated analysis of contemporary immigration policy reforms.

## Explicit, ethnic identity importance index

In this index, the children's self-reported ethnic identities were grouped into four categories: "1) a plain 'American' identity; 2) a hyphenated-American identity (e.g., Mexican-American, Vietnamese-American); 3) a national-origin identity (e.g., Filipino, Cuban, Jamaican); and 4) a pan-ethnic minority group identity (e.g., Hispanic, Latino, Chicano, Asian, Black)" (Aleinikoff and Rumbaut, 1998, p. 10). These categories are consistent with research studies designed to explore ethnic identity (Citrin & Sears, 2009) and are often found in segmented assimilation research, as well as in research pertaining to membership self-fulfilling prophecies that relied on the CILS data (Aleinikoff & Rumbaut, 1998; Gratton, Gutmann, & Skop, 2007; Portes, Fernandez-Kelly, & Haller, 2005; Portes & Zhou, 1994).

The American ethnic self-identity, within this context, represents upward assimilation into the United States mainstream of society, as well as lower interaction with prejudice and racism (Aleinikoff & Rumbaut, 1998). A hyphenated-American identity represents a bridge between the immigrant experience and the American identity (Aleinikoff & Rumbaut, 1998), and the pan-ethnic identity suggests an "identification with American racial minorities in contexts in which class and race play a more determinative role than culture and language" (Aleinikoff & Rumbaut, 1998, p. 15). These definitions facilitated the exploration of the relationship between the children's ethnic identity, and other segmented assimilation constructs included in this study, such as racial identification, experience of prejudice, perceived sociopolitical White Nativism, and mode of acculturation, among others.

Ashmore et al.'s (2004) theoretical definition and understanding of devaluation also informed this index. Although devaluation can be harmful and self-eroding, Ashmore, Deaux, and McLaughlin-Volpe (2004) suggest that devaluation does not invariably affect all individuals in a negative manner, explaining that its effects are contingent on the individual's social context, and on the importance the individual attaches to the devalued identity marker. To assess the level of importance an individual attributes to a specific devalued aspect of the self-concept, Ashmore et al. (2004) differentiate between explicit and implicit importance, where explicit importance is defined as: "the individual's subjective appraisal of the degree to which collective identity is important to her or his overall sense of self" (p. 87). The Explicit, Ethnic Identity Importance Index includes an explicit ethnic importance question to capture the importance the children attribute to their ethnic identity.

## Racial identification

The study includes a racial identity measure, since racial identity interacts with ethnicity, modes of acculturation (Berry, 2003; Gratton et al., 2007; Portes et al., 2005) and upward or downward segmented assimilation. Additionally, many Hispanic people define their racial identity in ethnic terms, rather than racially (Taylor, Lopez, Martinez, & Velasco, 2012), thus providing a complementary proxy measure for ethnic identity, while also controlling for what could be a confounding variable. This measure includes two questions from the 1995 and 2001 CILS questionnaires; the 1991 survey was not included as there was no equivalent question.

## Sociopolitical White Nativism

Sociopolitical White Nativism was measured at both the micro and macro levels, using the Experience of Prejudice Index (micro) and the Perceived Sociopolitical White Nativism Index (macro), defined as follows:

### *Experience of prejudice index*

This index measures the prejudice the children experienced within their immediate environment and was informed by Berry's (2003) theory of acculturation and by segmented assimilation theory (Portes & Rumbaut, 1994). Berry (2001, 2003) states that acculturation is comprised of various strategies chosen by an individual in an effort to adapt to his/her environment. At the same time, Berry (2001, 2003) also cautions that the strategies a non-dominant person may be able to choose, are not always freely chosen, and are influenced by the environment and attitude of the dominant group. Consistent with this perspective, segmented assimilation theory, [as discussed by Abraido-Lanza, Armbrister, Florez, and Aguirre (2006), Gratton, Gutmann, and Skop (2007), Portes & Rumbaut (1994) and Portes et al. (2005)] states that the assimilation process of immigrant groups is not only determined by the immigrant other, but is also determined by: (1) the particular characteristics of the host country; (2) the country's dominant sociopolitical discourse; (3) the country's structural policies; and (4) the dominant views of the ethnic group to which the immigrant other belongs. The Experience of Prejudice Index provides in this manner, a mechanism for capturing the children's perceived interactions with micro prejudice, which reflects one aspect of the dominant attitudes toward the children's parental ethnic group.

The Experience of Prejudice Index is also conceptualized and operationalized as a proxy measure of the White Nativist aggression directed toward "the American Hybrid other," and the increasingly White Nativist,[4] destructive, "exclusionary" and "marginalizing" behaviors toward the Mexican immigrant other. These behaviors, as discussed in the integrative analysis, are conceptually understood as "White Native," negative affect-laden, mother-me experiences, externalized onto "the American hybrid other;" an acceptable suitable target of externalization, necessary for the preservation of individual and collective "White Native" intrapsychic integration (Volkan, 1985, 2013).

### Perceived sociopolitical White Nativism index

This index measures the children's perceptions of the structural barriers present in their environment and in the country as a whole. The index uses questions belonging to Portes and Bach's Perceptions of Society and Discrimination Index (PSDI) and is informed by Huntington's (2004a) and Swain's (2002) definition of White Nativism and its implications.

## National belonging index

National belonging, as discussed in Chapter 4, "...is often defined in terms of 'ethnic' ancestry and 'civic' commitment (with the latter typically implying a more inclusive conception of belonging)" (Wakefield et al., 2001, p. 1). The National Belonging Index includes two separate and intersecting constructs discussed in the integrative immigration policy analysis: (1) Patriotism, as defined by Citrin and Sears (2009) and Kosterman and Feshbach (1989); and (2) Civic engagement as defined by Adler and Goggin (2005) and Putnam (1995, 2000); civic engagement comprises electoral and religious participation.

Patriotism, as discussed by Citrin and Sears (2009) and Kosterman and Feshbach (1989), can be understood as a measure of "the affective component of one's feelings toward one's country" (Kosterman & Feshbach, 1989, p. 271). This definition is also consistent with Volkan's (1985, 1998) conceptualization of the nation, and the relationship that exists between affective experiences and needs originating within the child–caregiver relationship, and the individual–nation relationship. In fact, Feshbach (1991) states, "In many ways, the nation provides adult individuals with feelings of security and vicarious feelings of approval and related rewards through identifications that were directly experienced in the early childhood situation" (p. 211).

Given Feshbach's (1991) conceptualization, question 47, "Which feels most like 'home' to you?" (CILS survey 2001), was used as a proxy measure for patriotism. This question also captures an important psychological metaphor between home and the nation, that of a secure base, linking this conceptualization to attachment processes and theory (Bowlby, 1988). This metaphor is often found in political literature (Feshbach, 1991), where the nation is referred to as the motherland or fatherland, and therefore conceptualized as a protector, or as a nurturer.

Yet, national belonging, as discussed in the integrative analysis, can also be conceptualized in terms of civic engagement, that is, level of individual community participation and integration (Adler & Goggin, 2005; Crowley, n. d.;

Putnam, 1995, 2000; Wakefield et al., 2011). Given this conceptualization, civic engagement was integrated as part of the National Belonging Index, and operationalized in terms of social capital, as any activity that fosters social capital, consistent with Putnam's (1995, 2000) definition. This conceptualization was also selected because it overlaps with the design of the CILS, which explored electoral and community participation as indicators of immigrant incorporation—upward or downward assimilation (Portes & Rumbaut, 2006). However, since civic engagement is tied to active expressions of citizenship[5] (Beltrandy y Rudquist, 2012) and not just interest in activities, the final operationalization of national belonging measured electoral affiliation and participation (Beltrandy y Rudquist, 2012). Religious participation was also included as a second measure of community participation and civic engagement, consistent with Putnam's (1995, 2000), Crowley's (n.d.) and Flanagan, Levine, and Setterson's (2009) conceptualization.

## Acculturation strategies index and scales

Five acculturation scales were developed to examine the acculturation processes of the children along five dimensions: Linguistic Assimilation: English Acquisition; Parental Native Acquisition; Linguistic Preference; Culture, Values and Behavior; and Ethnic Interaction. Only three of these five scales were integrated into the Acculturation Strategies Index, which was developed to measure the children's acculturation strategies along three central dimensions: (1) Linguistic Preference, as this measure was able to identify both English acquisition and acquisition/retention of parental native language; (2) the Ethnic Interaction Scale; and (3) the Culture, Values and Behavior Scale. The Acculturation Index was informed by Berry's (2003) acculturation model, where acculturation is understood as a process of adaptation along various dimensions of a person's culture, ethnic identification, values, beliefs, etc.; and by previous acculturation research that explored similar dimensions (Aleinikoff & Rumbaut, 1998; Citrin & Sears, 2009; Portes & Rumbaut, 1996; Portes et al., 2005).

The Acculturation Strategies Index provided a mechanism for measuring the children's acculturation strategies along Berry's (2003) continuum of assimilation, integration, separation and marginalization, consistent with a multilevel acculturation process. For example, a child could be acculturating to the dominant culture without decreasing his/her individual and psychological ties to his/her ethnic group culture (see Appendix C for further discussion).

## Sociopolitical immigration context between 1991 and 2003

### *Sociopolitical White Nativism*

To establish the nature of the sociopolitical context of the United States between 1991 and 2003, the secondary study explored the sociopolitical White Nativism perceived by the American-born children of Mexican immigrant parents. The presence of White Nativism was measured at both the micro, individual level, through the Experience of Prejudice Index; and at the macro, systemic level, through the Perceived Sociopolitical White Nativism Index.

### Experience of prejudice index

As can be seen in Table 6.2, over time the children did experience higher levels of prejudice.[6] In 1991, 65.99% of the children reported having experienced prejudice, whereas by 1995 this percentage had increased to 82.09%, rising again in 2001–2003 to 88.3%. The increase in experienced prejudice between 1991 and 1995, and between 1995 and 2001–2003 was statistically significant (symmetry, exact significance test, $p = .001$) and consistent with the integrative analysis' hypothesis of increasing sociopolitical White Nativism.

### Perceived sociopolitical White Nativism index[7]

This index, as previously mentioned, was designed to measure the children's perception of the structural barriers present in their environment and in the country as a whole. The index was developed using the questions belonging to the Portes and Bach's Perceptions of Society and Discrimination Index (PSDI), included within the 1991 and 1995, CILS survey questionnaires (see Appendix B for further discussion). The index was also informed by Huntington's (2004a) and Swain's (2002) operational definition of White Nativism and its implications (see Appendix C).

Table 6.3 summarizes the children's perception of the sociopolitical context in which they were growing up between 1991 and 1995–1996. Children were first asked whether there was racial discrimination in economic opportunity in the United States. While in 1991, 82.34% of the children agreed with this statement, in 1995–1996, 90.06% agreed, reflecting a substantial increase within a 4- to 5-year period. When it came to how the American

*Table 6.2* Experience of prejudice 1991, 1995 and 2001

| [b]*Experience of prejudice* | *1991* | | *1995* | | *2001* | |
|---|---|---|---|---|---|---|
| | *Frequency* | *%[a]* | *Frequency* | *%* | *Frequency* | *%* |
| Yes | 293 | 65.99 | 298 | 82.09 | 228 | 88.03 |
| No | 151 | 34.01 | 65 | 17.91 | 31 | 11.97 |
| Total | $N = 444$ | 100.00 | $N = 363$ | 100.00 | $N = 259$ | 100.00 |

a  Total percentages reflect the frequency distribution for the total sample per time period.
b  Experience of Prejudice: answers to question 81 in 1991 and 1995; and question 35 in 2001.

*Table 6.3* Perceived Sociopolitical White Nativism Index 1991 and 1995

| Index Questions | 1991 | | | | | 1995 | | | | |
|---|---|---|---|---|---|---|---|---|---|---|
| | N | 1 (%)[b] | 2 (%) | 3 (%) | 4 (%) | N | 1 (%)[b] | 2 (%) | 3 (%) | 4 (%) |
| | | *Likert Scale*[a] | | | | | *Likert Scale* | | | |
| [c]There is racial discrimination in economic opportunities in the U.S. | 436 | 168 (38.53) | 191 (43.81) | 57 (13.07) | 20 (4.59) | 362 | 163 (45.03) | 163 (45.03) | 28 (7.73) | 8 (2.21) |
| [d]The American way of life weakens the family | 430 | 32 (7.44) | 156 (36.28) | 172 (40.00) | 70 (16.28) | 360 | 58 (16.11) | 143 (39.72) | 117 (32.50) | 42 (11.67) |
| [e]There is much conflict between different racial and ethnic groups in the U.S. | 430 | 200 (46.51) | 161 (37.44) | 51 (11.86) | 18 (4.19) | 362 | 173 (47.79) | 144 (39.78) | 40 (11.05) | 5 (1.38) |
| [f]Non-whites have as many opportunities to get ahead economically as whites in the U.S. | 434 | 103 (23.73) | 123 (28.34) | 119 (27.42) | 89 (20.51) | 362 | 65 (17.96) | 121 (33.43) | 113 (31.22) | 63 (17.40) |
| [g]There is no better country to live in than the U.S. | 433 | 128 (29.56) | 133 (30. 72) | 112 (25.87) | 60 (13.86) | 359 | 135 (37.60) | 112 (31.20) | 74 (20.61) | 38 (10.58) |
| [h]Americans generally feel superior to foreigners | 434 | 181 (41.71) | 166 (38.25) | 67 (5.44) | 20 (4.61) | 361 | 150 (41.55) | 149 (41.27) | 51 (14.13) | 11 (3.05) |

a Likert Scale: 1 = Agree a lot; 2 = Agree a little; 3 = disagree a little; 4 = disagree a lot.
b (%) Percentages reported reflect the number of responses per Likert scale rating and question being reported.
c CILS 1991 and 1995: Question 79.
d CILS 1991 and 1995: Questions 80.
e CILS 1991 and 1995: Question 81.
f CILS 1991 and 1995: Question 82.
g CILS 1991 and 1995: Question 83.
h CILS 1991 and 1995: Question 84.

way of life affected the family, in 1991, 43.72% of the children reported that the American way of life weakened the family. By 1995, this percentage had increased to 55.83% – either a lot (16.11%) or a little (39.72%).

Children also reported perceiving more conflict among racial and ethnic groups in 1995 (87.57%) than in 1991 (83.97%). However, when children were asked if they had as many opportunities to get ahead as whites, their views appeared to be more positive, reflecting very little fluctuation. In 1991 (52.07%) and 1995 (51.39%), about 52% of the children agreed, either a lot or a little, that non-whites had as many economic opportunities for upward mobility as whites. In terms of living in the United States, in 1995, 68.89% of the children agreed, either a lot (37.60%) or a little (31.20%) that there was no better country to live in than the United States, reflecting an 8.8% increase from 1991. The children also noticed that Americans generally felt increasingly superior to foreigners. Whereas in 1991, 79.96% of the children reported that Americans felt superiority to foreigners, in 1995 this percentage had increased to 82.82%.[8]

The context described by the itemized responses of the Perceived Sociopolitical White Nativism Index is consistent with the overall, 1991 and 1995 index scores. The index's possible range of scores is between 6 and 22, where 6 indicates high-perceived sociopolitical White Nativism and 22, a very low perception. In 1991, 55.77% of the index scores clustered between the 12 to 15 range, whereas in 1995, 55.53% of the scores clustered between the 11 to 14 range. The paired t-test,[9] and Wilcoxon signed rank test ($p = .027$) confirmed these findings, indicating that over time, the children had indeed recognized the progressively White Nativist nature of the sociopolitical context in which they were growing up. These results were also consistent with the prejudice reported by the children in 1991 and 1995. When the relationship between sociopolitical White Nativism and prejudice was examined,[10] the findings revealed a statistically significant correlation between the Perceived Sociopolitical White Nativism Index and the Experience of Prejudice Index in both 1991 and 1995. Although this correlation was weak, it did show that an increase in experienced prejudice was indeed correlated with increasing perceived sociopolitical White Nativism, adding further validity to the White Nativist context captured by the analysis of the Sociopolitical White Nativism Index.

## Conclusion

### *Sociopolitical White Nativist context 1991–2003*

Overall, the findings provided empirical evidence and support for the sociopolitical and intrapsychic formulation of White Nativism and related White Nativist conceptualization of immigration reform policies enacted since 1996. The Perceived Sociopolitical White Nativism Index and Experience of Prejudice Index provided a mechanism for evaluating the presence of White

Nativism, as well as its effects on the American-born children of Mexican immigrant parents. The analysis also provided empirical evidence of a context marked by White Nativist aggression, that is, increasing prejudice, devaluation of the immigrant other, racial conflict and racially/ethnically driven, economic structural barriers (Crocker & Quinn, 2004; Miller & Garran, 2008).

The findings gave a unique window into the children's perception of the social context in which they were growing up between 1991 and 2003; especially as a majority of the children in the study resided in California at the time the CILS began. These children had grown up under the implementation of Operation Gatekeeper; the passing of Proposition 187 in 1994, which was subsequently halted and never implemented; and the implementation of IIRIRA and AEDPA in 1996. The children's responses, as captured by the micro and macro White Nativism indexes, are consistent with California's sociopolitical context between 1991 and 1995; and reflect the children's progressive interaction with an increasingly White Nativist context. Their responses also demonstrate the children's ability to detect and separate the micro[11] and macro[12] manifestations of an increasingly White Nativist, national, sociopolitical discourse. These findings are consistent with Portes and Zhou's (1994) research related to economic and sociopolitical risk factors associated with the downward assimilation of children of immigrants.[13]

The White Nativist sociopolitical context described by the children also clearly illustrates dynamics of power related to claims of White Nativist superiority and immigrant inferiority. The devaluation reported by the children, and exposed by the micro and macro sociopolitical White Nativism indexes, provides evidence, and is a concrete byproduct, of a White Nativist discourse, in which American-born Hispanic children are constructed as "other," as "too different" to be assimilated within the "White Native" identity due to their heritage. This devaluation is consistent with Huntington's (2004a) conceptualization of the "Hispanic other," as a threat to the American "White Native" identity, and especially the American-born Hispanic other, who is thought to be gradually "...[replacing] the white culture by black or brown cultures that are intellectually and morally inferior" (p. 41). The findings also show that American-born children of Mexican parents serve as "White Native," suitable targets of externalization, consistent with Volkan's conceptualization of synthetic nations and racism[14] (Volkan, 1985, 1998, 2013).

The characteristics of the children's social context certainly raises concern about the children's assimilation process, as well as about their ability to fully integrate into the mainstream of the sociopolitical and economic structure of the United States. The White Nativist context reported by the children makes explicit significant micro and macro risk factors that, as discussed by segmented assimilation theory (Abraido-Lanza et al., 2006; Gratton et al, 2007; Portes, 2006) and by Berry's (2003) acculturation strategies model, may thwart their integration and assimilation efforts. This next section will discuss the implications of this White Nativist context for the ethnic identity evolution and acculturation process of American-born children of Mexican immigrant parents.

## Sociopolitical White Nativism and ethnic identity development

### *Ethnic identity*

The cross tabulation analysis of the children's reported ethnic identities showed gradual changes; however, the two most predominant ethnic identities found were the hyphenated-American and pan-ethnic identities (see Table 6.4). In 1991, almost 75% of the children identified in hyphenated-American terms (39.32%) or as Mexican (35.45%). Although, by 1995, the hyphenated-American identity continued to be the most predominant identity (41.62%), the number of children identifying in a pan-ethnic manner had started to increase, from 20.91% in 1991, to 30.64%. By 2001, 76.86% of the children continued to identify primarily in a hyphenated-American (45.10%) and in a pan-ethnic manner (31.76%). Overall, the children's ethnic identity moved away from a Mexican ethnic identity and toward either a hyphenated-American or pan-ethnic identity, suggesting a move toward assimilation. However, whereas in 1991, 4.32% of the children identified as American, by 2001–2003 only 2.35% continued to do so. This change was statistically significant and suggests that while the children did move toward the assimilative plain, they were also moving away from an American, assimilative identity. Nonetheless, and consistent with White Nativist fears, the majority of the children in the secondary study did not identify as "American."

*Table 6.4* Ethnic identity 1991, 1995 and 2001

| Ethnicity | 1991 | | 1995 | | 2001 | |
|---|---|---|---|---|---|---|
| | Frequency | % | Frequency | % | Frequency | % |
| American[a] | 19 | 4.32 | 7 | 2.02 | 6 | 2.35 |
| Hyphenated American | 173 | 39.32 | 144 | 41.62 | 115 | 45.10 |
| Mexican | 156 | 35.45 | 89 | 25.72 | 53 | 20.78 |
| Pan-ethnic | 92 | 20.91 | 106 | 30.64 | 81 | 31.76 |
| Total | $N = 440$[b] | 100.00 | $N = 346$[c] | 100.00 | $N = 255$[d] | 100.00 |

a Ethnic identity: answers to question 78 in 1991; question 78 (a) in 1995; and question 33 in 2001.
b 1991 Total $N = 446$, missing values = 6.
c 1995 Total $N = 364$, missing values = 18.
d 2001 Total $N = 271$, missing values =16.

### Explicit importance of ethnic identity

When examining the explicit importance of the children's ethnic identity between 1995 and 2001, children who identified as "American" attributed the lowest level of importance to their ethnic identity, in contrast to children who identified as Mexican, who by 2001–2003, attributed the most importance to their ethnic identity (94.23%) (see Table 6.5). However, by 1995, the children who identified as hyphenated-American were the ones attributing the most importance to their ethnic identity, rather than those identifying in a Mexican or pan-ethnic manner. Despite some variation, the results indicate in a consistent, statistically significant manner, that children who identified in pan-ethnic terms, attributed less importance to their identity than those who identified in either Mexican or hyphenated-American terms.

### Racial identity

When the children's racial identity was examined, 82.05% of the children in 1995, and 75.29% in 2001, identified in ethnic terms, although by 2001 the number of children identifying racially had increased from 17.95% in 1995, to 24.71% in 2001. When the results were further examined, it became apparent that only the children who had identified as Latino/Hispanic in 1995 had continued to identify as such in 2001–2003. In fact, whereas the

*Table 6.5* Ethnic identity and level of importance, 1995 and 2001[a]

| | | | *Level of Importance*[b] | | | | | |
| | | 1995 (N = 344) | | | | 2001 (N = 253) | | |
| Ethnicity[c] | N | Not Imp. (%)[d] | Somewhat (%) | Very (%) | N | Not Imp. (%) | Somewhat (%) | Very (%) |
|---|---|---|---|---|---|---|---|---|
| American | 7 | 3 (42.86) | 3 (42.86) | 1 (14.29) | 6 | 1 (16.67) | 4 (66.67) | 1 (16.67) |
| Hyphenated-American | 144 | 7 (4.86) | 43 (29.86) | 94 (65.28) | 115 | 8 (6.96) | 38 (33.04) | 69 (60.00) |
| Mexican | 88 | 7 (7.95) | 22 (25.00) | 59 (67.05) | 52 | 3 (5.77) | 9 (17.31) | 40 (76.92) |
| Pan-ethnic | 105 | 14 (13.33) | 23 (21.90) | 68 (64.76) | 80 | 13 (16.25) | 20 (25.00) | 47 (58.75) |
| Total[e] | 344 | 31 (9.01) | 91 (26.25) | 222 (64.53) | 253 | 25 (9.88) | 71 (28.06) | 157 (62.06) |

a Fisher exact was calculated to determine differences between ethnic identity categories and level of importance for each time period. Associations were statistically significant at $p < .05$; for 1995, $p < .007$; and for 2001, $p < .010$.
b Level of importance: answers to question 78(b) in 1995; and question 34 in 2001.
c Ethnic identity: answers to question 78(a) in 1995; and question 33 in 2001.
d (%) The percentages reported reflect the frequency distribution of each ethnic identity and corresponding level of importance.
e Total percentages reflect the frequency distribution for the total sample per time period.

number of children identifying as Mexican had decreased from 35.33% in 1995 to 20% in 2001, the number of children identifying as Latino/Hispanic (pan-ethnic category) had only increased by 5.95%, to a total of 32.16%. Although these slight changes were not statistically significant, which will be later discussed in greater detail, they appear consistent with the children's ethnic identity evolution trend—moving away from a Mexican identity, and toward a pan-ethnic or a hyphenated-American identity.

### Sociopolitical White Nativism and ethnic identity

*Experience of prejudice and ethnic identity*

To determine if micro, sociopolitical White Nativism was in some way related to the ethnic identity outcomes of the American children of Mexican immigrant parents, the Experience of Prejudice Index was cross-tabulated with the children's ethnic identity in 1991, 1995–1996 and 2001–2003 (see Table 6.6).

The bivariate analysis of the 1991 Experience of Prejudice Index and the children's ethnic identity found some differences between the prejudice experienced and the children's ethnic identity outcome. As Table 6.6 shows, the children who identified in a pan-ethnic manner, were also the children who reported the highest experienced prejudice (67.39%), followed by those who identified as Mexican (64.68%), American (63.16%) and lastly, by those who identified in a hyphenated-American manner (57.80%).

Although bivariate results for 1995 (81.45%) and 2001 (87.65%) did indicate a substantial increase in the children's experienced prejudice, no statistically significant differences were found between ethnic identity outcomes and experienced prejudice in 1995 or 2001 ($p = .271$ and $p = 1.000$, respectively). This lack of association can be best explained as a function of the high incidence of prejudice experienced by the children in 1995 and 2001, making any comparison between ethnic categories and experienced prejudice negligible, as the majority of the children, regardless of ethnic identity, had experienced prejudice at some point by 2001.

*Micro and macro sociopolitical White Nativism and ethnic identity*

Given the preliminary bivariate analysis results, regression[15] analyses were conducted to explore whether or not Perceived Sociopolitical White Nativism, and/or Experiences of Prejudice, had any effect on the children's ethnic identity outcomes and their associated level of importance. Questions comprising the 1991, 1995 and 2001 Perceived Sociopolitical White Nativism Index,[16] the Experience of Prejudice Index and the Explicit, Ethnic Identity Index were included in the analyses (see Appendix C for the operationalization of each index).

Table 6.6 Experience of prejudice and ethnic identity, 1991, 1995 and 2001[a]

| | Experience of Prejudice[b] | | | | | | | | | | | |
|---|---|---|---|---|---|---|---|---|---|---|---|---|
| | 1991 (N = 344) | | | | 1995 (N = 345) | | | | 2001 (N = 251) | | | |
| Ethnicity[c] | No | %[d] | Yes | % | No | % | Yes | % | No | % | Yes | % |
| American | 7 | 36.84 | 12 | 63.16 | 3 | 42.86 | 4 | 57.14 | 0 | 0.00 | 6 | 100 |
| Hyphenated-American | 73 | 42.20 | 100 | 57.80 | 25 | 17.36 | 119 | 82.64 | 15 | 13.16 | 99 | 86.84 |
| Mexican | 39 | 35.32 | 115 | 64.68 | 14 | 15.73 | 75 | 84.27 | 6 | 11.16 | 45 | 88.24 |
| Pan-ethnic | 30 | 32.61 | 62 | 67.39 | 22 | 20.95 | 83 | 79.05 | 10 | 12.50 | 70 | 87.50 |
| Total[e] | N = 149 | 34.02 | N = 289 | 65.98 | N = 64 | 18.55 | N = 281 | 81.45 | N = 31 | 12.35 | N = 220 | 87.65 |

a Fisher exact was calculated to determine differences between ethnic identity categories and experience of prejudice for each time period. Associations were statistically significant at $p \le .05$ for 1991, $p \le .014$, but not for 1995, $p \le .271$ or for 2001, $p \le 1.000$.

b Experience of prejudice: answers to question 85 in 1991 and 1995; and question 35 in 2001.

c Ethnic identity: answers to question 78 in 1991: question 78 (a) in 1995; and question 33 in 2001.

d % The percentages reported reflect the frequency distribution of each ethnic identity and corresponding experience of prejudice category.

e Total percentages reflect the frequency distribution for the total sample per time period.

The regression analyses did identify a statistically significant relationship between Perceived Sociopolitical White Nativism and ethnic identity outcomes in 1991 and in 1995, but not in 2001. The findings associated a Mexican identity outcome with the highest level of perceived sociopolitical White Nativism, followed by a pan-ethnic identity outcome. The hyphenated-American identity outcome appeared to be associated with lower levels of perceived sociopolitical White Nativism. In terms of experienced prejudice and ethnic identity outcome, although the 1991 findings indicated an association between higher levels of experienced prejudice and some ethnic identity outcomes, similar findings were not found across time, consistent with the bivariate analysis previously reported. Lastly, no association was found between the children's ethnic identity, its explicit importance and experienced prejudice.

### Evolution and contextualization of ethnic identity between 1991 and 2003

At first glance, the evolution of the ethnic identity of the American-born children of Mexican parents in the study revealed a progressive move along the assimilation continuum. By 2001, the percentage of children who identified as Mexican had decreased, a category that is associated with the lowest assimilation level (Aleinikoff & Rumbaut, 1998), while at the same time the percentage of children identifying as hyphenated-American had moderately increased. These changes, as previously discussed, are consistent with a gradual progression toward "...the assimilative plain 'American' identity" (Aleinikoff & Rumbaut, 1998, p. 150).

However, other changes were also taking place, suggesting a different trajectory. By 2001–2003, the number of children identifying in a pan-ethnic manner had also increased, making this identity the second most frequent ethnic identity, after the hyphenated-American. The increasing prevalence of this ethnic identity by 2001–2003 is cause for concern, as it suggests that over time, an increasing number of children had developed what is considered to be a 'reactive ethnicity' (Aleinikoff & Rumbaut, 1998, p. 19). Although the trend toward a pan-ethnic identity is still consistent with a pattern of progressive assimilation, this ethnic identity is associated with downward assimilation rather than upward assimilation. In other words, a pan-ethnic identity, while reflecting a high acculturation level, and "...decreasing knowledge of, interest in, and attachment to the parental homeland, history and language..." (Aleinikoff & Rumbaut, 1998, p. 19), is also correlated with increasing exposure to prejudice, discrimination and structural racism, increasing the likelihood that children will identify with "...the socioeconomic status and family structure among native-born groups marginalized by racial or ethnic prejudice" (Gratton et al., 2007, p. 2).

The progressive move toward a pan-ethnic identity, coupled with the gradual, concurrent decrease in the number of children identifying as American, is inconsistent with what initially appeared to be a trend toward the assimilation end of the continuum. This bi-modal trend was also observed within the larger CILS study (Aleinikoff & Rumbaut, 1998), suggesting that the shift away from the plain American identity was not a function of the small sample size of the secondary study.

Given the somewhat contradictory evolution pattern of the children's ethnic identity, away from a plain American identity, rather than toward it, coupled with the increasing number of children identifying in a pan-ethnic manner, the data was further analyzed to determine if the children's racial identity needed to be included to better contextualize the ethnic identity trends reflected by the children.

## Ethnic identity and racial identity

Many Hispanic people, as previously mentioned, define their racial identity in ethnic terms, rather than according to established racial categories, for example, as Hispanic or Latino, rather than white, black, etc. (Taylor et al., 2012). The children in the secondary study were no exception; despite this tendency, over time there was a slight, statistically significant increase in the number of children who reported their racial identity in racial terms. Given the overlap between racial and ethnic identity within the Hispanic population, the children's racial identity evolution was used as a second opportunity to either confirm or reject the ethnic identity evolution pattern observed when the children were specifically asked about their ethnic identity.

The findings indicated that the evolution of the racial identity of the American-born children of Mexican parents paralleled some aspects of their ethnic identity evolution pattern. In 1995, Mexican and Latino/Hispanic were the two most predominant racial identifiers, while in 2001–2003, Latino/Hispanic, followed by both a Mexican racial and a multi-racial identity, were the two most predominant racial identifiers. In both, 1991 and 1995, Latino/Hispanic (pan-ethnic identity) was the most predominant racial identifier, confirming the ethnic identity evolution trend toward a pan-ethnic identity. In a similar fashion, the number of children identifying as Mexican decreased between 1995 and 2001, consistent with the ethnic evolution trend. However, the hyphenated-American identity did not emerge as a more frequent racial identity, contradicting previous ethnic identity evolution findings.

It is reasonable to presume, however, that this discrepancy can be due to some children having selected an either white or multiracial identifier, rather than identifying as hyphenated-American. Overall, it does seem appropriate to conclude that the racial identity evolution pattern was consistent with the ethnic evolution pattern; and that both trends show a decrease in the number of children identifying as Mexican, signaling an ethnic identity evolution toward increasing assimilation. Yet, the two evolution trends also point toward an increase in the number of children identifying in a pan-ethnic manner, suggesting a greater risk of downward assimilation over time.[17]

### White Nativist sociopolitical contextualization of ethnic identity, 1991–2003

When the children's ethnic evolution pattern is examined in relation to the White Nativist sociopolitical context, and not seen solely as a manifestation of particular individual inclinations or desires to assimilate or not assimilate, a more complex understanding of the evolution of the children's ethnic identity emerges: the increasing White Nativist nature of their interpersonal social and economic context had been interfering with their efforts to "ethnically" assimilate.

The contextualized findings show, as initially presented, that the evolution of the children's ethnic identity reflects both a move toward the plain American, assimilative end of the continuum (hyphenated-American identity) and also away from the mainstream assimilative plain. This trend, away from the assimilative plain, is illustrated by the increasing number of children identifying in a pan-ethnic manner by 2001–2003, suggesting a higher risk of downward assimilation, and by the decreasing number of children identifying as Mexican, as this identity reflects a complete move away from the assimilation continuum. However, the contextualization of this evolution revealed that both the Mexican and pan-ethnic identities were associated with an increasingly, perceived White Nativist sociopolitical context. These findings provide empirical evidence of a connection between increasing levels of White Nativism and the increasing likelihood of a reactive ethnic adaptation, either completely away from the assimilation continuum (Mexican identity) or toward downward assimilation (pan-ethnic).

What clearly emerges through the sociopolitical White Nativist contextualization of the children's ethnic identity evolution, is that over time, despite increasing interpersonal prejudice, and structural, political and economic White Nativism, more than a third of the children developed individual ways to upwardly assimilate into the mainstream of American society. This finding highlights the interactional/transactional quality of ethnic identity development, as discussed by Erikson (1968), Berry (2003) and by segmented assimilation theory (Portes & Rumbaut, 2006, 2014). When the American-born children of Mexican immigrant parents were faced with a context that increasingly devalued their parents' ethnic/national heritage, as well as their own heritage, coupled with the increasingly felt structural, political and economic White Nativist barriers, they still found a way to adapt and make meaning of themselves and their native country, the United States. This meaning-making process is consistent with attributional theory, where individual attributional processes are thought to function as potential protective factors for the development of individual self-concepts (Crocker & Major, 1989).

The findings clearly illustrate that what propels some children to ethnically identify toward the assimilative plain (hyphenated-American identity) and others away from assimilation (Mexican identity) or toward a downward assimilation path (pan-ethnic identity) is not just determined by the child's internal psychological and social understanding of the self and others. Rather, the ethnic identity evolution of the American-born children of Mexican parents is best conceptualized as a transactional process, contingent on and co-determined by the nature of the children's social context, the nature of its policies and the context's perception of the children's ethnic group (Abraido-Lanza et al., 2006; Berry, 2003; Portes & Rumbaut, 2006). The findings also strongly indicate that over time, the interaction with an increasingly White Nativist sociopolitical context fosters a hyphenated-American ethnic identity development, while also supporting a pan-ethnic identity development. The interaction appears to inhibit individual inclinations toward an American identification, while also fostering individual reactive adaptations to the experienced sociopolitical White Nativist aggression, as argued by segmented assimilation theory. Ethnic identity development, therefore, and that of the American-born children of Mexican immigrant parents, emerges as a highly contextual, interrelated process, consistent with Berry's (2003) acculturation model, which states that cultural integration cannot be attained unless there is "...a mutual accommodation..., involving the acceptance by both groups of the right of all groups to live as culturally different peoples within the civic framework of the larger society" (p. 24).

## Ethnic identity and level of importance, 1991–2003

A person's individual and collective self-concept becomes more salient depending on the context in which the person or group exists (Miller & Garran, 2008; Oyserman, 2004;[18] Tajfel, 1982). A discussion of the evolution of the ethnic identity of American-born children of Mexican immigrant parents would be incomplete without examining the importance the children attached to their ethnic identity, as well as its association with the children's increasingly White Nativist sociopolitical context.

Overall,[19] children who identified as American consistently assigned a lower level of importance to their identity than those who identified in ethnic terms; however, the importance the children ascribed to their ethnic identity changed in response (association) to the increasing White Nativist sociopolitical context in which they were growing up. Whereas in 1995, prior to the implementation of immigration reform policies, children who identified as hyphenated-American had ascribed the highest level of importance to their identity, followed by those identifying as Mexican and as pan-ethnic;[20] in 2001 it was the children who identified as Mexican that assigned the highest level of importance to their identity, coinciding with the increasingly anti-Mexican, White Nativist immigration sociopolitical context. These findings are consistent with social identity theory (Miller & Garran, 2008) and with Oyserman's (2004) conceptualization of the self-concept. The higher level of importance children ascribed to their Mexican identity can, therefore, be best understood in terms of the increasingly White Nativist social context in which they were growing up, which by 2001 was highlighting the salience of their Mexican identity—a part of the children' self-concept that was being targeted and devalued by White Nativists (Miller & Garran, 2008; Oyserman, 2004). These findings provide additional empirical support for the transactional quality of ethnic identity development and for the importance of contextualizing the children's ethnic identity evolution in relation to micro and macro sociopolitical White Nativism.

## Sociopolitical White Nativism and acculturation

The secondary study examined five acculturation dimensions: Linguistic Assimilation: English Acquisition; Parental Native Acquisition; Linguistic Preference; Culture, Values and Behavior; and Ethnic Interaction. Only three acculturation dimensions were included in the Acculturation Strategies Index: (1) Linguistic Preference, as this measure captured both English acquisition and acquisition/retention of parental native language; (2) Culture, Values and Behavior; and (3) Ethnic Interaction (see Appendix C for further explanation). This section will discuss the five-acculturation dimensions, as well as the findings of the Acculturation Index, to explore the acculturation process of American-born children of Mexican immigrant parents, as well as the effects of the White Nativist sociopolitical context in which they were growing up.

### *Dimensions of acculturation*

#### *Linguistic assimilation*

The children's linguistic assimilation was explored using three different Linguistic Assimilation Scales: (1) The English Acquisition Scale; (2) The Parental Native Language Acquisition Scale; and (3) The Linguistic Preference Scale (see Appendix C).

ENGLISH ACQUISITION

Overall, the analysis of the English Acquisition Scale showed that the children's English language competency and fluency increased over time. In 1991, 74.04% of the children reported speaking English very well, whereas by 1995, this percentage had increased to 79.12%, and to 88.64% in 2001. When it came to understanding English, results remained fairly stable over time and reflected a trend consistent with their English-speaking competency. The percentage of children who reported understanding English very well progressed overtime, from 79.01% in 1991, to 84.89% in 1995, and 91.64% in 2001.

The English reading competency also increased significantly over time. In 1991, 67.87% of children reported reading English very well, whereas by 1995 this percentage had increased to 73.08%, increasing again in 2001 to 89.77%. Children were also asked to rate their English writing skills which, as with their reading competency, had significantly increased over time; whereas in 1991, 62.75% of the children reported writing very well, in 2001 this percentage had increased to 81.30%. Symmetry, exact significance tests showed that although the descriptive differences observed between 1991 and 1995 were not statistically significant ($p = .5331$), those found between 1995 and 2001 were ($p = .0004$), confirming that the children's English competency and fluency had increased over time.

PARENTAL NATIVE LANGUAGE ACQUISITION: SPANISH

The cross tabulation results of the Parental Native Language Acquisition Scale questions reflected high levels of competency and fluency in Spanish across time; however, when compared to the English acquisition results, the children's English competency was higher than their Spanish competency.

In 1991, only 46.37% of the children reported speaking Spanish very well, this percentage increased to 48.43% in 1995 and to 58.73% in 2001. The children's ability to understand Spanish also increased over time. Where in 1991, 55.14% reported understanding Spanish very well, this percentage increased to 60.97% in 1995, and to 73.02% in 2001. In terms of reading ability, 30.37% of the children reported reading Spanish very well in 1991, increasing to 37.89% in 1995, and to 53.97% in 2001.

When asked about their Spanish writing ability, only 26.40% of the children reported writing Spanish very well in 1991. Although the children's Spanish writing ability increased significantly overtime, 28.21% in 1995 and 44.98% in 2001, it was significantly weaker than their speaking, understanding and reading abilities. Overall, symmetry, exact significance probability tests confirmed that the children's command of, and competency in, Spanish had gradually increased between 1991 and 1995 ($p = .0012$) and 1995 and 2001 ($p = .0000$).

LINGUISTIC PREFERENCE

The children's linguistic preference, as illustrated in Table 6.7, varied significantly across time unlike the results pertaining to English acquisition. In 1991, 55.41% of the children preferred to speak English most of the time, while 44.14% preferred Spanish; it is important to note that none of the children reported a preference for bilingualism in 1991. By 1995, children began to report some preference for bilingualism (26.70%), however, 53.41% continued to prefer the English language; the largest change was seen in

*Table 6.7* Linguistic preference, 1991, 1995 and 2001

| | 1991[a] | | 1995 | | 2001 | |
|---|---|---|---|---|---|---|
| | *In what language do you prefer to speak most of the time?* | | *In what language do you prefer to speak most of the time?* | | *In what language do you prefer to speak most of the time?* | |
| *Language categories* | *Frequency* | *%* | *Frequency* | *%* | *Frequency* | *%* |
| English | 246 | 55.41 | 188 | 53.41 | 115 | 44.92 |
| Spanglish | 2 | 0.45 | 0 | 0.00 | 0 | 0.00 |
| Bilingual/ both | 0 | 0.00 | 94 | 26.70 | 133 | 51.95 |
| Spanish | 196 | 44.14 | 70 | 19.89 | 8 | 3.13 |
| Total | N = 444 | 100.00 | N = 352 | 100.00 | N = 256 | 100.00 |

a   Question 59 in 1991 and 1995; Question 31 in 2001.

relation to the Spanish language, where only 19.89% of children reported preferring Spanish, down by 24.25% when compared to 1991. By 2001, this trend continued, while also changing toward bilingualism. Although 44.92% of the children continued to identify a preference for the English language, bilingualism saw a sharp increase, from 0% in 1991 to 51.95% in 2001. Symmetry, exact significance tests indicated that the changes observed were statistically significant (1991–1995, $p = .0000$; and 1995–2001, $p = .0000$), confirming that over time, the children preferred to be bilingual over monolingual (English only).

CONCLUSION

Overall, American-born children of Mexican parents reported a high command of English. Although the children reported increasing competency and fluency in Spanish, their command of English remained higher. However, despite lower competency in Spanish, the children preferred bilingualism (51.95%) to English only (44.92%).

## Culture, values and behavior

The 1991, 1995 and 2001 Culture, Values and Behavior Scales were used to explore whether American-born children of Mexican parents expressed a preference for the American culture, and were either raising, or wanted to raise, their children as bilingual (see Appendix C, Culture, Values and Behaviors Scale).[21] Cross tabulations analysis showed that in 1991, 91.82% of the children reported at least some preference for the American ways of doing things, either all the time (3.34%), most of the time (30.00%) or sometimes (58.18%); in 1995, no significant differences were observed (90.53%).

Table 6.8 Culture, Values and Behavior Scale, individual questions, 1991, 1995 and 2001

| How often do you prefer the American ways of doing things?[b] | 1991 (N = 260) | | | | | | 1995 (N = 243) | | | | | |
| | In what language do you hope to raise your children?[x][a] | | | | | | In what language do you hope to raise your children? | | | | | |
| | English only | % | Non-English | % | Both about the same | % | English only | (%) | Non-English | % | Both about the same | % |
|---|---|---|---|---|---|---|---|---|---|---|---|---|
| All of the time | 0 | 0.00 | 2 | 22.22 | 7 | 77.78 | 0 | 0.00 | 0 | 0.00 | 12 | 100.00 |
| Most of the time | 14 | 18.18 | 1 | 1.30 | 62 | 80.52 | 15 | 27.27 | 0 | 0.00 | 40 | 72.73 |
| Sometimes | 10 | 6.41 | 2 | 1.28 | 144 | 92.31 | 8 | 5.23 | 6 | 3.42 | 139 | 90.85 |
| Never | 1 | 5.56 | 2 | 11.11 | 15 | 83.33 | 0 | 0.00 | 1 | 4.35 | 22 | 95.65 |
| Total | 25 | 9.62 | 7 | 2.69 | 228 | 87.69 | 23 | 9.47 | 7 | 2.88 | 213 | 87.65 |

a  Question 32 in the 2001 CILS survey.
b  Question 98 in the 1991 and 1995 CILS surveys.
c  Fisher's exact test for the 1991 and 2001 results were found to be statistically significant, p = .001. They were also found to be statistically significant for 1995 and 2001. Fisher's exact test, p = .001.

Cross tabulation analysis of the 1991 Culture, Values and Behavior Scale, and question 32, 2001 CILS survey, which asked children to identify the language in which they wanted to raise their children, indicated that 87.69% of them wanted to raise their children in both English and Spanish; and 97.81% of them expressed at least some preference for the American ways of doing things (see Table 6.8). Overall, the 1995–2001 cross tabulation results were similar to the 1991–2001 results. The percentage of children who reported wanting to raise their children in both English and Spanish remained almost unchanged (87.65%). However, within this category, the percentage of children who reported at least some preference for the American ways of doing things decreased from 97.81% in 1991 to 89.67% in 1995. The percentage who preferred the American ways most of the time also decreased from 27.19% to 18.77% in 1995. Yet, all of the children ($N = 12$, 4.94%) who reported preferring the American ways of doing things all the time, consistently reported wanting to raise their children in both languages ($N = 12$,100.00%). These descriptive differences were statistically significant (Fisher's exact test, $p = 0.001$).

It is, therefore, reasonable to say, that overall, the large majority of American-born children of Mexican parents in the study expressed at least some preference for the American ways of doing things, wanting to raise their children as bilingual (81.92% in 1991 and 78.60% in 1995). The findings also showed the children's acceptance of some of the "American" culture and values, as well as their desire to maintain some aspects of their parental cultural heritage, such as the Spanish language.

### Ethnic interaction

The Ethnic Interaction Scale was developed to examine the children's level of integration across ethnic groups, including within the White dominant group. This acculturation domain was one of the three domains included in the Acculturation Index (see Appendix C, Ethnic Interaction Scale). In 1991, cross tabulation analysis showed that only 4.87% of the children reported that none of their friends had foreign-born parent(s), 49.19% indicated that some of them did have foreign-born parent(s), while, 45.94% reported that most of their friends had foreign-born parent(s). By 1995, the children's ethnic interaction pattern had changed, reflecting a 7.27% increase in the percentage of children whose friends did not have foreign-born parents (12.14%), consistent with upward assimilation.

In 2001, the children who had now become young adults, were asked to identify the language they used when speaking with their closest friends, indirectly also capturing the degree of ethnic interaction with other groups, as manifested in their closest friendship circle (see Appendix C, 2001 Ethnic Interaction Scale for further information). 56.49% of the young adults reported speaking with their closest friends only, or mostly, in English, while 37.40% reported speaking in both Spanish and English; only 6.11% of young adults identified Spanish as the primary language spoken with their closest friends.

Thus, over time, the ethnic interaction pattern of the American-born children of Mexican parents reflected greater interaction with non-immigrant groups—a 4.61% increase between 1991 (54.06%) and 1995 (58.67%) in the number of children reporting only, or some friends whose parents were not foreign born. As they grew older, the now young adults, also reported greater preference for socializing in English (56.49%), indirectly reflecting their ongoing socialization with a variety of immigrant and non-immigrant groups.

### Acculturation strategies index

The Acculturation Strategies Index was used to explore the acculturation process of the American-born children of Mexican immigrant parents in the study. Three acculturation dimensions were included in the Acculturation Strategies Index: (1) Linguistic Preference; (2) Culture, Values and Behavior[22]; and (3) Ethnic Interaction (see Appendix C for further explanation). These dimensions still capture the complexity of Berry's acculturation model (2003), while also preventing methodological overlap. The operational definition of Berry's (2003) four acculturation strategies was as follows:

1   Assimilation: Relationships with other groups are sought (Ethnic Interaction Scale) + maintenance of heritage culture decreases (Linguistic Preference; Culture, Values and Behavior Scale)
2   Integration: Relationships with other groups are sought (Ethnic Interaction Scale) + maintenance of heritage culture is sought (Linguistic Preference; Culture, Values and Behavior Scale)
3   Separation: Relationships with other groups are not sought as much (Ethnic Interaction Scale) + maintenance of heritage culture is sought (Linguistic Preference; Culture, Values and Behavior Scale)
4   Marginalization: Relationships with other groups are not sought (Ethnic Interaction Scale) + maintenance of heritage culture is not sought (Linguistic Preference; Culture, Values and Behavior Scale)

These initial acculturation strategies were expanded upon when additional styles were observed after conducting a preliminary analysis of the Acculturation Index. The final acculturation strategies categories were as follows: assimilation; assimilation/separation; integration; integration/assimilation; integration/separation; marginalization; and separation (see Appendix C, Acculturation Strategies Index for further information).

In 1991, as Table 6.9 illustrates, the children's two most predominant acculturation strategies were separation (37.94%) and integration/assimilation (26.23%), followed by assimilation (15.93%) and marginalization (12.88%). By 1995, some changes appeared to have taken place: integration/assimilation had become the children's most predominant acculturation strategy (31.53%), followed by separation (22.82%), integration (22.52%) and

*Table 6.9* Acculturation Strategies Index,[a] 1991, 1995 and 2001

| Acculturation categories | 1991 | | 1995 | | 2001 | |
|---|---|---|---|---|---|---|
| | Frequency | % | Frequency | % | Frequency | % |
| Assimilation | 68 | 15.93 | 55 | 16.52 | 43 | 16.86 |
| Assimilation/ separation | 12 | 2.81 | 7 | 2.10 | 2 | 0.78 |
| Integration | 2 | 0.47 | 75 | 22.52 | 78 | 30.59 |
| Integration/ assimilation | 112 | 26.23 | 105 | 31.53 | 120 | 47.06 |
| Integration/ separation | 16 | 3.75 | 3 | 0.90 | 0 | 0.00 |
| Marginalization | 55 | 12.88 | 12 | 3.60 | 1 | 0.39 |
| Separation | 162 | 37.94 | 76 | 22.82 | 11 | 4.31 |
| Total | N = 427 | 100.00 | N = 333 | 100.00 | N = 255 | 100.00 |

a   Changes over time, between 1991 and 1995, and between 1995 and 2001 were found to be statistically significant; symmetry, exact significance probability tests $p \leq .0001$ for both time intervals.

assimilation (16.52%). The most significant change occurred within the marginalization strategy, which decreased from 12.88% in 1991 to 3.60% in 1995.

In 2001, additional changes were observed; integration/assimilation continued to be the children's most predominant acculturation strategy (47.06%) reflecting a 20.83% increase when compared to 1991. The percentage of children using the separation and the integration strategies had also substantially changed; in 1991, only 0.47% (2 children) used an integration strategy, whereas by 2001, 30.59% did so, making integration the children's second most prevalent acculturation strategy. The reverse trend was observed in regard to the separation and marginalization strategies. Whereas in 1991, separation (37.94%) was the children's most predominant acculturation strategy, by 2001, this percentage had decreased significantly to 4.31%, along with the assimilation/separation strategy (0.78%); a very infrequent strategy over time (2.81% in 1991; 2.10% in 1995). As for the marginalization strategy, whereas in 1991 marginalization was the children's third most frequent acculturation strategy (12.88%), by 2001, only one child continued to use this strategy. The percentage of children using an assimilation strategy remained mostly unchanged—15.93% in 1991 and 16.86% in 2001. The gradual acculturation strategy changes were found to be statistically significant (Symmetry, exact significance probability test for paired items ($p \leq .0001$)). To clarify the direction of the children's acculturation process, toward or away from the assimilation continuum, cross tabulation of paired items analyses were conducted, comparing the 1991 and 1995, and the 1995 and 2001 data.

The 1991–1995 results showed that 32.61% of all the children who used an assimilation strategy in 1991, continued to use this strategy by 1995, with

39.13% changing to an integrated/assimilated strategy. Of concern was the observed downward shift toward separation and marginalization, where 17.39% of the children changed from an assimilated strategy to either a separation (8.70%) or a marginalization (8.70%) strategy. All of the children who used an assimilated/separation strategy moved away from the separation end of the continuum and toward either integration (30%) or integration/assimilation (60%).

On the other hand, 48.28% of the children who used an integration/assimilation strategy, continued to use it in 1995, while 41.38% moved between the assimilation (16.09%) and integration (22.99%) continuum; only 9.20% changed to a separation strategy. The percentage of children who used a marginalization strategy decreased significantly, as only 12.82% of the children continued to use this strategy by 1995. The largest percentage changed to an integrated/assimilated strategy (35.90%), while 20.51% moved to an assimilated one; the remainder of the children shifted to an integration (12.82%) or a separation strategy (12.82%). Within the separation strategy, only 41.32% of the children continued to use this strategy, largely shifting to either an integrated (30.58%), or an integrated/assimilated strategy (15.70%); only 8.26% began to use an assimilation strategy. Overall, between 1991 and 1995, the children seemed to move away from a purely assimilated acculturation strategy, away from marginalization, and to a lesser extent also away from the separation strategy, moving primarily toward full integration, followed by the integration/assimilation strategy. This trend was statistically significant ($p = .0001$).

The 1995–2001 results showed that 30.77% of the children who used an assimilation strategy in 1995 continued to do so in 2001, while 56.41% changed to an integrated/assimilated strategy. However, unlike in 1991–1995, of the children who used an assimilation strategy in 1995, only 2 shifted toward a separation (2.56%), or a marginalization (2.56%) strategy, indicating a more positive direction in the acculturation process than the one observed between 1991 and 1995 for children within this category. In terms of the assimilation/separation strategy, as in 1991–1995, all of the children previously using this strategy moved away from the separation end of the continuum (100%), toward either an integration/assimilation (60%) or integration (20%) strategy.

As for the children who had used an integration strategy in 1995, 48.94% of them continued to use it in 2001, while 40.43% changed to an integration/assimilation strategy. Within the integration/assimilation strategy, 61.76% of the children who had used this strategy in 1995 continued to use it in 2001; while 17.65% changed to an assimilation strategy, followed by integration (14.71). In terms of the marginalization strategy, all of the children who used a marginalization strategy in 1995, shifted either to an integrated/assimilated strategy (75%) or an assimilated strategy (25%) in 2001. Lastly, in regard to the separation strategy, only 6.00% of the children continued to use this strategy in 2001. Most of them, as in 1991–1995, either changed to an integrated strategy (58.00%), or an integrated/assimilated strategy (34.00%). Overall, between 1995 and 2001, the children appeared to move away from a purely assimilated acculturation strategy, and almost completely away from the marginalization and separation strategies, primarily changing toward integration/assimilation, followed by an integration strategy. This trend was statistically significant ($p = .0001$). These findings were consistent with the direction of the children's acculturation trend observed between 1991 and 1995.

### Sociopolitical White Nativism and acculturation strategies

To determine if micro and/or macro, sociopolitical White Nativism were in some way related to the acculturation outcomes of the American children of Mexican immigrant parents, the Experience of Prejudice Index and the Perceived Sociopolitical White Nativism Index were examined in conjunction with the Acculturation Strategies Index. The analysis, which will be subsequently presented, confirmed that perceived sociopolitical White Nativism did affect the acculturation strategy outcome used by the children in the study, while also identifying the nature of the association[23] between the acculturation strategy categories and perceived sociopolitical White Nativism. Experienced prejudice was only found to be associated with the children's acculturation outcome in 1991. Since perceived sociopolitical White Nativism emerged as the best predictor variable for the acculturation outcome from the two examined here, the analysis of macro and micro sociopolitical White Nativism will be reported concurrently.

Kruskal-Wallis test analyses were used to examine whether perceived sociopolitical White Nativism affected acculturation outcomes. In 1991, the range of the perceived sociopolitical White Nativism mean values was between 12.77 and 19, from a possible range of 6–22, where lower scores indicate higher levels of perceived sociopolitical White Nativism. The analysis yielded statistically significant differences between the medians of perceived sociopolitical White Nativism and acculturation outcomes ($X^2 = 16.497$; $df = 6$; $p \leq .0113$). Overall, the assimilation/separation ($M = 12.77$) and separation strategies ($M = 13.13072$) were associated with higher levels of perceived sociopolitical White Nativism ($M = 13.13072$), while lower levels were associated with the assimilation strategy ($M = 14.2656$).

In 1995, statistically significant differences between the medians of perceived sociopolitical White Nativism and the respective acculturation strategies were also found ($X^2 = 19.277$; $df = 6$; $p < .00037$) and were consistent with the 1991 findings. The separation strategy ($M = 11.8667$) was associated with the highest levels of perceived sociopolitical White Nativism, followed by the integration/assimilation ($M = 13.09$) and assimilation strategies ($M = 13.33$). It is important to note that the range of the

1995, perceived sociopolitical White Nativism mean values had significantly decreased, changing from 12.77–19 in 1991 to 11.86–15.83, reflecting the children's interaction with an increasingly White Nativist sociopolitical context, consistent with the sociopolitical context in California and the larger nation.

The 2001 analysis did not yield any statistically significant results ($X^2 = 2.744$; $df = 5$; $p < .7393$) however, it is important to consider that the results for perceived sociopolitical White Nativism had been imputed, using a univariate imputation sampling method based on multiple regressions (see Appendix C, 2001 Perceived Sociopolitical White Nativism Index). Hence, it was difficult to discern if the lack of statistical significance was related to the imputation method, or due indeed to a lack of difference between perceived sociopolitical White Nativism and acculturation outcomes. To further clarify the findings, Wald Chi-square tests and regression analyses were performed. The Wald Chi-square tests[24] found a statistically significant effect between perceived sociopolitical White Nativism and acculturation outcomes. The 1991, 1995 and 2001[25] regression analysis provided a more detailed window into the relationship between sociopolitical White Nativism and acculturation. The regression analysis showed that an assimilation strategy was a more likely acculturation outcome when perceived sociopolitical White Nativism decreased, and a separation strategy was a more likely outcome when perceived sociopolitical White Nativism increased, consistent with the Kruskal-Wallis tests' findings. The integrated strategy was found to be a more likely outcome when perceived sociopolitical White Nativism increased, than the marginalization strategy, but both were less likely than the separated strategy as sociopolitical White Nativism increased.

In terms of experienced prejudice and acculturation outcome, the findings showed an effect and association between experienced prejudice and acculturation outcome, in 1991, but not in 1995 and 2001. In 1991, when 65.98% (21.67% less than in 2001) of the children reported having experienced prejudice, both the Wald chi-square test (Wald $\alpha^2$ (5,397) = 11.35, $p = .0449$) and regression analysis found a statistically significant effect between experienced prejudice and acculturation strategy outcome. Overall, the findings suggest that the children in the study seemed to be able to separate individual and personal experiences of prejudice (87.65% answered yes by 2001) from experiences related to the larger sociopolitical, cultural context of the nation. However, since by 2001, 87.65% of the children reported having experienced prejudice, the inability to find an effect between prejudice and acculturation outcome in 1995 and 2001, seems to reflect an inability to detect the latent effect of experienced prejudice due to its pervasiveness, rather than a lack of effect or association between these two variables. What the findings do clearly and consistently show is that perceived sociopolitical White Nativism seems to be the best predictor variable for acculturation outcome.

## White Nativist sociopolitical contextualization of acculturation, 1991–2003

The exploration and sociopolitical contextualization of the evolution of the acculturation process of American-born children of Mexican immigrant parents revealed both the nature of the cultural transformation feared by White Nativists and the transactional quality of the acculturation pattern of the children. The findings indicated that over time, American-born children of Mexican immigrant parents acquired and developed high English competency skills and expressed at least some preference for the American culture. However, the findings also indicated that the children were not giving up their parental, Mexican, cultural linking symbols, developing instead a loyalty toward both languages, English and Spanish. The findings also showed that the children wanted to raise, or were raising, their children as bilinguals within a family environment that had accepted some, but not all, of the cultural values, and behaviors considered by "White Natives" to be "American." These findings, therefore, confirm the White Nativist fears discussed in the integrative immigration policy analysis. In other words, the "White Native" cultural amplifiers (Volkan, 2013), which symbolically maintain a "White Native," collective intrapsychic sense of "we-ness," emerged as being indeed transformed through the acculturation process of the American-born children of Mexican immigrants.

At the same time, the transactional quality of the acculturation process of the American-born children of Mexican immigrant parents also emerged clearly, consistent with Berry's acculturation strategies model (2003). The findings provided empirical evidence of the association between the structural level of sociopolitical White Nativism and acculturation strategies. They also empirically supported the conceptualization of sociopolitical White Nativism as a significant predictor of the acculturation strategies outcome. The separation and marginalization acculturation strategies were seen to be positively associated with sociopolitical White Nativism, followed by the integration strategy, while the integration/assimilation and assimilation strategies were seen to be negatively associated with sociopolitical White Nativism.

Overall, the acculturation process of the American-born children of Mexican immigrant parents reflected the effects of the increasingly White Nativist sociopolitical context in which they were growing up. Although, over time, the children moved toward the assimilated end of the acculturation continuum, as reflected by the significant increase in the percentage of children using an integrated/assimilated strategy and an integrated strategy by 2001–2003, the percentage of children using an assimilated acculturation strategy did not increase between 1991 and 2003. This evolution toward and away from the assimilated acculturation strategy[26] is consistent with the association found between higher levels of sociopolitical White Nativism and the integrated acculturation strategy, as well as with lower levels of sociopolitical White Nativism and the assimilated acculturation strategy.

However, the evolution of the acculturation process of the American-born children of Mexican immigrant parents appeared more hopeful than their ethnic identity evolution, which had suggested an increasing risk toward downward assimilation, given the number of children identifying in a pan-ethnic manner. Despite the connection found between higher sociopolitical White Nativism and the separated acculturation strategy, the percentage of children using this strategy, as well as the marginalization strategy, decreased significantly over time.

These findings highlight the transactional nature (Berry, 2003) of the acculturation process, clearly illustrating how the acculturation strategy adopted by an individual is a product of the interaction between the individual's particular characteristics and the country's historical and sociopolitical context in relation to the individual's ethnic group (Abraido-Lanza et al., 2006). Consistent with this transactional conceptualization of acculturation, the exploration of the acculturation process of American-born children of Mexican immigrant parents also revealed an association between increasing levels of experienced prejudice and the acculturation strategies outcome, where increasing levels of experienced prejudice were found to hinder the children's efforts to fully integrate into the American society through an assimilated adaptation style.

Most importantly, the findings make explicit the effects of the White Nativist, "[Hispanic] social or public self-fulfilling prophecies" (Aleinikoff & Rumbaut, 1998, p.1) while also providing empirical evidence to refute White Nativist claims related to the assimilative failure of the Hispanic other. In other words, although over time, American-born children of Mexican immigrant parents have indeed been moving along the assimilation continuum, "White Natives" did not experience/perceive the American-Hispanic other, as progressing along this continuum, when compared to the historical assimilation pattern of immigrants between 1890 and 1920, often referred to as the "classic case." Instead, "White Natives" continued to hold onto a long accepted myth, the Hispanic other as unassimilable, persisting in conceptualizing the adaptation of the American-Hispanic other as an assimilation failure, because their adaptation does not fully reject all aspects of their Hispanic, and in this case Mexican, heritage (Huntington, 2004a, 2004b; Swain, 2002). This perception, that reflects underlying sociocognitive constructions, related to and informed by a White Nativist ideology, fueled the development of interior control immigration policies, embedded within White Nativist aggression.[27] As this study has shown, this legal and covert aggression has affected and derailed the acculturation process of the "American-born, Hispanic other," producing what White Nativists fear most: an increasing number of American-born children of Mexican immigrant parents, who although moving along the assimilation continuum, are unable to fully assimilate into American society, due to the effects of the White Nativist structural barriers they and their families have encountered along the way. Where White Nativists (Huntington, 2004a, 2004b) attribute and locate the "assimilation problem" within the Hispanic other, this study has provided a different explanation. American-born children of Mexican immigrant parents are not refusing to "assimilate," but rather it is the White Nativist social context, and associated structural forces that are exerting pressure on the nature of their assimilation path (Citrin & Sears, 2009; Gratton et al., 2007).

Chapter 7 will continue to present the findings of the secondary study of the CILS. It will examine the children's sense of national belonging, and the implications of the White Nativist sociopolitical context in which they were growing up. The chapter will also examine the interaction between the children's ethnic identity and acculturation styles, and their sense of national belonging.

## Notes

1 The CILS project was directed by Alejandro Portes, from Johns Hopkins University and by Ruben G. Rumbaut, from San Diego State University, in collaboration and through grants from The National Science Foundation; Russell Sage Foundation; Andrew W. Mellon Foundation; Hewlett Foundation; and Spencer Foundation (Portes & Rumbaut, 2005).
2 The term "second-generation immigrant children" is understood within the CILS study and in this chapter as referring to "U.S.-born children with at least one foreign-born parent or children born abroad but brought at an early age" (Center for Migration and Development).
3 Sample attrition: Given the level of attrition present in the first and second follow-up samples used for this study, the attrition level and its possible implications were evaluated across two of the study's central variables: ethnic identity and experience of prejudice. Cross tabulations, Chi-square and/or Fisher Exact tests were performed for each variable, between time periods, to assess whether or not the missing subjects were missing at random (Schafer & Graham, 2001). Results indicated that the subjects were missing at random, thus no attrition/sample bias correction methods were used.
4 For construct definition/clarity, "White Nativism" was understood as defined by Huntington (2004) and Swain (2002): a recent "new white racial advocacy" (Swain, 2002, p. 15) movement that has gained force within the United States since the 1990s due to, the changing demographic composition of the United States; and to the impact of the exodus of high wage, non-skilled jobs overseas, increasing competition between white unskilled workers and immigrant workers (Huntington, 2004; Swain, 2002). "White Nativists" advocate for race-preservation instead of racial supremacy, "affirming that culture is a product of race" (Huntington, 2004, p. 41) and cautioning that "...the shifting U.S. demographics foretell the replacement of white culture by black or brown cultures that are intellectually and morally inferior" (Huntington, 2004, p. 41).
5 Individual desire to participate in the democratic life of the nation and in its community.
6 Unlike the Perceived Sociopolitical White Nativism Index, which could not be reported for 2001–2003, as the questions pertaining to the index were not included in the 2001–2003 CILS survey, the questions pertaining to the Experience of Prejudice Index were included in the three CILS data collection periods.
7 The index measure was operationalized using questions from the 1991 and 1995 CILS surveys, as no equivalent questions could be found in the 2001 CILS survey

questionnaire. The questions comprising this index measure for 1991 and 1995 were as follows:

> Question 79: There is racial discrimination in economic opportunities in the U.S.
>
> Question 80: The American way of life weakens the family.
>
> Question 81: There is much conflict between different racial and ethnic groups in the U.S.
>
> Question 82: Non-whites have as many opportunities to get ahead economically as whites in the U.S.
>
> Question 83: There is no better country to live in than the United States.
>
> Question 84: Americans generally feel superior to foreigners.

8 This perception is particularly important, given the sociopolitical climate in California in 1995, where the majority of the children resided.

9 Paired $t$-test (1991 ($M$ = 13.47774, SD = 2.617525) and 1995 ($M$ = 12.9911, SD = 2.838392); $t$ (337) = 2.4960, $p$ < .0130 of −0.5 points.

10 The Spearman's Rho correlation coefficient test, 1991 ($r$, (415) = −.2963, $p$ < .0001) and 1995 ($r_s$ (355) = −0.2625, $p$ < .0001).

11 Experience of Prejudice Index.

12 Perceived Sociopolitical White Nativism.

13 Downward assimilation places American-born children of Mexican immigrant parents at risk of joining "reactive subcultures as a means of protecting their sense of self-worth" (pp. 27–8) after "…seeing their parents and grandparents confined to menial jobs, and [becoming, as they get older] increasingly aware of discrimination by white mainstream…" (Portes & Zhou, 1994, pp. 27–8).

14 As postulated in the theoretical formulation of this study, and consistent with Volkan's conceptualization of suitable targets of externalization, synthetic nations, racism and thus, the individual and collective intrapsychic need for enemies (1985, 1998 and 2013) experienced prejudice provided a proxy measure for the White Nativist aggression directed toward the "American born children of Mexican immigrant parents."

15 Multinomial logistic regression analyses.

16 Since the 2001, CILS questionnaire did not include the questions comprising the Perceived Sociopolitical White Nativism Index, values were imputed, using a univariate imputation sampling method based on multiple regressions (see Appendix C). The 1991, ethnic identity level of importance was also imputed, carrying backward the 1995 data, as the 1991, CILS survey did not include the corresponding question.

17 Both, a national origin and a pan-ethnic identity are considered, in segmented assimilation theory, to be two different manifestations of the child's reactive adaptation to a societal context marked by prejudice, discrimination and racism (Aleinikoff & Rumbaut, 1998). While the Mexican identity suggests a lack of assimilation into American society, the pan-ethnic identity suggests a downward assimilation (Aleinikoff & Rumbaut, 1998; Portes, 2006).

18 As postulated by Oyserman (2004), "social contexts enable, elicit, and scaffold certain selves while disenabling, suppressing, and dismantling others even in the face of what might appear to be objective evidence of these self-dimensions" (p. 13).

19 The evolution of the ethnic level of importance could only be explored for the 1995 and 2001–2003 CILS survey periods, as the question corresponding to the ethnic identity level of importance was not included in the 1991 CILS survey.

20 These differences were found to be statistically significant ($p$ = .007).

21 While the 1991 and 1995 Culture, Values and Behavior scale (Question 98, CILS) evaluated the children's level of preference for the American way of life, question 32 from the 2001 Culture, Values and Behavior scale asked children to identify the language in which they were hoping to raise their children. Question 30, CILS 2001 was not included here, and only used for the Acculturation Strategies Index.

22 Culture, Value and Behavior variable, 2001: since not all respondents were parents in 2001, a new variable was developed, combining the answers to question 30c and 32 due to the number of missing values when only using question 32. 2001 CILS, Question 30c: "In what language do you speak with your children?" (CILS 2001). Question 32: "In what language do you hope to raise your children?" (see Appendix C, Culture, Values and Behavior Scale).

23 Multinomial logistic regression analyses provided results consistent with the literature review, and specifically with Berry's acculturation conceptualization (2003).

24 Wald Chi-square tests: 1991, Wald $\alpha^2$ (5,397) = 14.26, $p$ = .0140; 1995, Wald $\alpha^2$ (5,325) = 17.03, $p$ = .0044; and 2001 using 1995 carry forward data, Wald $\alpha^2$ (3,226) = 9.16, $p$ = .0273.

25 2001, Multinomial logistic regression analyses were conducted inputting/carrying forward the 1995 Perceived Sociopolitical White Nativism Index data.

26 While the marginalization and separation strategies almost disappeared by 2001, higher levels of sociopolitical White Nativism were seen to thwart the development of an assimilation strategy, fostering instead an integrated or integrated/assimilated strategy, if the level of White Nativism decreased.

27 As reflected in the level of experienced prejudice and sociopolitical White Nativism reported by the children overtime.

# 7 Secondary study of the children of immigrants longitudinal study

## National belonging

### Introduction

This chapter will continue to present the findings of the secondary study, focusing on the sense of national belonging of the American children of Mexican immigrant parents, who by 2001–2003 had become young adults. The interaction between the children/young adults' ethnic identity, acculturation and their sense of national belonging will be explored. This discussion will examine White Nativist claims that have sociocognitively constructed ethnic and/or cultural particularisms as undermining, individual, and thus collective, notions of American national belonging. The young adults' sense of national belonging will also be contextualized within the increasingly contemporary, White Nativist sociopolitical context of the United States.

### National belonging

The sense of national belonging of the American-born children of Mexican immigrant parents was explored through the National Belonging Index, which examined the children's sense of national belonging along two dimensions, patriotism and civic engagement. Each of the dimensions will be presented separately, and later contextualized in relation to ethnic identity, acculturation and sociopolitical White Nativism.

### *Patriotism*

Question 47, CILS, 2001–2003, "which country feels more like home?" was used to explore the children's affective tie to the United States, as well as their possible perception of the United States as a home, a safe base from which to explore the world (Bowlby, 1988). Cross tabulation analysis showed that an overwhelming majority of the now young adults, 84.23%, felt more like home in the United States, while 15.77% felt equally at home in both, the United States and Mexico. None of the young adults reported feeling at home only in Mexico, or not feeling at home in either country.

### Civic engagement

Civic engagement was subdivided into community/religious participation and electoral participation. Question 39 ("What is your current religion?") and question 40 ("About how often do you attend religious services?") of the 2001 CILS survey, were used to explore the young adults' community/ religious participation. Initial cross tabulation analysis showed that the vast majority of the young adults had a religious affiliation, 70.83% identified as protestant or catholic, and 14.39% reported other religious affiliations.

When the young adults' religious affiliation (question 39) was cross tabulated[1] with their religious participation (question 40), 45.42% of those who had identified as protestant or catholic reported the highest religious participation, attending religious activities often or some of the time. Young adults with other religious affiliations reported significantly lower religious involvement, only 9.54% attended religious activities often or some of the time. However, some young adults who identified no religious affiliation (1.53%), reported participating in religious activities sometimes or often.

Electoral participation[2] was explored both in terms of voting registration (questions 42, "Are you registered to vote?"), and political affiliation (question 43, "What is your political party preference or affiliation?"). Cross tabulation analysis showed that the large majority of young adults in the study (73.41%) were registered to vote, regardless of whether or not they reported belonging to a political party, indicating a high level of electoral participation. However, the largest percentage, 48.41%, belonged to a political party and were registered to vote. Only 26.59% of young adults were not registered to vote, whether they belonged to a political party (7.54%) or not (19.05%).

### Conclusion

Overall, the preliminary analysis of the sense of national belonging of the young adult children of Mexican immigrant parents revealed a strong sense of belonging and patriotism, as all of them felt the United States was their home, with only a small percentage reporting feeling at home in both the United States and Mexico, 15.77%. In terms of civic engagement, a large number of the young adults identified a religious affiliation, and reported being actively engaged within their religious community. Their electoral engagement also reflected significant participation within the civic life of the United States, with 73.41% of the young adults being registered to vote, regardless of established political affiliation.

Although this preliminary analysis provided a small window into the young adults' sense of national belonging, it did not allow for a more complex and nuanced contextualization. The next three sections will examine the interaction between ethnic identity, acculturation and sociopolitical White Nativism, and the young adults' sense of national belonging. The analysis will also explore White Nativist, sociocognitive, discursive constructions that posit that ethnic identifications other than American, and acculturation strategies other than assimilation, weaken individual and collective notions of American national belonging.

## National belonging and ethnic identity

Analyses were conducted using the 2001–2003[3] Explicit Ethnic Identity Importance Index and the National Belonging Index to examine the effect of ethnic identity, and its explicit importance on the three components of national belonging.

### *Patriotism*

Regression analyses identified a statistically significant ($p = .05$) negative association between ethnic identity and patriotism. The findings showed that an American identity predicted feeling at home in the United States 100% of the time, while other ethnic identities did so at a lesser rate. However, it is important to highlight that although ethnic identity did affect the patriotism outcome, 84.23% of the young adults reported feeling more at home in the United States than in Mexico, and none of the youth reported not feeling at home in the United States. While all non-American ethnic identities were less likely to feel at home only in the United States, a Mexican identity was found to have a stronger negative association with (lower patriotism) patriotism than a hyphenated-American or pan-ethnic one. However, the explicit importance of the young adults' ethnic identity was not found to be a predictor for greater or lesser levels of patriotism.

### *Civic engagement*

Regression analyses did not show that ethnic identity or its explicit importance were statistically significant predictors of political participation; however, ethnic identity was found to be a predictor for religious participation.

### *Religious participation*

Regression analyses[4] showed a statistically significant ($p = .05$) positive association between ethnic identity and its explicit importance, and religious participation. An American identity was found to be negatively associated with religious participation, whereas the hyphenated-American and Mexican identities were found to be positively associated with religious participation, that is, higher religious participation. Differences were nonetheless observed within the non-American ethnic identities and the level of religious participation. Youth who identified as Mexican had lower religious participation levels than those who identified as hyphenated-American, but higher than those who identified as American. The explicit importance of the young adults' ethnic identity was consistently found to be positively associated with higher levels of religious participation ($p = .05$); and, in fact, the two ethnic categories associated with the highest levels of explicit importance, hyphenated-American and Mexican, were the two identities that best predicted religious participation ($p = .05$).

## National belonging and acculturation

Regression analyses[5] were performed using the National Belonging and the Acculturation Strategies Index to examine how acculturation strategy categories affected the sense of national belonging of American-born children of Mexican parents.

### *Patriotism*

Regression analyses showed a statistical significant association between acculturation strategies and patriotism outcomes ($p = .05$). Overall, the analyses showed that an assimilated strategy was positively associated with feeling more like home only in the United States (higher patriotism), while an integrated strategy was negatively associated with patriotism; hence, youth who used an integrated strategy were more likely to feel more like home in both the United States and Mexico than only in the United States. These findings appear to be congruent with the conceptual definitions of both acculturation strategies (Berry, 2003). However, in regards to the assimilation strategy, although the effect was statistically significant, the range of the confidence interval raised some questions as to the usefulness of the significance. This was not the case in terms of the integrated strategy, which appeared to have a consistent, statistically significant effect on the patriotism outcome, with moderately discrete confidence interval ranges.

### *Civic engagement*

Regression analyses[6] showed a statistically significant association between acculturation strategies and level of electoral participation ($p = .05$). Results showed that a separated acculturation strategy was negatively associated with electoral participation; youth who used a separated strategy, relative to the integrated/assimilated strategy were found to be less likely to engage in high electoral participation.[7] The reverse finding was also observed; youth who used an integrated/assimilated strategy were more likely to display higher electoral participation than those who used a separated strategy.[8] However, regression analyses did not show any statistically significant effect or association between acculturation strategies and religious participation.

## Ethnic identity, acculturation and sociopolitical White Nativism: Effects on national belonging

Regressions analyses[9] were conducted to examine in one single model the relationship between: (1) ethnic identity; (2) explicit importance of ethnic identity; (3) experienced prejudice; (4) perceived sociopolitical White Nativism;[10] (5) acculturation strategy categories, and national belonging. Overall, the analyses findings were consistent with those previously reported pertaining to ethnic identity, acculturation strategies, and national belonging. However, experienced prejudice and perceived sociopolitical White Nativism were not found to be associated with any of the components of national belonging. These findings were consistent across regression analyses, regardless of the imputation method used for the 2001 Perceived Sociopolitical White Nativism Index (see Appendix C).

## Contextualization of national belonging: Ethnic identity, acculturation and White Nativism

This study examined both ethnic identity and acculturation, in addition to sociopolitical White Nativism, as possible predictors of national belonging, given White Nativist sociopolitical discourses that have increasingly questioned whether "it is possible to foster loyalty to and identification with one's own ethnic [and cultural] particularism and, at the same time, maintain shared national values and a sense of common national identification" (Sidanius, Feshback, Levin, & Pratto, 1997, p. 103). Given White Nativists concern with both the ethnic identity and acculturation process of "the Hispanic other;" and having predicted that both of these constructs would be associated with, and affected by, the level of White Nativism present in the social context of the American-born children of Mexican immigrant parents, the study included both ethnic identity and acculturation as possible predictors of the sense of national belonging of the children. This conceptualization and methodological design allowed for the exploration of sociopolitical White Nativism, as both an indirect and direct factor for the sense of national belonging of the children.

Overall, the findings indicated that micro and macro sociopolitical White Nativism did not have a direct effect on the national sense of belonging of American-born children of Mexican immigrant parents. However, sociopolitical White Nativism (at the micro and macro level) was found to have an indirect effect on national belonging, due to its effect on the ethnic identity development and acculturation process of the American-born children of Mexican immigrant parents, both of which were found to have an effect on the children's sense of national belonging.

The exploration of national belonging along two dimensions, patriotism and civic engagement, showed that despite the increasingly White Nativist sociopolitical context in which the children were growing up, American-born children of Mexican immigrant parents had developed a strong primary, affective tie and attachment to the United States as reflected in their level of patriotism, interpreted according to Feshbach (1991) and Kosterman and Feshbach's (1989) definition. Along civic engagement, the children displayed a high to moderate level of civic engagement, consistent with Adler and Goggin's (2002) and Putnam's (1995) conceptualization of community participation and integration. By 2001–2003, the now young adults reported a high to moderate level of active electoral participation, and a high to moderate religious participation, consistent with Portes and Rumbaut's (2014) CILS research findings.

In terms of ethnic identity and national belonging, the findings revealed a statistically significant effect on patriotism. An American identity was found to be a perfect predictor of patriotism, predicting a sole affective tie toward the United States, while all other ethnic categories were associated with some likelihood of a dual affective tie toward both the United States and Mexico. The Mexican ethnic identity was found to have the strongest negative association with a sole affective tie toward the United States, indicating a greater likelihood of a dual affective tie toward both countries, than the hyphenated-American or pan-ethnic identities.

Ethnic identity was also found to be associated with religious participation. An American identity was found to be negatively associated with religious participation, whereas the hyphenated-American, Mexican and pan-ethnic identities were found to be positively associated with higher levels of religious participation. Within this context, the explicit importance of the ethnic identity was also found to be positively associated with higher religious participation. The association found between ethnic identity, its explicit importance and higher religious participation is particularly important, given that religious institutions have historically supported the acculturation process of immigrant parents. These institutions often help immigrant parents understand the American social context in which they are raising their children, thus facilitating the integration of these children into American society (Portes & Rumbaut, 2014; Putnam, 1995).

Given the mediating role that religious institutions play on the acculturation process of parents and families, the association between the Mexican and pan-ethnic identities and lower religious participation, relative to the hyphenated-American ethnic identity is of concern. This association suggests a higher disengagement from the natural, community support systems that could foster the assimilation and integration process of these youth, protecting against a reactive adaptation (Aleinikoff & Rumbaut, 1998). In line with this interpretation, the hyphenated-American identity and its association with higher religious participation are congruent with both its higher assimilation level and the mediating role of religious participation for the acculturation and social integration of immigrant families. Putnam (2000) and Crowley (n.d.), in fact, identified religious participation as a leading indicator of community participation and integration, while also cautioning that the level of civic engagement is not only determined by a person's motivation, but also "by the civic infrastructure" (p. 344) of his/ her environment.

In terms of acculturation and its effect on the sense of national belonging of American-born children of Mexican immigrant parents, acculturation was found to be associated with the nature of the patriotism outcome. An assimilated strategy was found to be positively associated with higher levels of patriotism, a sole affective tie toward the United States; while an integrated strategy was found to be negatively associated with patriotism, reflecting a greater likelihood of a dual affective attachment toward both countries. Acculturation was not found to have a consistent, conclusive effect on electoral participation, and did not appear to have an association with religious participation.

These findings bring us, in a hermeneutic manner, to the initial question posited by Sidanius et al. (1997), "...is it possible to foster loyalty to and identification with one's own ethnic particularism and, at the same time, maintain shared national values and a sense of common national identification?" (p. 103). As shown by the effects of ethnic identity and acculturation on national belonging, all the American-born children of Mexican immigrant parents reported having an affective tie and attachment to the United States, regardless of their ethnic identification, or acculturation style/strategy. However, a smaller percentage reported having a dual affective tie to both the United States and their parents' native country, Mexico. Hence, the children's sense of belonging to the United States nation-state was clearly illustrated by the findings.

Yet, the findings presented in Chapter 6 also concurrently showed that ethnic identity formation and acculturation processes are affected by the presence of sociopolitical White Nativism, which in turn fosters ethnic identifications away from the assimilative plain, as well as cultural adaptations away from assimilation; and, in a circular manner, both ethnic identity and acculturation were found to have an effect on patriotism, as well as civic engagement. Consequently, although in a reductionist manner, it can be said that as posited by White Nativists (Huntington, 2004a, 2004b; Swain, 2002), an ethnic identity and/or acculturation strategy other than the American identity and the assimilated acculturation strategy, have a negative effect on the patriotic, national sense of belonging of an individual.

However, this study provided empirical evidence for a more complex understanding of the national sense of belonging of American-born children of Mexican immigrants, as related to patriotism. What the findings revealed was a highly transactional process, consistent with segmented assimilation (Gratton, Gutmann, & Skop, 2007; Portes and Rumbaut, 2014) and Berry's (2003) acculturation model, in which the characteristics of a person's environment can either hinder or foster individual characteristics and inclinations, leading to particular types of ethnic identity formation and acculturation processes. Hence, as the study has shown, environments marked by sociopolitical White Nativism due to their micro and macro level aggression toward specific ethnic and racial groups, such as toward the American-born children of Mexican immigrant parents, exert pressure on the nature of the ethnic identity and assimilation path that the group will follow (Citrin & Sears, 2009; Gratton et al., 2007).

What is perhaps most significant, is that the secondary study of the CILS exposed the otherwise obscured implications of the White Nativist ideology and associated contemporary sociopolitical context for the American-born children of Mexican immigrant parents. It thereby provided empirical evidence that refutes simplistic attributional, decontextualized claims that hold the Hispanic other solely responsible for his/her presumed failure to assimilate. This perceived and presumed failure, as the study revealed, is better understood as part of a White Nativist, collective social myth, fueled by the intrapsychic annihilatory fear induced by the gradual transformation of the "White Native," cultural amplifiers (Volkan, 2009, 2013). In fact, what the findings clearly show is that, despite the micro and macro White Nativist aggression, the American-born children of Mexican immigrants in this study felt that this country was their home and where they belonged.

## Limitations of the study

Since this was a secondary analysis, the conceptual operationalization of the variables was limited to the existing questions that had been included in the CILS survey questionnaires. In some instances variables had to be developed/created anew, as in the case of the experience of prejudice index. In addition, there was sample attrition between the first, second and third phases of the CILS study, which was also reflected in the study's subsamples. Although the sample attrition between the study's first and second phases was within normal limits, consistent with the original CILS study, the sample attrition in the third phase was more significant. To evaluate for possible sample bias due to attrition, two of the study's variables were examined: ethnic identity and experience of prejudice. The sample attrition analysis along ethnic identity and the experience of prejudice variables yielded similar results, indicating that, despite attrition, the study's samples had not been affected by possible sample bias.

In addition to sample attrition, there were also missing item responses in all the variables, which required the use of a "listwise deletion method" (Howell, 2012); however, there were also variables that were missing from one survey period to another, as was the case with the 1991 ethnic identity level of importance, and the 2001 perceived sociopolitical White Nativism.[11] The univariate sampling imputation method used for this later variable, produced a mean that was artificially higher (higher values reflect lower levels of sociopolitical White Nativism) than expected, due to the effect of the 1991 data included in the univariate sampling method, placing all values slightly above those reported by the children in 1995. This inflation may have led to a loss of statistical effect for the predictor variables that were most sensitive to fluctuations in the perceived sociopolitical White Nativism index, acculturation and electoral participation, 2001.

It is also important to note that many of the variables were either nominal/categorical or ordinal, thus limiting the types of statistical measures that could be used, especially as pertaining to regression. This study used multinomial logistic regression analyses to predict the categorical outcomes of various dependent variables. While this type of analysis is "...more flexible and versatile than discriminant analysis..." (Metter & Vanatta, 2005, p. 313), it is sensitive to outliers and high correlations among independent variables, and may produce results that have little statistical power (Metter & Vanatta, 2005). However, given sample attrition in the third CILS survey period, and due to the number of missing responses, statistical analyses conducted with the 2001–2003 data did reflect an unavoidable lack of power due to the smaller number of observations available for analysis. As a result, some of the statistical significance of some predictor variables for national belonging, such as, acculturation, was lost largely due to the lower number of observations available. In addition, the generalizability of the findings is also limited by the study's sample size, and by the geographical characteristics of the children in the sample, since a large percentage resided in California at the time of the CILS study.

Lastly, it is important to note, that although the study's findings provided empirical support for the sociopolitical and psychological formulation of White Nativism as it pertained to the Hispanic immigrant other and their American-born children, none of the measures used in the study were able to tap directly into the connection between White Nativism and immigration policy. Yet, given that: (1) most of the children in this study resided in San Diego, CA (95.29% in 1991; 95.50% in 1995; and 95.94% in 2001); and that (2) this state began to experience significant anti-immigrant sociopolitical changes and tension starting in 1994,—first due to Operation Gatekeeper and Proposition 187, followed by the implementation of IIRIRA and AEDPA in 1996—it seems reasonable to conclude that the social context described by the American-born children of Mexican immigrant parents in this study must have been permeated by the effects of these sociopolitical changes,[12] as well as by the deportation rates affecting their community since 1994.

## Integrated immigration policy reform analysis and research application

The research study presented in this chapter and in Chapter 6 emerged from the conclusions derived from the integrated sociopolitical and psychological analysis of contemporary American immigration reforms, specifically IIRIRA and AEDPA. The analysis began with a critical discourse historical analysis of immigration policy that served to contextualize current immigration reform policies. This analysis examined the historical dynamics of dominance, subjugation, inclusion and exclusion that led to the creation of the "native American" and the American nation-state. The critical discourse historical analysis uncovered the sociocognitive processes by which both the "native American" and the racialized, immigrant Hispanic, Mexican other were constructed, exploring the racial paradigm in which they were created. The analysis exposed the sociocognitive and legal processes implicated in the creation and maintenance of the White Nativist ideology.

Within this context, the origin of the contemporary, White Nativist racial, codifying categories that delineate who is and isn't "American," was historically traced back to the country's dissociated "native American" history of occupation, territorial expansion, conquest, colonization, enslavement and genocide that birthed and legitimized the "White Natives' claim" to what is now the American nation-state. Immigration policy emerged at that point, as constitutive to the maintenance of the "White Native" identity, that is, as a legal, sociocognitive mechanism by which "White Natives" established and reinforced their constructed, large collective, idealized, national synthetic identity (Volkan, 2013). The Immigration Act of 1924 emerged within this historical context as the central legal mechanism by which contemporary, racialized, national origin categories were birthed, effectively preserving "White Native" dominance while recasting Mexicans as racialized others through the creation of the Mexican race (Ngai, 1999, 2014).

The Immigration Act of 1924, however, was also instrumental in constructing the Mexican racialized other as illegal and criminal, and thus as unwanted and unlawful (Ngai, 1999, 2014). This sociopolitical construction, eventually legitimized the early 1930s, mass deportation of the Mexican other, along with their American citizen children (Hernandez, 2010). In this manner, immigration policy and deportation emerged as a White Nativist legal mechanism that allowed "White Natives" to create and protect their synthetic, idealized group identity (Volkan, 2013) and culture from a feared impending transformation, due to the national origins of the incoming immigrant population. These new immigrants had not only been racialized, but also constructed as unassimilable into the "White Native" identity and culture.

The integration of a critical analysis of globalization, capitalism and demographic change, partially informed by Wallerstein's world-systems analysis model (Wallerstein, 2002, 2003), exposed immigration policy as a "White Native" legal mechanism by which to regulate and control the presence of the Hispanic, Mexican immigrant other. This Mexican immigrant other was needed as a means of production within the American capitalist economic system and yet unwanted as a permanent member of American society (Massey, Durand, & Malone, 2002) on grounds of unassimilability and criminality that fueled a growing nationalist and protectionist sociopolitical rhetoric during the 1980s and early 1990s, which has again re-emerged. This analysis also exposed immigration policy as a White Nativist sociopolitical mechanism by which to overtly regulate Mexican immigration, while in a complicit and covert manner creating an "undocumented de facto" cheap labor force (Massey et al., 2002) necessary to maximize production and wealth creation in the United States.

The psychological framework, presented as part of the integrated analysis model, complemented the sociopolitical analysis framework. The psychological analysis, informed by Winnicott's object relations theory (1965), Volkan's conceptualization of "suitable targets of externalization" (1985), synthetic nations (2013) and cultural amplifiers (2009, 2013), and Freud's work on Mourning and Melancholia (1917), examined the individual and collective affective linking processes that bind "White Natives" to each other, while legitimizing the White Nativist ideology of entitlement. The psychological analysis illustrated how the externalization of affective, good and bad "mother–me" unintegrated aspects of the individual self onto acceptable collective "suitable targets of externalization" (Volkan, 1985, 2013), provides "White Natives" with an unconscious mechanism by which to maintain their individual and group identity. This externalization process also legitimizes affect-driven behavior, as it supports and legitimizes sociocognitive constructions of "White Native" superiority that maintain the "White Native" idealized synthetic national identity and the necessary subjugation of the other. This part of the analysis illustrated the importance of conceptualizing American immigration policy as an external, sociocognitive manifestation of psychological, conscious and unconscious collective group efforts aimed at preserving the "White Native," mythical, idealized, shared identity and culture, and its related cultural amplifiers (Volkan, 2013), from their inevitable transformation due to capitalist labor demands. This conclusion informed a complex inquiry into identity contestation, aggression, collective loss and mourning.

Immigration reform policies enacted since 1996 emerged ultimately as a legal, sociocognitive process, embedded in and informed by an intricate, conscious and unconscious intrapsychic defense system, aimed at protecting the "White Native" individual and group psyche from a frightening realization: their "White Native" culture has already changed and cannot be preserved. The inability to engage in and complete a normal mourning process (Volkan, 2009), which would require mourning the synthetic nature of the "White Native" identity, prevents "White Natives" from integrating all aspects of their individual and collective selves. As the analysis discussed, "White Natives" remain locked in a position of forced, unconscious narcissistic idealization and concurrent sociocognitive devaluation of those constructed as other, in this case the Mexican other. This failure to engage in a collective mourning process prevents "White Natives" from processing the racial, ethnic and cultural collective trauma that led to the creation of the 'native American' identity and the nation-state. Thus, it precludes "White Natives" from achieving a different, more adaptive and integrated psychological and sociocognitive individual group "American self," that no longer requires the idealization of one group and the subjugation of the other. This new identity could free "White Natives," and the racialized other, from perennial social, large group, racial enactments in which members of each group have to adopt the position of perpetrator, victim or helpless bystander, with the associated feelings of fear, shame, humiliation and guilt that each of these positions may evoke (Volkan, 2009, 2013). In this manner, the new identity would reflect a reality-based affective and sociocognitive construction of the individual and collective self, devoid of the fear and anxiety that fuel contemporary immigration policy efforts to preserve an identity that never existed other than as affectively imagined.

Instead, the inability to mourn the mythical and idealized synthetic nature of the "White Native" identity, keeps "White Natives" engaged in a process of identity preservation and contestation, due to the ongoing demographic population changes taking place in the United States—a demographic change that is no longer being brought about by immigration but rather by the increasing number of American children born to the immigrant, often Mexican, other. These efforts at preserving the "White Native" identity and culture have been manifesting in increasing White Nativist sociopolitical discourses, that have led to increasingly exclusionary immigration policy reforms with a focus on interior enforcement and deportation, IIRIRA and AEDPA.

These two acts have had devastating and harmful effects on the American children of Hispanic immigrant parents and, in particular, children of Mexican immigrant parents often living in mixed status families. The "Mexican other" has been disproportionately affected by contemporary immigration policy reforms that began with IIRIRA and AEDPA, as they shifted immigration enforcement from border to interior enforcement and deportation (Hagan, Castro, & Rodriguez, 2010, p. 1809). The financial and emotional hardship experienced by American children of Mexican immigrant parents, due to the apprehension and permanent deportation of one or both caregivers, has been well documented (Enchautegui, 2013; Fix & Zimmermann, 1999; Hagan et al., 2010); as well as the effects on the children's developmental trajectory. However, no study had sought to explore how the current American immigration sociopolitical context, reflected in deportation reform policies enacted since 1996, was affecting the ethnic identity, acculturation and sense of national belonging of American-born children of Hispanic immigrant parents. This study sought to provide answers to this question.

Overall, this study provided empirical evidence for the integrated sociopolitical and psychological analysis and formulation of White Nativism and immigration policy reforms enacted since 1996, in particular IIRIRA and AEDPA. The study showed that over time, the increasingly White Nativist sociopolitical context, reflected in immigration reform policies enacted since 1996, had indeed affected the ethnic identity development, acculturation process and sense of national belonging of these children. Furthermore, as the findings illustrated, the increasingly White Nativist sociopolitical context in which the children were growing up, was found to thwart their ethnic identity development and acculturation process, interfering with their progression toward the assimilative plain. However, this study also provided evidence of the children's desire to integrate themselves within the American mainstream of society, as despite the effects of the increasingly White Nativist sociopolitical context in which they were growing up, over time they were seen to move toward higher levels of the assimilation continuum. Most importantly, the findings clearly reflected the children's affective tie and emotional attachment to the United States. Their level of patriotism clearly illustrated their sense of American national belonging, despite immigration policies that have significantly impacted the survival of their family units, with the emotional and financial effects of parental deportation and often-permanent division of family units (Enchautegui, 2013; Fix & Zimmermann, 1999; Hagan et al., 2010). The empirical evidence provided by this study: (1) raises the need to question the current White Nativist sociopolitical discourse of this country in regards to immigration policy, and the American-born "Hispanic hybrid other"; and also (2) provides a different etiological understanding for the ethnic identity development and acculturation process of American-born children of Mexican immigrant parents.

White Nativists, as discussed by Huntington (2004b), have been increasingly concerned about the Hispanic other's perceived failure to assimilate, leading to the implementation of immigration reform policies that have increasingly threatened the existence of the Hispanic other, their families, and the ability of their American children to often remain within the United States (Chaudry et al., 2010). However, the secondary data analysis study of the CILS, points toward a different understanding of the assimilation trajectory of the Hispanic other.

Assimilation has been taking place, although thwarted in its progression by the effects of the White Nativist discourse, which has manifested both in increasing interpersonal experienced prejudice and structural, White Nativist social and economic barriers (Gratton et al., 2007; Portes, Fernandez-Kelly, & Haller, 2005). However, because White Nativists have held a different perspective—one fueled by the fear of losing their "White Native" culture as originally conceived—immigration reform policies enacted since 1996, with their increasing focus on interior enforcement and deportation, have been indeed producing what White Nativists feared: an American-born child, of Mexican immigrant parents, who despite efforts to assimilate, has been unable to fully move along the assimilation continuum due to the effects that the White Nativist sociopolitical discourse has had on the self and his/her family unit. The etiological understanding provided by this study therefore highlights, as discussed by Aleinikoff and Rumbaut (1998), a different problem, one related to the effects of a "...social or public self-fulfilling prophecy that goes far toward explaining the dynamics of ethnic and racial conflict in the America of today" (p. 1), dynamics that have been felt by the American-born children of Mexican immigrant parents, and that this study sought to explore and illustrate.

## Notes

1  The subcategories of questions 39 and 40 were rank ordered as follows: 1 = No religion, No attendance; 2 = Other religion, No attendance; 3 = Protestant/ Catholic, No attendance; 4 = Attendance (any), No religion; 5 = Other religion, Attendance rarely; 6 = Protestant/Catholic, Attendance rarely; 7 = Other religion, Attendance somewhat; 8 = Protestant/Catholic, Attendance somewhat; 9 = Other religion, Attendance often; and, 10 = Protestant/Catholic, Attendance often. Total N for the cross-tabulation was 262.
2  Question 42 was designed as a nominal level variable, where 1 = Yes and 2 = No. Question 43 was designed as a nominal level variable, where: 1 = Democratic; 2 = Republican; 3 = Other; 4 = No party preference or affiliation. Levels 1, 2 and 3 were combined under 1 = political affiliation; level 4 maintained its current level, 4 = No party preference.
3  Logistic regression and ordinal logistic regression analyses were conducted using the 2001–2003, Explicit Ethnic Identity Importance Index and the National Belonging Index.
4  Ordinal logistic regressions.
5  Logistic regression and ordinal logistic regressions were conducted.
6  Ordered logistic regression analyses.
7  OR = 0.2978465, 95% CI (0.0920535, 0.9637063), $p = 0.043$.
8  OR = 3.357434, 95% CI (1.037661, 10.86325), $p = 0.043$.
9  Logistic and ordinal logistic regressions analyses were conducted.
10  Analyses were conducted using both imputation methods described in Appendix C pertaining to Perceived Sociopolitical White Nativism.
11  In terms of the 1991, ethnic identity level of importance variable, the corresponding 1995 data values were carried backward to compute the statistical analysis required for certain hypotheses across time. In terms of the 2001, Perceived Sociopolitical White Nativism Index, two different imputation methods were used to compute the required statistical analysis: (1) a simple carry forward method, where the 1995, perceived sociopolitical White Nativism values were carried forward; and, (2) a univariate imputation sampling method (see, Perceived Sociopolitical White Nativism, Appendix C). The univariate sampling method, based on multiple regressions, unavoidably clustered all values around the predicted mean, thus collapsing the range in the data of the 2001 index.
12  This theoretical explanation was also provided by Portes and Rumbaut (2006) when discussing the larger CILS study.

# 8 Immigration policy reforms

## Implications for clinical practice and policy development

### Introduction

This chapter will begin by discussing the clinical implications of contemporary immigration policy reforms on American-born children of Mexican immigrant parents, connecting macro level social and immigration policy to micro level clinical practice. The chapter will conclude by discussing future policy directions consistent with the findings of the integrated sociopolitical and psychological analysis of contemporary immigration policy reforms. This last section will link the secondary study's research findings to the proposed future policy directions. The chapter will also present the new immigration executive orders implemented by President Trump as of January 2017, examining their implications for mixed status families and their American children, with an emphasis on the long-term implications for American society.

### Contemporary immigration policy and deportation: Implications for clinical practice

The integrated analysis of contemporary immigration reform policy exposed current policies as a legal, conscious and unconscious White Nativist mechanism by which to both preserve and protect the existing "White Native" identity and culture from its impending transformation. However, this transformation cannot be averted due to the gradual and progressive demographic changes taking place in the United States population, which were initially propelled by the Immigration Act of 1965. However, as the integrative analysis of contemporary immigration policy reforms has shown, the current demographic change is not taking place due to immigration but, rather, due to the increasing number of children being birthed by the immigrant other, who is often a Hispanic, Mexican, immigrant other. Within this context, contemporary immigration policy reforms emerged not only as a White Nativist mechanism for controlling the immigrant other but also as a legal mechanism for removing American-born children of Hispanic, often Mexican, immigrant parents from their birth country, the United States. The secondary study presented in Chapters 6 and 7 explored and presented the effects that the current American, White Nativist, immigration sociopolitical context, with its reliance on deportation, is having on the ethnic identity development, acculturation and sense of national belonging of American-born children of Mexican immigrant parents. The integrated analysis of immigration policy also examined the short- and long-term effects of parental deportation on children, such as financial hardship, behavioral and emotional difficulties, as well as educational problems, among others (Capps, Castaneda, Cahudry, & Santos, 2007; Chaudry et al., 2010). However, the children of deported parents are not the only ones who experience short-term and long-term emotional, educational and behavioral problems (Capps et al., 2015). Children who have not been directly exposed to parental deportation are also affected by the uncertainty and anxiety experienced by parents, extended family members and friends, who may themselves fear a possible deportation, or may know someone who has been deported (Yoshikawa, 2011). Given the short-term and long-term effects of parental deportation, and the anxiety deportations have induced in predominantly immigrant communities and their children, it is important that social workers that provide clinical (mental health) services to "mixed status" families are able to provide clinical services informed by an integrated psychological and social justice framework.

An integrated psychological and social justice clinical framework highlights the need to acknowledge within the clinical treatment process, the White Nativist ideology present in the American, national immigration discourse, and its anti-immigrant, anti-Hispanic rhetoric, as well as its macro and micro level effects. Within this context, attention needs to be paid to the individual's experience of the self, and associated self-concept constructions and narratives, whether the client is an adult, adolescent or young child. As the findings of the secondary research study showed, it is particularly important for social workers to pay attention to the ethnic identity formation and acculturation processes of their clients, especially due to the correlation between higher levels of assimilation and declining mental health outcomes, reflected in research related to the Hispanic paradox (Oppedal, Roysamb, & Heyerdahl, 2005). Although both the integrated analysis and the secondary research study have examined dynamics pertaining to assimilation due to the White Nativist focus on the assimilability, or lack thereof, of the Hispanic other, the privileging of assimilation over all other modes of acculturation is conceptually problematic and misleading. Assimilation also entails psychological risks and can lead to forced cultural erasure, and thus constitutes a form of colonization (Oppedal et al., 2005; Rogler, Cortes, & Malgady, 1991; Wadsworth & Kubrin, 2007). Consequently, clinical social workers working with immigrant families, regardless of migratory status, need to be familiar with acculturation dynamics to explore individual and family acculturation processes and examine dynamics that privilege certain forms of acculturation, such as assimilation. The acculturation processes of family members and children need to be sociopolitically contextualized and explored as adaptations that either facilitate or hinder individual and/or family functioning ability. Within this framework, special attention needs to be paid to dynamics related to reactive identity formation and its associated risk factors for children and young adults (Aleinikoff & Rumbaut, 1998). In addition, transferential and countertransferential dynamics that may re-enact or highlight clients' experiences of marginalization and exclusion, especially within therapeutic dyads in which the clinician is, or is perceived as, a member of "the White Native" majority, need to be recognized and carefully explored to successfully address dynamics of power and subjugation, promoting therapeutic change and growth.

A clinical approach that fails to integrate a social justice framework could not only replicate the marginalization inherent in the current American national immigration discourses, but also runs the risk of pathologizing or "psychologizing" "the Hispanic other." In so doing, mental health providers could interpret the emotional and behavioral presentation of "Hispanic American children" and their "mixed status families" as reflective of intrapsychic processes or negative family dynamics that discount or negate the hurtful, and "aggressive" national context in which these families and children live. Within this "psychological context," mental health providers can inadvertently become social "White Native" tools of oppression. In other words, "the other" is "diagnosed" due to behavioral and emotional reactions that emerge in response to experienced interpersonal prejudice and to interactions with structural, White Nativist barriers, while the "White Nativist" ideology and its manifestations, continue to operate in an "unnamed" and disavowed manner.

## Immigration policy and clinical social work practice with mixed status families: The case of Ana and Rosa

This section will present a clinical vignette to illustrate the effects of current immigration policy and deportation, on the life of a young American child, born to Mexican undocumented immigrant parents, and the integrated psychological and social justice approach used to guide the therapeutic relationship and clinical work.

At the time I met Ana and her young child Rosa, I had been working in a local community mental health agency in the northeast of the United States. IIRIRA and AEDPA had been in effect for three years. The number of immigrant deportations had been increasing since their inception and worry and anxiety had started to spread within immigrant communities. Amidst these tensions, anxiety and uncertainty Ana, a 30-year-old, Mexican woman, arrived to the mental health agency where I was working, after being referred to the agency by her daughter's pediatrician. Her daughter, Rosa was four years old at the time that treatment began. Ana could speak some English, enough to navigate daily life, but she wasn't comfortably fluent. To facilitate engagement and treatment, she was assigned to me, as I was one of the few

Spanish-speaking, bilingual, bicultural clinicians working for the agency at the time. Ana was clearly worried about Rosa but also visibly anxious.

I was an immigrant to the United States and had recently become a permanent resident. I had initially arrived to the United States to attend college in the early 1990s under a student, F-1 visa, and had changed my visa status several times, between student visas and H1-B visas until I married, becoming a permanent resident in the late 1990s. Through the years living in the United States I had become very familiar with the immigration system, both personally and through my work with the immigrant community. Our immigration trajectories were certainly different and set us apart in pronounced ways, although at the same time our commonalities, shared immigration and language, facilitated the initial encounter.

Ana and I started to work together on what would be a four-year journey. Given the immigration context in which we found one another, I explained to Ana the importance of learning some initial information regarding her life and that of her daughter Rosa, but also clarified the limits of confidentiality, explaining that although knowing her immigration status would be helpful in understanding her current situation, I would not document any information provided in that regard. It had become standard practice not to document a client's immigration status in the clinical record, in order to protect clients, instead, essential aspects of the client's immigration context, including pre- and post-migration history, were summarized in a broad manner (Falicov, 2014).

Ana was tired and felt overwhelmed, doubting her capacity to take care of herself and her daughter without her husband, Jose. Ana had met Jose in Mexico when he was 22 years old; Ana was 18 years old at the time. Ana and Jose married in Mexico, and a year after, Jose decided to migrate to the United States, where he hoped to establish himself and to then bring Ana. A year after his arrival to the United States, Jose had managed to secure a job with a local company and an apartment where he and Ana could live together. He had also saved money to bring her over and at age 20, Ana migrated to the United States to join her husband. The crossing had been difficult and traumatic. Ana did not initially discuss what had happened; however, a year into therapy it became clear that Ana had been raped during the crossing. Once in the United States, Ana had been determined to forget what happened, focusing on building a new life with Jose. Ana started to secure jobs cleaning houses, and through word of mouth, was able to financially establish herself, until she became pregnant with Rosa. With Rosa's birth, Ana stopped working to raise Rosa, relying on Jose as their primary provider. They struggled financially, but both were hopeful, and despite difficulties, they felt their daughter would have a better life in the United States. However, their life completely changed after Jose's arrest and subsequent conviction.

On the day of his arrest, Jose had gone to work, as he typically did, deciding to visit a friend after work. His friend offered to drive Jose back to his house, and Jose accepted as he relied on public transportation, however they were pulled over by the police while driving. The police found drugs in the car and, both Jose and his friend were charged with drug trafficking. Jose had not been involved in drug trafficking, but he seemed to have just been in the wrong place at the wrong time. The implications of this charge were significant, as Jose had now been charged and convicted with an aggravated felony under AEDPA regulations that, together with IIRIRA, made him subject to an expedited deportation, without the possibility of a cancellation of removal. In addition, due to the changes introduced by IIRIRA to the hardship clause pertaining to dependent family members, it would be difficult for Jose to substantiate the need to stay in the United States. To appeal his removal orders, Jose needed access to legal counsel, and although a lawyer had been appointed to represent him in the criminal court, he hadn't attained legal immigration counsel, falsely believing that after serving his time he would be released, and would then be able to address any immigration proceedings. Jose believed that because he had lived in the United States for about ten years and had built a life together with his wife and child, Rosa, immigration authorities would allow him to stay without prioritizing his possible removal. It is also important to highlight that Jose was primarily Spanish speaking and had limited schooling, including literacy skills.

It was unclear at the time whether Ana understood the implications of Jose's conviction. However, it was clear from Ana's report that Jose did not fully grasp the need to seek immigration legal counsel, or if he did and understood the implications, may have been partially denying the seriousness of his situation and also protecting Ana from the frightening reality that awaited them. Regardless, Ana believed, or needed to believe, that Jose would join the family upon his release from prison.

After Jose's arrest, Ana started to work again, but she was limited in her ability to do so as she lacked resources and needed to take care of Rosa. Ana had returned to some of her previous employers, cleaning houses again on a regular basis, and picking up some extra work in a restaurant as a dishwasher; however, her income was limited. Despite her efforts, two months after Jose's incarceration, Ana could no longer pay for the apartment they had been living in, moving in with friends. By the time I met Ana and Rosa, they had moved ten different times, and were now renting a small room.

Ana had enrolled Rosa in their local Head Start Program, but over the last three months, Ana had gotten multiple calls from Rosa's teachers due to behavioral problems. Rosa, who according to Ana had been a pleasant, although somewhat willful child, had recently gotten into fights with peers, hitting some of them. Most recently she had tried to run out of the program, almost running into traffic. The teachers expressed ongoing concern, adding that Rosa's verbal communication seemed to have regressed, and her behavior seemed to be most consistent with that of a young toddler. The teachers urged Ana to take Rosa to a counselor, adding that if Rosa's behavior did not improve she could be suspended. Ana was fearful and worried about Rosa's recent behavior but was hopeful that the problems would end in a year, upon her husband's release from prison.

Ana did not have insurance but Rosa was insured through Medicaid, as she had been born in the United States, and was an American citizen. A decision was made to see Ana and Rosa for family therapy, while also providing individual sessions for Ana every other week. During Ana's individual sessions the focus of therapy was on stabilizing the family situation. Ana had been afraid to access social services such as food stamps and subsidized housing, due to her undocumented status; however, the living conditions were very hard on both Ana and Rosa, which were manifesting in increasing behavioral problems at Head Start. In addition, Ana was significantly depressed. She struggled to be a sole provider and caregiver, especially as she had a pre-migration, trauma history that had been exacerbated when she was raped crossing over to the United States. Ana had repressed much about what happened, but at times struggled with flashbacks and was unable to sleep, while also feeling very guilty about Rosa's current problems, often blaming herself for her daughter's difficulties. The clinical treatment was complex and will not be discussed in its entirety here. Instead, the review of the clinical treatment will be limited to the family's immigration status, and to the effects of the current immigration deportation policies.

As the clinical relationship unfolded, Ana began to consider ways in which she could improve her living situation; significant time was spent discussing available subsidized housing resources, as well as other services she could access on behalf of Rosa, including food stamp benefits and food pantries in the area. Therapy focused on addressing Ana's fears and practicing how she would apply for the resources she needed, while protecting her undocumented status. While we worked together on coaching Ana to interface with the safety network for children and families, sessions also focused on Rosa's developmental needs, and Ana and Rosa's relationship. As Ana was more able to process her guilt in relation to their life circumstances, she started to feel less conflicted in setting age appropriate limits for Rosa. While, in the beginning, Rosa did not appreciate the new rules, over time they provided Ana and Rosa with a predictable structure, that served to help Rosa regulate her feelings with greater ease while at Head Start. In addition, Ana and I worked together with Head Start, first by discussing the information that Rosa's teachers needed to have, and the information that Ana did not have to disclose, including her undocumented status. After practicing in session how she wanted to address the school, Ana felt ready to meet with Rosa's teachers and to collaborate with them, without the fear she had felt due to her undocumented status. Although Rosa's teachers felt strongly that Rosa had Attention Deficit and Hyperactivity Disorder (ADHD) and needed to take medication, Ana was able to discuss Rosa's behavior within a frame of multiple housing transitions, financial stressors and parental separation. Gradually, Ana developed more confidence and felt more control over her life and her ability to advocate for her daughter, who in turn was responding to Ana's efforts to assert herself more. Despite sporadic requests from Head Start to medicate Rosa, Ana continued to work with the school, while declining medications for Rosa, feeling confident that Rosa was not struggling with ADHD, but rather with sadness and anxiety. Rosa's pediatrician was also helpful in advocating on behalf of Rosa, writing a letter to the Head Start program where he spoke about the importance of waiting until Rosa became older to then consider pharmacological interventions if Rosa's anxiety and behavioral difficulties had not improved.

During the joint sessions with Ana and Rosa, Rosa sometimes spoke about her father, and brought in pictures she had drawn for him. Ana maintained regular contact with Jose and although visiting him was difficult due to lack of transportation, Ana and Rosa did attend family visits at least once a month. Ana was also more able to answer Rosa's questions during the therapy sessions, talking in an age-appropriate manner about where Rosa's father was and her hope that very soon he would join them again. This provided them both with comfort, although I worried about the implications of this hope, both wanting to support their hope while knowing that the possibility of being reunited was quite small. However, how does one take away the one thing that is helping a family continue to struggle through hardship? I knew Ana was not ready to completely admit to herself that Jose would most likely be deported, and she was certainly unable to discuss this with Rosa, who often drew pictures of her family as it was, prior to her father's arrest.

Ana's situation, nonetheless, continued to improve. Eventually she was able to move into a small one-bedroom, subsidized apartment, and was receiving food assistance as well as fuel assistance. Although in the beginning she had feared applying, over time, she had grown more confident and small successes had paved the way for ongoing efforts to access the help they needed in order for Rosa to thrive as much as she could. Ana was also a very resourceful woman, and had found free activities they could attend in the community, often visiting the library with Rosa to get books, videos, etc., which Rosa thoroughly enjoyed. As their world got larger and their living environment improved, Rosa continued to feel less anxious and her behavioral outbursts at Head Start were now sporadic, although she certainly needed clear structure and was sensitive to small changes and deviations from her daily routine; these were all sequels of the many changes Rosa and Ana had endured together, as well as directly related to the sudden separation from her father. As life continued to move forward, Jose's expected release date was soon approaching.

Ana began to think about his return more intently, and eventually the sessions focused on Jose's undocumented status, and increasing fear of a possible deportation. Ana could at times speak about this reality, but only briefly, while Rosa continued to speak about her father coming home. Rosa had started to count down the months left for "papi" to come home, and had been going through her closet finally selecting what she described as "the prettiest dress and shoes" because she wanted to have a party with "papi." It wasn't only Rosa or Ana who were hoping, but so was Jose, who kept urging Ana to have faith, despite having gotten his removal order, indicating that upon completion of his current sentence he would be transferred to the custody of what is now ICE, to await deportation to Mexico. Ana had begun to look for legal resources, and in therapy various legal organizations were identified that could provide free guidance and consultation. Ana wanted to seek legal advice but feared hearing there was nothing that could be done.

Individual therapy continued to be a space where Ana could speak about her worries and anxiety, and discuss legal information, without having to worry about Rosa being present. However, as it became increasingly clear that Jose would not be granted the cancellation of his removal, Ana started to become increasingly depressed. Rosa was, in turn, noticing her mother's sadness and tried to engage her in play, but soon Rosa's behavior began to deteriorate; at first, she appeared more restless at school, and eventually at home as well. Rosa and Ana soon got caught up in a vicious cycle, one in which Ana did not feel capable of comforting Rosa, due to the "secret" she was keeping from her. Rosa was now attending an elementary school, and her teachers had also noticed the change.

Eventually, during one of Ana's individual sessions, her denial, which had until then protected her, broke; she knew she needed to face Jose's impending deportation and that Rosa needed to know this too; it could no longer be avoided. A number of sessions were used to help Ana process what was happening while supporting her efforts to contact Jose's case manager to learn the reality of their situation. The next step was to support Ana in speaking with Rosa about her father's removal. Ana was restless and did not want to pierce Rosa's hopes, but she also understood that Rosa was asking more questions and knew something was happening, which was now manifesting in her agitated and angry behavior. A plan was developed in therapy to support Ana in discussing with Rosa what was about to happen. In family therapy Ana discussed with Rosa that "papi" could not stay in the United States and would have to leave very soon. Rosa was first in disbelief, and ignored what was being said, but as the session progressed, both Ana and Rosa could acknowledge what was happening, allowing for their emotions to emerge. What had initially been a discussion about family reunification was now a discussion about loss and grief, and of planning how to say goodbye.

Rosa stayed home from school the day after the family therapy session, and the school was contacted to explain that the family had learned Rosa's father would not be staying in the United States. A plan was also developed with Ana and the school, in the form of a 504 educational plan, to implement educational and behavioral accommodations in a proactive rather than reactive manner. The plan included meetings with the school's adjustment counselor and periodic breaks where Rosa could have a few minutes away from peers to de-escalate her anxiety while engaging in "special chores" assigned by her teacher. These "special chores" were introduced as a positive reward and helped Rosa feel helpful and important, at a time when her world was forever changing.

Rosa had also started to have problems sleeping, and returned to using her favorite teddy bear for comfort, having difficulty leaving it at home when going to school. Eventually a plan was developed with the schoolteacher, where Rosa could bring "Laura" (her beloved transitional object) and upon arrival at school, her teacher would place "Laura" in a special spot where she would be "safe" while Rosa learned in class. Separations from Ana had also become very difficult for Rosa, as she was worried about Ana and sometimes about the possibility that Ana would also go away. Whereas before Rosa had been able to sleep in her own bed, now at night, Rosa would quietly "sneak" into her mother's bed; given the level of anxiety and sadness they were both enduring, this regression was understood as appropriate and normalized. In therapy, after obtaining permission to speak with Jose's prison's case manager, and with Ana present, I called to discuss how to set up a final visit for Ana and Rosa with Jose prior to his transfer. During this conversation, information was also obtained to ensure that Jose, Ana and Rosa could maintain contact with each other until Jose's deportation; addresses, as well as names and numbers of personnel within the receiving facility, were obtained.

The family therapy sessions leading up to Jose's transfer were used to prepare Rosa and Ana for their final visit with Jose. Rosa and Ana worked together on a letter they wanted to give him, that Rosa had filled with drawings and hearts, tucking in a big picture of Ana and Rosa together. As the day approached, although filled with pain and fear, Ana felt able to support her daughter in saying goodbye.

After Jose's transfer and subsequent removal, Rosa's behavior escalated, and her educational performance deteriorated, often appearing distracted or "unwilling" to complete her class work. Her educational plan was again adjusted, and although the suggestion of prescribing medications came to the fore once more, a decision was made against this. Although Rosa was referred for a psychiatric medication evaluation to discuss the benefits and risks of pharmacological intervention, in the end the psychiatrist wrote to the school stating that Rosa's reaction was a normal reaction to some very difficult family losses, recommending instead additional modifications to Rosa's school day, to provide further structure and needed containment. He also recommended a small dose of Benadryl if Rosa was having too much difficulty sleeping at night. Over time, Rosa progressively returned to her previous functioning level, as did Ana, but the road back had been difficult and very painful. However, Jose's ongoing involvement with Ana and Rosa over phone calls, and cards with pictures, helped them to continue to move forward. Over the year that followed, significant time was spent exploring with Ana the possibility of returning to Mexico. Although she wanted to join her husband, they had both decided to remain apart until he could secure employment, and a place where they could all live together.

Rosa eventually settled into school again, and her grades began to improve. She continued to display some anxiety and worry about her mother, but overall, she felt reassured by her father's ongoing engagement with them, and was now instead thinking about a day when they could all live together again. Although Rosa had imagined a life with Jose and Ana in the United States, through the cards she received from her father and other relatives, she had started to consider that a life in Mexico could be "ok" after all, and there could be some "pluses" because she could also get to meet "abuelo and abuela, and all my cousins." However, the immigrant's wish to return home can be a powerful wish that often perseveres despite barriers that prevent a return, as Akhtar (1995) discusses,

> This can at times manifest itself in the immigrant's fervent plans to "someday" (Akhtar, 1991, 1994) return to his homeland; [these] fantasies... [of some day, soon, next year] are versions of this wish temporally displaced even further. With such a dynamic shift, the future comes to be idealized, robbing the present of full commitment. Often these "if only" and "some-day" fantasies coexist, with nostalgia providing the fuel for the hope of return.
>
> (p. 1065)

In Ana's and Rosa's case a return to Mexico continued to be a longed-for wish, but one that, with the passage of time, seemed more distant, as Jose was struggling to establish himself and Ana and Jose were beginning to confront the possibility that a life together in Mexico would not happen, at least in the foreseeable future.

## Conclusion

As Ana's and Rosa's case well illustrates, policies have very real consequences that enter private and personal spaces, transforming them and the people within them in a lasting manner. In Ana's and Rosa's case AEDPA and IIRIRA changed their family and way of life in a permanent manner. This is one of the many families that have been affected by the current immigration reform policies that have persisted for the last 20 years, and unfortunately, many families like this one will continue to be permanently broken apart unless congress is able to implement a comprehensive immigration reform that addresses the reality of mixed status families and their American children. Rosa was a small child, who lived in a two-parent home; both parents were committed to each other and to Rosa. Jose worked to support his family, and although living within very modest means, he and Ana had built a life together. Rosa was described as a happy, willful child, who was developing in an age-appropriate manner. However, unlike other American citizen children, her fate and that of her family was other, due to her father's undocumented status. Whereas prior to Jose's arrest and conviction, Ana and Rosa had had a stable living environment, soon thereafter they found themselves homeless although prevented from complete homelessness by friends who offered them shelter and support. Whereas prior to Jose's incarceration and subsequent deportation Rosa was developing without difficulties, upon parental separation she began to regress, and struggled with emotional and behavioral difficulties, that eventually interfered with her educational development. Jose was a victim of circumstances; he was not trafficking drugs but his inability to communicate effectively and his limited education, together with his undocumented status, intersected in a regrettable manner that rendered him a criminal, an aggravated felon who was also an illegal immigrant. It is important to clarify at this point what constitutes "drug trafficking" under the law in some northeastern states. Massachusetts General laws, Title XV, Chapter 94 C, Section 32 E states,

> (1) Eighteen grams or more [of cocaine] but less than 36 grams, be punished by a term of imprisonment in the state prison for not less than 2 nor more than 15 years… a fine… may be imposed but not in lieu of the mandatory minimum term.
>
> (The 190th General Court of the Commonwealth of Massachusetts, para. 7)

Thus Jose's sentence, which at first glance can construct him as a criminal, and drug dealer, upon review reflects a different reality, one pertaining to existing laws governing the possession and trafficking of illegal substances that group together those with substantiated histories of illegal trafficking with those who are in possession of minor amounts, such as in the case of Jose's friend. Jose's case unfortunately is one of many "drug [related] deportations tearing families apart," ("U.S. Drug deportations," 2015, para. 1) that organizations such as the Human Rights Watch Organization have been documenting in an advocacy effort on behalf of these families. However, laws are broad and certainly cannot be designed to address each individual situation, but certain laws, such as AEDPA and IIRIRA are restrictive in nature and aim to narrow exceptions reducing legal flexibility and excluding many. If Rosa's father had been an American citizen, after serving his sentence, he would have been able to return to his family. Jose served time for an offense he had not committed but could not prove, but faced a double penalty, that of deportation.

This case also illustrates the clinical flexibility required of social workers who provide services to immigrant families and children, in which both a psychological and a social justice approach need to be held concurrently to address the effects that oppression, subjugation and marginalization can have on families. Social workers not only function as treatment providers but also as legal and cultural brokers who provide families with legal resources and information to access and navigate the immigration and safety net system, as well as the educational, medical and mental health system of care.

This case also highlights the importance of conducting a thorough, biopsychosocial and cultural assessment that contextualizes families and children within the sociopolitical realities of their environment. By beginning to assess the sociopolitical context of the family to then move inward, that is from the external to the internal, it becomes easier to de-pathologize individual symptomatology. In so doing, structural forces and their effects, in this case the White Nativist ideology manifesting in immigration policies of exclusion and marginalization and its aggression toward the immigrant other, mixed status families and their American citizen children become more visible. Through this process, the perils of diagnosing children like Rosa can be avoided, recognizing instead the structural violence inflicted against them (Demmers, 2012). While it could have been compelling to diagnose Rosa in some way, given the pressure exerted by the educational system to label her as a child with Attention Deficit and Hyperactivity Disorder and thus subject to medication, Rosa's struggle was one of grief, loss and profound uncertainty. While the Diagnostic and Statistical Manual of Mental Disorders, DSM 5, can be a helpful tool, it is one that can be inadvertently misused to locate within the individual, societal and systemic problems. In such instances, the DSM and the social workers' power to diagnose, allow dynamics of oppression and subjugation to continue to operate unquestioned, in a hegemonic manner. Rosa's response was a normal response to an incomprehensible situation, that is, the division of an intact family unit due to exclusionary, White Nativist policies despite extensive child development research that suggests that children thrive when they are raised in stable, caring and nurturing family environments (Davies, 2011).

## Integrated analysis of contemporary immigration policy reforms: Implications for policy development

This section will present three separate policy directions informed by the conclusions derived from the integrated analysis of contemporary immigration policy reforms implemented since 1996 and the subsequent secondary study presented in Chapters 6 and 7. The first policy direction will address the conscious and unconscious effects of the White Nativist ideology, as it continues to operate in a partially disguised manner informing sociopolitical discussions about the "White Native" identity and that of the immigrant other. Hence, this policy direction will address the collective, affective processes fueling existing identity-based sociocognitive constructions that include some, while subjugating others as second-class citizens. This section will incorporate a discussion of unresolved collective racial trauma that prevents the mourning of the mythical, synthetic, "native American" identity. The second policy direction will present an alternative policy by which to provide a legalization path to millions of undocumented parents of American citizen children. The third policy direction will focus on a "harm reduction" approach to at least temporarily mitigate the effects that the contemporary immigration policy reforms are having on some of the most vulnerable members of American society, its children.

## First policy direction: The recognition and healing of collective historical racial trauma

As the integrative analysis showed, immigration policy is a legal mechanism by which "White Natives" have sought to preserve and protect their "White Native" identity and culture from being transformed by the increasing presence of the Hispanic, immigrant "other." However these efforts, which proved insufficient prior to 1996, as evidenced by the racial and ethnic demographic population trends of the United States, led to a number of interior immigration enforcement policies that have been breaking up stable immigrant families, while also forcing American children of immigrant parents to leave their birth country. The children who do stay, face significant financial and emotional hardships that interfere with their development (Capps et al., 2015; Koball et al., 2015) and integration within the mainstream of the American society, exerting pressure toward a reactive identity formation and downward assimilation path (Aleinikoff & Rumbaut, 1998). These policies stem from partially unconscious and conscious affective and sociocognitive processes that support the 'native American' identity. This mythical identity served to synthesize differences that had previously divided Nordic European immigrants from Southern and Eastern European immigrants under one shared, large group identity (Volkan, 2013). These collective identity formation processes legitimized the subjugation and exploitation of the Indigenous peoples native to this land, the enslavement of the African "other" for the plantation economy, with its long-standing societal legacy, as well as the exploitation of the Mexican immigrant "other" for wealth maximization and production within the American capitalist system. Thus, before discussing political structures that can provide a remedy by which to address the long-standing American social inequality created by a White Nativist politic of exclusion and subjugation, it is necessary to speak about the need to process the still partially unacknowledged, and often dissociated and disowned effects of the historical racial collective trauma upon which this nation has been built (Bashir & Kimlicka, 2008; Volkan, 1998).

While a discussion of the different models that exist to address the collective, racial, historical traumas of large groups, is beyond the scope of this book, some of the premises of these models will be briefly introduced, focusing on two primary aspects: reconciliation and forgiveness. This frame seems particularly pertinent, given the current societal polarization of the United States, due to the 2016 presidential elections. The election brought to the surface in a very visible manner, the previously obscured White Nativist ideology, and the unresolved nature of the historical, racial collective trauma that has been fueling American immigration sociopolitical rhetoric since the 1990s, also partially responsible for President Trump's electoral win.

President Trump's election has come to represent new hope and long-needed validation for some groups, such as White Nativists. For others, his election represents a regression, the re-opening of old historical wounds that had never really healed, giving way to complex and difficult emotions that have reawakened old, dormant, collective traumas (Volkan, 2013). After President Trump's election and inauguration, political conversations entered many personal and private spaces, from family gatherings and secondary and higher education classrooms, to all types of mainstream media. Regardless of the setting, emotions were difficult to contain and manage for many, resulting in many acts of public protest and civil activism. Families suddenly found themselves divided, unable to speak to those who may have supported or not supported President Trump, depending on their convictions. What is certain is that President Trump's right-wing nationalist, political platform, embedded in a subjugating ideology of entitlement (Volkan, 2013), opened the door to, and fueled, increasing expressions of White Nativist aggression and anger toward groups that had long been constructed as other within the history of this country, including immigrants and refugees. School lunchrooms were suddenly spaces in which children overtly harassed each other, and chanted "build that wall" intimidating Latino students. Similar incidents occurred in college campuses, where students of color felt unwelcomed in some of their classrooms, or endured racial slurs that would not have been articulated out loud prior to this election.

The question is, how does this nation move forward now that these dormant wounds have been awoken? Can we indeed move forward, now that these old, unprocessed and often repressed and dissociated historical racial wounds have re-emerged? Given this context, examining what a frame of reconciliation and forgiveness may contribute toward the societal healing of this nation, and any subsequent social policies, is both necessary and pertinent. A sociopolitical frame of reconciliation and forgiveness is also consistent with the integrated analysis of contemporary immigration policy reforms, as the analysis exposed latent dynamics of identity contestation and intergroup conflict, particularly pertaining to Hispanic immigrants and their American children. However, although much has been written about reconciliation and forgiveness, what does it mean to speak about reconciliation? And can reconciliation exist without forgiveness? Bloomfield (2003) defines reconciliation as "a process that includes searching for truth, justice, forgiveness and healing" (p. 12). In its simpler form, reconciliation may mean to coexist (Kohen, 2009). Yet, coexistence is not the same as tolerance, rather, coexistence "seeks to promote" (Kohen, 2009, p. 399) tolerance and may eventually lead to trust. At a social level, reconciliation can be conceptualized as "a process through which a society moves from a divided past to a shared future" (Bloomfield, 2003, p. 12).

Social reconciliation can also be understood as a process that fosters inter-group reciprocal dialogue. This type of dialogue can open new avenues for conflict resolution and ultimately heal social wounds (Kohen, 2009). However, are reconciliation and forgiveness one and the same?

Kohen (2009) makes a distinction between personal and political reconciliation, clarifying that "Personal reconciliation... is not required for either the success of restorative practices or the achievement of political reconciliation" (p. 400). However, he does suggest that for reconciliation to occur, forgiveness has to happen. Yet, forgiveness is a slow process and can often be thwarted. As noted by Kohen (2009) and Luskin (2003):

> Some of us confuse forgiveness with condoning unkind actions... some of us are afraid to forgive because we think we will not be able to seek justice. Some think that forgiveness has to be a precursor to reconciliation. Some of us think that forgiveness means we forget what happened.
> (p. 68)

Instead Kohen (2009) and Tutu (1999) propose that forgiveness should be conceptualized as a process of healing and empowerment. Zehr (2015) concurs with Kohen (2009) and Tutu (1999), describing forgiveness as: "letting go of the power the offense and offender have over a person" (p. 53). In this manner, forgiveness is an act of self-liberation that is not contingent on the offender and his/her ability to acknowledge any wrongdoing, or to accept responsibility. The act of forgiveness is in this manner an act by which a victim can regain control and self-determination, and provides for a path toward a new future.

In a similar, and yet slightly different manner, Bloomfield (2003) cautions that reconciliation is not "An excuse for impunity; only an individual process; in opposition to/an alternative to truth or justice; a quick answer; a religious concept; perfect peace; an excuse to forget; nor, a matter of merely forgiving" (p. 14). Instead Bloomfield (2003) proposes that reconciliation entails,

> Finding a way to live that permits a vision of the future; the rebuilding of relationships; coming to terms with past acts and enemies; a society-wide, long-term process of deep change; a process of acknowledging, remembering, and learning from the past; and, voluntary.
> (p. 14)

The path toward reconciliation and forgiveness therefore, creates an opportunity for the healing of old historical wounds, at the center of conscious and partially unconscious intergroup conflict (Bloomfield, 2003). This process of mourning (Freud, 1917), allows for the integration of emotions that were previously overwhelming and repressed, while always close to the surface (Volkan, 2009b, 2013). In fact, trying to bypass this affective working through will eventually derail any possible reconciliation efforts.

New immigration policy initiatives that seek to integrate immigrants and their children, especially Hispanic, Mexican immigrants and their American-born children, into the mainstream of American society will be limited in scope and effectiveness, unless public policy first promotes a social collective mourning process. This process needs to acknowledge the historical racial and cultural collective trauma endured in the building of the American nation-state, while concurrently providing an avenue where a new American collective identity can be envisioned. Public policies informed by a reconciliation and forgiveness framework would foster intergroup dialogue at all societal levels, and would also result in a reshaping of the educational curriculum from primary and secondary education to higher education. By introducing a different historical curriculum early on, one that deconstructs the "native American" as native, while acknowledging the historical wounds inflicted and endured in the building of the American nation-state, there is a possibility to foster a new generation that will begin to have a different sociocognitive and affective relationship to their past. At the same time, the process of dismantling the mythical, synthesized nature of the "White Native" identity will also foster and create a different vision and experience of the ties that bind all American children, not only to their group but also to all other societal groups. As Bashir (2008) states:

> Reconciliation involves the effort to restore a previous state of harmony or amity... But in many cases of political reconciliation, such as slavery and colonialism [and other forms of subjugation] there is no prior state of harmony to be restored. Rather, the historic relationship began as one of oppression, denial, and misrecognition. In this case, the goal of reconciliation is not to restore a lost harmony, but to bring into existence a new relationship, a new state of affairs yet to be realized.
>
> (p. 19)

## Second policy direction: Reform of IIRIRA and AEDPA, and legalization of undocumented parents of American citizen children

As the integrated analysis of contemporary immigration policy reforms illustrated, IIRIRA and AEDPA marked a shift toward interior enforcement, aimed at facilitating the identification, arrest and deportation of the immigrant other, while also reinforcing existing constructions that cast the Hispanic other as criminal and illegal, and thus as unwanted and deportable. While IIRIRA increased the hardship threshold that immigrants with dependent family members have to meet to qualify for cancelation of removal, based on the effects that their deportation could have on their children, spouses, etc., AEDPA expanded the range of offenses that could qualify as aggravated felonies, including crimes of moral turpitude, as qualifying grounds for deportation (see Chapter 5). Although these two acts have facilitated the identification and deportation of many undocumented immigrants with American-born children, it is important to highlight that they have also caused the deportation of permanent residents. Permanent residents charged with or convicted for a qualifying aggravated felony are rendered deportable. Those convicted of a crime of moral turpitude are also subject to deportation, depending on the number of years they have resided in the United States prior to the alleged offense, and whether or not a previous offense of moral turpitude had occurred. The time frame that can trigger deportation for permanent residents, due to the charges and convictions, ranges between five and ten years. Thus IIRIRA and AEDPA do not only affect undocumented family members in mixed status families, but also permanent residents within these families.

All in all, there are currently an estimated 4.1 million American-born children living in mixed status families (Capps et al., 2016; Menjivar & Gomes Cervantes, 2016), where one or both parents are undocumented, thus rendering them vulnerable to deportation under IIRIRA and AEDPA. These two acts, as previously discussed, paved the way for other interior enforcement programs, such as the 287(g) program and the Secure Communities Program (see Chapter 5) that were reinstated by President Trump in 2017. Given that the number of deportations drastically increased as a result of the changes introduced by IIRIRA and AEDPA, a review and amendment of these policies is warranted.

Canceling IIRIRA's changes to the hardship clause, which currently states that immigrants have to show evidence of hardship to dependent family members beyond the level of hardship that could be expected as a result of deportation, would certainly provide many parents of American-born children with a mechanism for remaining in the United States. Redefining hardship to dependent family members as constituting hardship incurred due to parental deportation and not beyond what is expectable would be a responsible measure, consistent with existing research that has extensively documented the short-term and long-term, adverse effects of parental deportations on children. In addition, inserting language into ICE directives that prevents the expedited deportation of immigrant parents, mandating instead individual immigration court hearings, in which immigrants must not only be offered, but given access to legal counsel and representation, is also important. This mandate would give parents of American-born children a mechanism for accessing immigration legal counsel, as well as the right to an immigration court hearing where their unique circumstances could be considered, even if falling under categories that would render them subject to expedited deportations. Currently, under programs such as Secure Communities, deportations in general are expedited without giving immigrants access to counsel or to an immigration court hearing in many instances (Kohli et al., 2011).

In addition, the existing language that expanded the definition of aggravated felonies under immigration law, and that includes crimes of moral turpitude as grounds for deportation, needs to be amended to de-criminalize the immigrant "other," who is often Hispanic. The expansion of what constitutes an aggravated offense under immigration law, together with the inclusion of crimes of moral turpitude, have been two of the legal mechanisms that have not only reinforced existing, criminal, White Nativist constructions of the Hispanic other, but that, due to their broad and often times vague definition, have successfully constructed many immigrants as deportable.

Programs, such as the Priorities Enforcement Program (PEP), instituted during President Obama's administration, also provide another mechanism for the decriminalization of the immigrant "other," by narrowing ICE's enforcement authority. Whereas PEP, only authorized ICE to detain immigrants with existing criminal convictions, programs such as the Secure Communities Program expand this authority, further criminalizing the immigrant "other." Under Secure Communities' guidelines, for example, ICE can detain immigrants without criminal convictions or probable cause, in violation of the Fourth Amendment to the United States Constitution (ACLU, 2014), reinforcing sociopolitical constructions that cast the immigrant other as both criminal and deportable. In addition, programs such as PEP also serve to protect mixed status families and their children, as they decrease the risk of parental deportation due to suspected criminality; in fact, under PEP the number of parental deportations decreased.

A program similar to the Deferred Action for Parents of American and Lawful Permanent Residents, DAPA, although halted indefinitely due to the Supreme Court's inconclusive ruling in 2016, is also a program that would provide American children of immigrant parents with additional time until comprehensive immigration reforms, aimed at maintaining their mixed status families together and intact, could be enacted.

Lastly, as the integrated analysis illustrated, the contemporary "immigration problem" is a problem that the United States government allowed and helped create, as it met the interests of the American capitalist economy (Massey, Durand, & Malone, 2002). As discussed in Chapter 5, the 1965, 1980 and 1990 immigration policy reforms allowed the United States government to hide and deny their active participation in the creation of the "Mexican immigration problem," under an overt policy of racial neutrality and border control. Thus, while the previously proposed policy reforms could alleviate the fears of many mixed status families, and protect the welfare of American-born children of immigrant parents, they fail to address the governmental, capitalist, dynamics that fostered the creation of a largely "de facto" undocumented cheap labor force (Massey & Prenn, 2012). To this aim, new policies need to be developed that provide existing undocumented immigrants with a mechanism for regularizing their status, as long as they can provide evidence of continuous long-term residency beyond a reasonable period. A restructuring of the current H-2 visa program could certainly facilitate the regularization of these undocumented workers, while also addressing the American employers' labor demands. A restructuring of the H-2 visa program, with the goal of facilitating its use, accessibility and flexibility, would allow employers to meet their production and labor needs in a timely and efficient manner, while also addressing their existing criticism of the current H-2 visa programs (American Immigration Council, 2013; Chishti, Meissner, & Bergeron, 2011). However, before the H-2 visa programs can be restructured, the extent of the labor performed by undocumented immigrants in this country has to be accurately acknowledged and reflected in American, governmental, official economic reports. In so doing, the ways in which certain American business sectors have grown and expanded, primarily due to undocumented labor such as the agricultural, construction and hospitality sector (Gitis & Vargas, 2016), would be openly recognized within mainstream socioeconomic and political debates. By acknowledging the realistic labor needs of the United States, and its dependency on immigrant, Hispanic labor, the existing H-2A (agricultural) and H-2B (non-agricultural) temporary worker visa programs could be restructured and expanded with mainstream, societal support.

Although the current H-2A visa program is not capped, its filing requirements and fees make it difficult for agricultural employers to use, interfering with their ability to meet labor demands in a flexible manner (American Immigration Council, 2013; Chishti et al., 2011). The current H-2B visa program is capped at an annual 66,000 visas, which significantly reduces employers' ability to hire necessary immigrant labor during times of growth and expansion, thus ultimately turning to the "de facto undocumented labor force" (Massey et al., 2002). The reforms suggested here would create an overt, legal labor system that would provide undocumented workers with a mechanism to regularize their immigration status. These reforms would also eliminate the need to foster a hidden, "de facto undocumented labor supply" (Massey et al., 2012) underneath a governmental overt rhetoric of border control that has historically, and covertly, enabled the profiting from, and the exploitation of, the undocumented labor force created by the government. This process of acknowledgment and accountability, would result in an accurate estimate of the needed, immigrant temporary labor, rather than its under-reporting; and in combination with the restructuring of the current H-2 visa programs, would socially recast Hispanic immigrant workers as needed and essential to the economic growth of the United States, rather than as unwanted, criminal and illegal (Edwards & Ortega, 2016; Gitis & Varas, 2016; Pager, 2017). Most importantly, this new, more realistic account of the necessary immigrant labor required to maximize production would show that the Hispanic immigrant other is performing jobs that "White Natives" do not want even if available, rather than benefiting from the job displacement of native workers (Pager, 2017). The exploitative quality of the current H-2A visa program is best captured by the Farmworker Justice Organization:

> Most significantly, H-2A workers are often valued... [because they] can be treated as a commodity: a captive workforce that will work to the limits of human endurance to please their employers, that can be returned home if they do not meet expectation. U.S. workers should not have to compete with that.
>
> (Farmworker Justice, n.d., p. 2)

As the Farmworker Justice Organization states, albeit in a manner that pits immigrant workers against native workers, immigrant workers do not "take advantage of the system" as often posited in current, White Nativist sociopolitical immigration debates. These workers are exploited for the benefit of the American employer and economic system. A reform of the H-2 temporary worker visa programs would also have to address the working conditions of these temporary workers, while also providing a legal mechanism for the existing, undocumented immigrants to transition into the H-2 temporary worker program and access permanent residency, after providing evidence of their previous, long-standing, continuous residence in the United States. There are currently an estimated 11.3 million undocumented immigrants in the United States, of whom 7 million are estimated to be workers (Edwards & Ortega, 2016). These existing undocumented immigrants are therefore not meeting a temporary labor need, but rather a permanent need. In fact as Krogstad, Passel and Cohn (2016) explain:

> In 2014, unauthorized immigrant adults had lived in the U.S. for a median of 13.6 years, meaning that half had been in the country at least that long. Only 7% of Mexican unauthorized immigrants had been in the U.S. for less than five years in 2014.
>
> (A Rising Share of Unauthorized
> Immigrants section, para. 1)

The recognition of the actual labor being provided on a consistent basis by the existing undocumented population can produce an estimate of the number of existing undocumented workers that can be absorbed on a permanent basis, thereby accurately meeting the existing labor demands necessary to maintain current GDP levels (Edwards & Ortega, 2016). A mass deportation of the undocumented other, according to existing research estimates, would "reduce the nation's GDP... ultimately by 2.6 percent, and reduce cumulative GDP over 10 years by $4.7 trillion ...[these] effects ...amount to two-thirds of the decline experienced during the Great Recession" (Edwards & Ortega, 2016, The Main Findings of this Report section, para. 1). These economic figures, which will be subsequently expanded upon, suggest that many undocumented immigrants are currently performing jobs essential to the economic growth of the United States, and that exceed what is typically constructed as temporary work. Within this context, a path toward the legalization of undocumented parents of American children is not only an issue of children and social welfare, but also one of economic welfare that can no longer be ignored.

The proposed reforms outlined in this section are consistent with those formulated by entities such as the American Immigration Council (2013) and the U.S. Chamber of Commerce, Labor, Immigration and Employment Benefits Division. A report issued by this chamber on 2016, that sought to separate immigration myths from facts when discussing immigration reform, advocated for a plan similar to the one just outlined:

> Immigration reform that includes a pathway to legal status for undocumented immigrants already living in the country, with the creation of flexible avenues for future immigration (through temporary worker programs) and mandatory employment verification, would enhance border security and reduce illegal immigration.

(p. 13)

## Third policy direction: Harm reduction approach for American children of deported parents

As the integrated immigration policy analysis exposed, contemporary immigration policy is not just a legal mechanism by which the United States has sought to regulate immigration, but rather a legal, protectionist mechanism fueled by sociocognitive schemas and affective ties that bind "White Natives" to a shared identity and culture, embedded within a historical White Nativist ideology. This White Nativist ideology that operates in a common sense normalizing manner (Van Dijk, 2002) is deeply embedded within American society, and emerged in a very explicit and overt manner during the 2016 elections. In order for any comprehensive, inclusionary, American immigration reform policy to be accepted within the existing sociopolitical context, it is necessary to first engage in a social, deliberative[1] policy (Bashir, 2008) of collective mourning, related to a history of racial unprocessed trauma and identity contestation. As discussed in the psychological policy analysis section of this book, and consistent with the first proposed policy framework of social reconciliation and forgiveness, this deliberative policy process would give way to a new and different American self-concept and identity that does not require the idealization of the "White Native" and hence, the subjugation of the racialized other. However, since the 2016 presidential elections, the possibility of moving forward toward a new, more adaptive, and inclusive American identity seems to be more elusive and distant than in recent years. Hence, this third proposed policy direction has been included in acknowledgment of the increasingly White Nativist, anti-immigrant, sociopolitical climate that continues to persist in the ongoing criminalization of the Hispanic immigrant other, and in the construction of the American children of Hispanic, primarily Mexican, immigrants as second-class citizens.

Given President Trump's executive immigration orders implemented in January 2017 which reinstated Secure Communities, and expanded the 287(g) program, deportations of both undocumented and documented immigrant parents of American-born children can be expected to increase substantially. A harm reduction model that seeks to mitigate the known short-term and long-term effects of parental deportation on children informs the policies that are being proposed in this section. These policy suggestions represent a call toward collective action, and require that American society takes an active role in supporting and stabilizing mixed status families and children affected by current deportation immigration laws. These policies, therefore, ultimately ask the larger American society to afford these children the protection and care to which all other American children have access, by virtue of their American citizenship.

Given the well-documented effects of parental deportation on mixed status families and children, and since more parents of children will be deported in the near future, it is important for local and state governments, as well as for the federal government, to consider a system of care that provides children with deported caregivers access to emergency, basic financial, medical and educational resources. Access to these types of resources could mitigate the initial instability experienced by mixed status families and their children, after the arrest and eventual deportation of one or both parents.

Within this context, developing a continuum of social services that American children of deported parents can access is essential. Since these children are minors, services would be accessed on their behalf, which would require guidelines that protect the confidentiality of caregivers and that include provisions by which providers administering these services would not inquire as to the immigration status of the adult requesting access to services on behalf of the child or children. Since many mixed status families face financial hardship upon the deportation of one or both parents, the social service continuum should have the capacity to provide divided families with access to financial resources to prevent imminent homelessness, as well as assistance in accessing affordable and/or subsidized housing when families are unable to remain in their current homes. In addition, provisions should be instituted to assist caregivers in accessing other aspects of the existing safety net for families and children on behalf of the child or children; for example, assistance in filing for supplemental nutrition benefits, fuel assistance and other forms of vouchers or in-kind benefits, while also expediting the approval process.

Given that children and adults experience a number of short-term and long-term emotional and behavioral difficulties, and since the adult that may have remained with the child or children may fear coming into contact with existing providers, the social service continuum should include case-management services to support the adult caregiver in accessing necessary mental health care to stabilize the family unit, child/children and adult. To this aim, after-school programs and day care services need to be made available to facilitate the remaining caregiver's ability to work and function as a single parent. In addition, access to this type of programming would support and facilitate the ongoing integration of the child/children within the community, serving as a buffer against the risks of downward assimilation and a reactive identity formation (Aleinikoff & Rumbaut, 1998).

In addition, schools need to be integrated as part of the continuum of care to modify the child's learning environment in a preventative manner, rather than a reactive one. This will require ensuring that school personnel inform parents that they will not report their immigration status, emphasizing that they will work with the remaining family members to support the educational progress of the child/children. School-based counseling services, 504 educational plans or Individual Educational Service Plans, are some of the possible supports schools can use to respond to the children's changing emotional and educational needs.

The above recommendations are a general overview of the societal supports that could be implemented in response to the existing research pertaining to the deportation of caregivers, but it is not intended as an all-encompassing or exhaustive list of the array of services that could be necessary post parental deportation. However, the implementation of an array of public, social services aimed at addressing the effects of parental deportation is a necessary remedy if current immigration reform aimed at protecting the welfare of American children living in mixed status families continues to be elusive (Capps et al., 2016; Koball et al., 2015). Failure to either mitigate the effects of parental deportation, or to engage in a comprehensive reform of current deportation policies, can lead to a future generation of marginalized American citizens who, despite efforts to integrate into the American society, and despite calling this country their home, have been socially excluded by an ideology of entitlement (Volkan, 2013) and a politic of fear, embedded in a rhetoric of nationalism and protectionism (Wodak, 2015).

## Generalizability of the integrated sociopolitical and psychological analysis model

This book introduced the reader to an integrated sociopolitical and psychological analysis model that was later applied to the analysis of contemporary immigration policy reforms implemented since 1996. The model, informed by existing social welfare policy models, critical discourse historical analysis (Reisigl & Wodak, 2001; Wodak, 2015) and psychodynamic individual and group collective processes, provided a systematic and comprehensive analysis process by which to examine social welfare policy. This comprehensive process can facilitate, as illustrated by its application to the analysis of contemporary immigration policy reforms, the examination of the complex affective and sociocognitive individual and collective processes that lead to the development of social welfare policy, regardless of the policy's specific subject matter. However, the integrated model is particularly useful in examining policies pertaining to historically marginalized and subjugated groups within any specific society. The model, due to its sociopolitical and psychological nature, and critical discourse historical analysis framework, is well suited to identify the covert, power relations and dynamics that have facilitated the historical exclusion of any specific societal group. The comprehensive and systematic nature of the analysis process is able to expose and identify the underlying historical, affective, sociocognitive and ideological processes implicated in the subjugating social dynamics, linking these processes to particular social, public policies that either intentionally or unintentionally reinforce existing social inequalities. The integrated policy analysis model is, in this manner, well positioned to identify additional or complementary new social policies that are better able to address the complex social dynamics that have maintained and reinforced social inequality.

## New immigration policy directions: Immigration executive orders, 2017

As this book was coming to a close, President Trump signed into law the 2017 Border Security and Immigration Enforcement Improvements, Executive Order; and, the Enhancing Public Safety in the Interior of the United States, Executive Order. The first order terminated the Priorities Enforcement Program (PEP) enacted by President Obama's administration in 2015, which narrowed immigration enforcement efforts, by prioritizing the identification and arrest of immigrants "convicted of a criminal offense and others who pose a danger to public safety" (ICE, 2014, para.1). The 2017 Executive Immigration Order replaced PEP and reinstated the previous Secure Communities Program, despite the significant criticism this program had faced from local and state lawmakers, police departments and social justice advocate groups (see Chapter 5) in part due to supported violations of the Fourth Amendment to the Constitution, and because it led to expedited deportations without giving immigrants the opportunity to have access to legal counsel or to an immigration hearing (Kohli et al., 2011). The order also broadened the immigration enforcement focus, ordering ICE to "detain individuals apprehended on suspicion [not conviction] of violating Federal immigration law, pending further proceedings regarding these violations" (Executive Order, 2017a, para. 7); and, expanded the use of the 287(g) program, which enables "state and local police to identify and turn over to ICE any suspected criminal immigrants…" (Hagan, Castro, & Rodriguez, 2010, p. 1807). This order also allocated funding for the hiring of 5,000 additional immigration border enforcement officers, and ordered into law the construction of a border wall between the United States and Mexico, in addition to the existing one (Executive Order, 2017a). The second Executive Order (2017b) reinforced language included in the first Executive Order and also created the Office for Victims of Crimes Committed by Removable Aliens Office, further constructing the immigrant other, who is implicitly assumed to be Hispanic, as an illegal, criminal, dangerous other.

These two Executive Orders effectively reinforce IIRIRA and AEDPA, and expand the 287(g) program enacted as part of IIRIRA, and the Secure Communities Program implemented in 2008. Since the implementation of these immigration enforcement mechanisms in 1996, 4,681,000 immigrants have been deported from the United States between 1996 and 2013. This figure includes both border-related and interior enforcement deportations and was compiled with data obtained from the Bipartisan Policy Center (2014) and the Pew Research Center (Gonzalez-Barrera & Krogstad, 2014). It is thus reasonable to conclude that by returning to the same conditions that facilitated this number of deportations, and by having further expanded the programs that facilitated them, the expected number of deportations will continue to follow a similar trajectory. The new reforms introduced by Present Trump place mixed status families, their 4.1 million American-born children, as well as the undocumented children living in these families, at greater risk than ever before, with devastating consequences for all involved, but especially to the children who lack protection and have no voice.

The fear that has been spreading throughout immigrant communities is certainly not unfounded. In fact during a raid conducted in 11 states after the two Executive Orders were signed into law, 600 people were arrested by ICE ("ICE arrests 600", 2017). President Trump in fact characterized the raids as a "military operation" (Meridia, 2017) evoking reverberations of a not so distant militarized operation, Operation Wetback, that led to the mass deportation of Mexican immigrants, along with their families and children, regardless of whether or not they were American citizens by birth (Hernandez, 2010; Ngai, 2014). Although the characterization of the February 2017 raids as a militarized operation was later "corrected," there is reason for concern as there are certainly militarized historical precedents against the immigrant "other," and the perceived immigrant "other" (Hernandez, 2010; Ngai, 2014).

However, as many have been cautioning, the mass deportation of the immigrant "other" from the United States "could cost the economy trillions" (Covert, 2017). As Gitis and Vargas (2016) explain: "Depending on how the government conducts its apprehensions, it would need to spend $100 billion to $300 billion arresting and removing all undocumented immigrants residing in the country" (p. 3). The mass deportation of the immigrant other "would [also] cost the federal government nearly $900 billion in lost revenue over 10 years" (Edwards & Ortega, 2016, p. 2), and would affect some economic business sectors in particularly detrimental ways, such as the agriculture, construction and hospitality sectors. In addition, although the nation's GDP would initially decrease by 1.4%, subsequent gradual decreases estimate a cumulative GDP reduction of $4.7 trillion after a ten-year period (Edwards & Ortega, 2016, p. 2). Contrary to arguments that suggest that current jobs held by undocumented immigrants would be allocated to "native American" workers, reducing native unemployment, Gitis and Varas' research study (2016) found that the deportation of "approximately 6.8 million employed undocumented immigrants" (p. 9) would cause a labor shortage of 4 million people. As Gitis and Varas' (2016) explain, the number of available native and permanent legal resident workers that could offset the decrease in manpower is insufficient to counteract the deportation effects.

As the integrated analysis of contemporary immigration policy has illustrated, the current, American White Nativist sociopolitical discourse has cast the Hispanic immigrant other as illegal, criminal and unwanted. As the number of American children birthed by the Hispanic immigrant "other" began to rise, immigration policy increasingly focused on interior enforcement, albeit under overt sociopolitical claims of increasing undocumented immigration. However, as the integrated analysis of immigration policy showed, since the early 2000s, birthing replaced immigration as the primary factor fueling Hispanic population growth in the United States. Since 1996, interior enforcement immigration policies have led to the mass deportation of the Hispanic, Mexican immigrant "other;" however, they have also led to the departure of an estimated 550,000 American citizen children from their birth country, the United States, to be able to continue to live with their parents in Mexico after parental deportation (Homeland Security News Wire, 2016). Many more children are staying behind with their remaining caregiver, other family members or in the foster care system; the consequences these policies have had, and are still having, devastating effects.

President Trump's political discourse is marked by nativist, protectionist language, that is best captured by a single slogan: America first and Americans first (Dunn, 2016). However, who are the Americans that President Trump is speaking about? Who is an American within this sociopolitical context? The answer to this question will fundamentally affect the social, public policies that will be enacted under Donald Trump's presidency. In invoking "Americans first" President Trump is implicitly defining who is and is not American, who will belong and who will be excluded. However, where does this leave the 4.1 million estimated American-born children, who live in mixed status families, as well as their siblings? Much of the current sociopolitical discourse has focused on the undocumented immigrant and the undocumented children. There is reason for this focus and emphasis, yet the absence of a discussion of the rights of the American-born children living in mixed status families renders them invisible at a dangerous time, and reinforces existing White Nativist constructions that cast the Hispanic "other," as immigrant, often undocumented, and certainly as not American. The absence of political debates that pertain to the American citizen children of Hispanic documented and undocumented immigrants inadvertently contributes to erase their existence, in a different yet similar manner to the ways in which parental deportation has been silently removing them from their birth country. Yet, as the secondary study of the CILS showed, for these children the United States is their home; it is the country that they are affectively attached to and where they feel they belong. However, they are getting lost within a sociopolitical discourse that conflates them with the "undocumented other." This conflation is implicitly maintaining existing White Nativist constructions where one is American, if born to the "White Native," and "other," if born to the Hispanic immigrant "other" within the United States; thus, never American enough and always "immigrant."

If President Trump wants to put America and Americans first, then including legislation that protects the rights of American citizen children of Hispanic immigrant parents to grow up in the United States, and to do so with their families regardless of parental immigration status, is indeed placing America and Americans first. Failure to do so has the potential to fracture the well-being of American society, not only due to the long-term consequences of parental deportation, but also due to the detrimental effects that a politic of exclusion and marginalization has on children. As the integrated analysis of immigration policy reforms argued, and as the secondary study of the CILS later illustrated, the way in which this country treats its American children of immigrant parents will affect how they come to integrate themselves within the mainstream of American society. Ethnic identity formation and acculturation, as it has been shown, are not one-directional processes determined primarily by the individual in question. Instead, they are highly transactional processes, largely co-determined by how individuals, and their families, are treated and thought about within the country in which they are growing up. The failure to protect and nurture the well-being of American children of Hispanic immigrant parents, regardless of migratory or citizenship status will have long-lasting societal implications. Who America will become will have much to do with whether or not the United States government decides to protect all of its children, or only some, thus neglecting, hurting, and "deporting" some of "its own."

## Note

1 Deliberative policy is interpreted within this context as a collective, social policy process, by which "all those who are affected by [the decision-making process] have the right to participate in deliberation, as free and equal persons, about their content" (Bashir, 2008, p. 60).

# References

Abdelal, R., Herrera, Y., Johnston, A., & McDermott, R. (2009). Identity as a variable. In R. Abdelal, Y. Herrera, A. Johnston, & R. McDermott (Eds.), *Measuring identity: A guide for social scientists* (pp. 17–32). New York: Cambridge University Press.

Abraido-Lanza, A. F., Armbrister, A. N., Florez, K. R., & Aguirre, A. N. (2006). Toward a theory-driven model of acculturation in public health research. *American Journal of Public Health, 96*(8), 1342–1346. doi:10.2105/AJPH.2005.064980

ACLU, American Civil Liberties Union. (2014, November 13). *ICE detainers and the fourth amendment: What do recent federal court decisions mean?* Retrieved from www.aclu.org/other/backgrounder-ice-detainers-and-fourth-amendment-what-do-recent-federal-court-decisions-mean.

Adler, R., & Goggin, J. (2005). What do we mean by civic engagement? *Journal of Transformative Education, 3*(3), 236–253. doi:10.1177/1541344605276792.

Akhtar, S. (1995). A third individuation: Immigration, identity and the psychoanalytic process. *Journal of the American Psychoanalytical Association, 43*, 1051–1084.

Alba, R., & Nee, V. (2003). *Remaking the American mainstream: Assimilation and contemporary immigration.* Cambridge, MA: Harvard University Press.

Aleinikoff, A., & Rumbaut, A. (1998). Terms of belonging: Are models of membership self-fulfilling prophecies? *Georgetown Immigration Law Journal, 13*(1), 1–24.

American Hispanics (2015, March 12). [Special Issue]. *The Economist.* Retrieved from www.economist.com/news/special-report/21645996-one-american-six-now-hispanic-up-small-minority-two-generations-ago.

American Immigration Council. (2016). *Understanding the legal challenges to executive action.* Retrieved from www.americanimmigrationcouncil.org/research/legal-challenges-executive-action-on-immigration.

American Immigration Council. (2013). *Built to last: How immigration reform can deter unauthorized immigration. Fact Sheet.* www.americanimmigrationcouncil.org/research/built-last-how-immigration-reform-can-deter-unauthorized-immigration.

American Immigration Council. (2011). *Secure Communities. Fact Sheet.* Retrieved from www.americanimmigrationcouncil.org/research/secure-communities-fact-sheet.

Antiterrorism and Effective Death Penalty Act of 1996. Pub. L. No. 104-132, 110 Stat. 1214. (1996). Retrieved from www.uscis.gov/sites/default/files/ocomm/ilink/0-0-0-8598.html.

Applegate, J., & Bonovitz, J. (2004). *The facilitating partnership: A Winnicottian approach for social workers and other helping professionals.* New York: Rowman & Littlefield Publishers, Inc.

Argueta, C. N. (2016). *Border security: Immigration enforcement between ports of entry.* Congressional Research Service. Retrieved from https://fas.org/sgp/crs/homesec/R42138.pdf

Arizona et al. v. United States. 641 F. 3d 339 (AR, 2012). Retrieved from www.law.cornell.edu/supremecourt/text/11-182.

Ashmore, R., Deaux, K., & McLaughlin-Volpe, T. (2004). An organizing framework for collective identity: Articulation and significance of multidimensionality. *Psychological Bulletin, 130,* 80–114. doi:10.1037/0033-2909.130.1.80.

Baker, P., & Davenport, C. (2017, January 24). Trump revives Keystone XL, Dakota access pipelines rejected by Obama. *The Boston Globe.* Retrieved from www.bostonglobe.com/news/nation/2017/01/24/trump-advance-keystone-dakota-access-pipelines/ozRWsCjgkWiiR55H5OgQ0H/story.html.

Barusch, A. S. (2015). *Foundations of social policy: Social justice in human perspective* (5th ed.). Stanford, CT: Cengage Learning.

Bashir, B. (2008). Accommodating historically oppressed social groups: Deliberative democracy and the politics of reconciliation. In W. Kymlicka & B. Bashir (Eds.), *The politics of reconciliation in multicultural societies* (pp. 48–69). New York: Oxford University Press.

Bashir, B., & Kymlicka, W. (2008). Introduction: Struggles or inclusion and reconciliation in modern democracies. In W. Kymlicka & B. Bashir (Eds.), *The politics of reconciliation in multicultural societies* (pp. 1–24). New York: Oxford University Press.

Bell, D. (2013). After we're gone: Prudent speculations on America in a postracial epoch. In R. Delgado & J. Stefancic (Eds.), *Critical race theory: The cutting edge* (3rd ed., pp. 9–14). Philadelphia, PN: Temple University Press.

Beltrandy y Rudquist, M. (2012) Creating a civic national identity: Integration through immigrant political participation. *Macalester International, 30*(6), 1–21. http://digitalcommons.macalester.edu/macintl/vol30/iss1/6.

Benen, S. (2016, June 23). *Supreme Court blocks Obama admin's immigration policy.* Retrieved from www.msnbc.com/rachel-maddow-show/supreme-court-blocks-obama-admins-immigration-policy.

Berry, J. W. (2005). Acculturation: Living successfully in two cultures. *International Journal of Intercultural Relations, 29*(6), 697–712. Retrieved from https://isites.harvard.edu/fs/docs/icb.topic551691.files/Berry.pdf.

Berry, J. W. (2001). A psychology of immigration. *Journal of Social Issues, 57*(3), 615–631. doi:10.1111/0022-4537.00231.

Berry, J. (2003). Conceptual approaches to acculturation. In K. Chun, P. Organista, & G. Marin (Eds.), *Acculturation: Advances in theory, measurement, and applied research* (pp. 17–37). Washington, DC: American Psychological Association.

Bipartisan Policy Center. (2014). *Issue brief: Interior immigration enforcement by the numbers.* Retrieved from http://bipartisanpolicy.org/wp-content/uploads/sites/default/files/files/Interior%20Immigration%20Enforcement.pdf.

Bloomfield, V. (2003). Reconciliation: An introduction. In D. Bloomfield, T. Barnes, & L. Huyse (Eds.), *Reconciliation after violent conflict: A handbook* (pp. 10–28). Stockholm, Sweden: International Institute for Democracy and Electoral Assistance, IDEA.

Blommaert, J., & Bulcaen, C. (2000). Critical discourse analysis. *Annual Review of Anthropology, 29,* 447–446.

Branscombe, N., Schmitt, M., & Harvey, R. (1999). Perceiving pervasive discrimination among African Americans: Implications for group identification and well-being. *Journal of Personality and Social Psychology, 77*, 135–149.

Bodkin-Andrews, G., O'Rourke, V., & Craven, R. (2010). The utility of general self-esteem and domain-specific self-concepts: their influence on indigenous and non-indigenous students' educational outcomes. *Australian Journal of Education, 54*(3), 277–306.

Bowlby, J. (1988). *A secure base: Clinical applications of attachment theory.* New York: Routledge.

Brodkin Sacks, K. (1999). How did Jews become white folks? In M. Adams & J. Bracey (Eds.), *Strangers and neighbors: Relations between Blacks and Jews in the United States* (pp. 500–519). Amherst, MA: University of Massachusetts Press.

Capps, R., Castaneda, R. M., Cahudry, A. & Santos, R. (2007). *Paying the price: The impact of immigration raids on America's children.* Washington, DC: The Urban Institute. Retrieved from http://www.urban.org/sites/default/files/publication/46811/411566-Paying-the-Price-The-Impact-of-Immigration-Raids-on-Americas-Children.PDF.

Capps, R., Koball, H., Campetella, A., Perreira, K., Hooker, S., & Pedroza, J. M. (2015). *Implications of immigration enforcement activities for the well being of children in immigrant families.* Washington, DC: The Urban Institute and the Migration Policy Institute. Retrieved from file:///Users/wsu/Downloads/ASPE-ChildrenofDeported-Lit%20Review-FINAL%20(1).pdf.

Capps, R., Fix, M., & Zong, J. (2016, January). A profile of U.S. children with unauthorized immigrant parents. Fact Sheet. *Migration Policy Institute.* Retrieved from www.migrationpolicy.org/research/profile-us-children-unauthorized-immigrant-parents.

Carpini, M. (2000). Gen. com: Youth, civic engagement, and the new information environment. *Political Communication, 17*, 341–349. doi:10.1080/10584600050178942

Castro, F., Garfinkel, J., Naranjo, D., Rollins, M., Brook, J., & Brook, D. (2007). Cultural traditions as protective factors among Latino children of illicit drug users. *Substance Use & Misuse, 42*, 621–642. doi:10.1080/10826080701202247.

Cave, D. (2013, May 9). In immigration bill, deportees see hope for second chance in U. S. *The New York Times.* Retrieved from www.nytimes.com/2013/05/09/us/politics/in-immigration-bill-deportees-see-hope-for-second-chance.html

Center for Migration and Development. The Children of Immigrants Longitudinal Study (CILS). Retrieved from www.princeton.edu/cmd/data/cils-1/.

Chambers, H. L. (2013). Slavery, free blacks and citizenship. *Rutgers Law Journal, 43*, 486–513.

Chandler, M., & Proulx, T. (2008). Personal persistence and persistent peoples: Continuities in the lives of individuals and whole cultural communities. In F. Sani (Ed.), *Self-continuity: Individual and collective perspectives* (pp. 213–2260). New York: Taylor & Francis Group.

Chaudry, A., Capps, R., Pedroza, J., Castaneda, R., Santos, R., & Scott, M. (2010). *Facing our future: Children in the aftermath of immigration enforcement.* Washington, DC: The Urban Institute. Retrieved from www.urban.org/publications/412020.html.

Chin, G. J., & Villazor, A. C. (2015). Introduction. In G. J. Chin & A. C. Villazor (Eds.), *The Immigration and Nationality Act of 1965: Legislating a new America* (pp. 292–482) [Kindle for Mac]. New York: Cambridge University Press. Retrieved from Amazon.com.

Chishti, M., Meissner, D., & Bergeron, C. (2011, November 11). At it's 25th anniversary, IRCA's legacy lives on. *Migration Policy Institute*. Retrieved from www.migrationpolicy.org/article/its-25th-anniversary-ircas-legacy-lives.

Citrin, J., & Sears, D. (2009). Balancing national and ethnic identities: The psychology of e pluribus unum. In R. Abdelal, Y. Herrera, A. Johnston, & R. McDermott (Eds.), *Measuring identity: A guide for social scientists* (pp. 145–174). New York: Cambridge University Press.

Coatsworth, J., Maldonado-Molina, M., Pantin, H., & Szapocznik, J. (2005). A person-centered and ecological investigation of acculturation strategies in Hispanic immigrant youth. *Journal of Community Psychology, 33*(2), 157–174. doi:10.1002/jcop.20046.

Cohen, E. (2007). Carved from the inside out: immigration and America's public philosophy of Citizenship. In C. Swain (Ed.), *Debating immigration* (pp. 32–45). New York: Cambridge University Press.

Cohen, G., & Garcia, J. (2005). I am us: Negative stereotypes as collective threats. *Journal of Personality and Social Psychology, 89*, 566–582. doi:10.1037/0022-3514.89.4.566

Collins, C., & Nieves, E. (2016). The ever growing gap: Without change, African-American and Latino families won't match white wealth for centuries. *CFED & Institute for Policy Studies.*

Cordell, K., & Wolf, S. (2010). *Ethnic conflict.* Malden, MA: Polity Press.

Crenshaw, K., Gotanda, N., Peller, G., & Thomas, K. (1995). *Critical race theory: The key writings that formed the movement.* New York: The New Press.

Crocker, J., & Major, B. (1989). Social stigma and self-esteem: The self-protective properties of stigma. *Psychological Review, 96*, 608–630. doi:10.1037/0033-295x.96.4.608.

Crocker, J., & Quinn, D. (2004). Psychological consequences of devalued identities. In B. Brewer & M. Hewstone (Eds.), *Self and social identity* (pp. 124–146). Malden, MA: Blackwell Publishing.

Crowley, (n. d.). *Summary of youth engagement strategy.* Woburn, MA: Social capital, Inc.

Davies, D. (2011). *Child development: A practitioner's guide* (3rd ed.). New York: The Guildford Press.

Davies, P., Steele, C., & Markus, H. (2008). A nation challenged: The impact of foreign threats on America's tolerance for diversity. *Journal of Personality and Social Psychology, 95*, 308–318.

Deschamps, J. (1982). Social identity and relations of power between groups. In H. Tajfel (Ed.), *Social identity and intergroup relations* (pp. 85–98). New York: Cambridge University Press.

Decker, R. J. (2013). The visibility of Whiteness and immigration restriction in the United States, 1880–1930. *Critical Race and Whiteness Studies, 9*(1), 1–20.

Delgado, R., & Stefancic, J. (Eds.) (2013). *Critical race theory: The cutting edge* (3rd ed.). Philadelphia, PN: Temple University Press.

Demmers, J. (2012). *Theories of violent conflict.* New York: Routledge.

Department of Homeland Security. (2009, January). *Removals involving illegal alien parents of United States citizen children.* Retrieval from www.oig.dhs.gov/assets/Mgmt/OIG_09-15_Jan09.pdf.

Department of Homeland Security. (2014a). *Deportation of aliens claiming U.S.-born children: First semi-annual calendar year 2013*. Retrieved from http://big.assets.huffingtonpost.com/2013report1.pdf.

Department of Homeland Security. (2014b). *Deportation of aliens claiming U.S.-born children: Second semi-annual calendar year 2013*. Retrieved from http://big.assets.huffingtonpost.com/2013report2.pdf.

Derrida, J. (1984). *Margins of Philosophy* (A. Bass, Trans.). Chicago, IL: The University of Chicago Press.

Diehl, M., & Hay, E. (2007). Contextualized self-representations in adulthood. *Journal of Personality, 75*, 1255–1284.

Diller, E. (2001). Citizens in service: The challenge if delivering civic engagement training to national service programs. *Corporation for National Service*. Retrieved from www.nationalserviceresources.gov/online-library/items/r2091.

Donald Trump speech, debates and campaign quotes. (2016, November 9). *Newsday*. Retrieved from www.newsday.com/news/nation/donald-trump-speech-debates-and-campaign-quotes-1.11206532.

Dreby, J. (2012). *How today's immigration enforcement policies impact children, families, and communities: A view from the ground*. Washington, DC: Center for American Progress. Retrieved from www.americanprogress.org/wp-content/uploads/2012/08/DrebyImmigrationFamiliesFINAL.pdf.

Dreby, J. (2015). U. S. immigration policy and family separation: The consequences for children's well-being. *Social Science & Medicine Journal, 132*, 245–251. doi:10.1016/j.socscimed.2014.08.041.

Dunbar-Ortiz, R. (2015). *An indigenous peoples history of the United States* [Kindle for Mac]. Retrieved from Amazon.com.

Dunn, S. (2016, April 28). Trump's 'America first' has ugly echoes from U. S. history. *CNN*. Retrieved from www.cnn.com/2016/04/27/opinions/trump-america-first-ugly-echoes-dunn/.

Edwards, R., & Ortega, F. (2016, September, 21). *The economic impacts of removing unauthorized immigrant workers*. Washington, DC: Center for American Progress. Retrieved from https://cdn.americanprogress.org/wpcontent/uploads/2016/09/20120917/massdeport1.pdf.

Enchautegui, M. (2013). *Broken immigration policy: Broken families*. Washington, DC: The Urban Institute. Retrieved from www.urban.org/publications/412806.html.

Erikson, E. (1968). *Identity: Youth and crisis*. New York: Norton.

Ethier, K., & Deaux, K. (1994). Negotiating social identity when contexts change: Maintaining identification and responding to threat. *Journal of Personality and Social Psychology, 67*, 243–251.

Executive Order: Border Security and Immigration Enforcement Improvement. (2017a, January 25). *The White House: Office of the Press Secretary*. Retrieved from www.whitehouse.gov/the-press-office/2017/01/25/executive-order-border-security-and-immigration-enforcement-improvements.

Executive Order: Enhancing Public Safety in the Interior of the United States (2017b, January 25). *The White House: Office of the Press Secretary*. Retrieved from www.whitehouse.gov/the-press-office/2017/01/25/presidential-executive-order-enhancing-public-safety-interior-united.

Fairclough, I., & Fairclough, N. (2012). *Political discourse analysis: A method for advanced students*. New York: Routledge.

Falicov, C. J. (2014). *Latino families in therapy* (4th ed.). New York: The Guilford Press.

Farina, M. (2013). Failure to mourn White Nativism: Impact of deportation on Hispanic American born children and mixed status families. *Smith College Studies in Social Work*, *83*(2–3), 139–169. doi:10.1080/00377317.2013.803362

Farina, M. (2015). *Immigration reform: Impact of sociopolitical context on the ethnic identification, acculturation and sense of national belonging of American born Hispanic youth* (Unpublished doctoral dissertation). Smith College, School for Social Work, Northampton, MA. Retrieved from www.tandfonline.com/doi/abs/10.1080/00377317.2015.1067009?src=recsys&journalCode=wscs20.

Farmworker Justice Organization. (n.d.). *Questions and answers about the H-2A agricultural guestworker program*. Retrieved from www.farmworkerjustice.org/sites/default/files/documents/H-2A%20Factsheet%207-30-2012.pdf.

Ferguson, R. A. (2007). Race. In B. Burgett & G. Hendler (Eds.), *Keywords for American Cultural Studies* (pp. 191–196). New York: New York University.

Ferguson-Bohnee, P. (2015). The history of Indian voting rights in Arizona: Overcoming decades of voter suppression. *Arizona State Law Journal*, *47*, 1099–1144.

Fix, M., & Zimmermann, W. (1999). *All under one roof: Mixed-status families in an era of reform*. Washington, DC: The Urban Institute. Retrieved from www.urban.org/publications/ 409100.html.

Flanagan, C., Levine, P., & Setterson, R. (2009). *Civic engagement and the changing transition to adulthood*. Medford, MA: CIRCLE: The Center for Information and Research on Civic Learning and Engagement. Retrieved from www.civicyouth.org/civic-engagement-and-the-changing-transition-to-adulthood/.

Feshbach, S. (1991). Attachment processes in adult political ideology: Patriotism and nationalism. In J. Gewirtz & W. Kurtines (Eds.), *Intersections with attachment* (pp. 207–226). Hillsdale, NJ: Lawrence Erlbaum Associates.

Fortuny, K., & Chaudry, A. (2009). *Children of immigrants: Immigration trends. Fact Sheet No. 1*. Washington, DC: The Urban Institute. Retrieved from http://files.eric.ed.gov/fulltext/ED508244.pdf.

Freud, S. (1917). Mourning and Melancholia. In J. Strachey (Ed. & Trans.), *The standard edition of the complete psychological works of Sigmund Freud*, (Vol. 14, pp. 237–258). New York: W. W. Norton & Company.

Frum, D. (2015, December 11). America's immigration challenge. *The Atlantic*, 1–16. Retrieved from www.theatlantic.com/politics/archive/2015/12/refugees/419976/.

Garza, R., Falcon, A., & Garcia, F. (1996). Will the real Americans please stand up: Anglo and Mexican-American support of core American political values. *American Journal of Political Science*, *40*(2), 335–351.

Gitis, B., & Varas, J. (2016, May 5). *The labor and output declines from removing all undocumented immigrants*. Washington, DC: The American Action Forum. Retrieved from www.americanactionforum.org/research/labor-output-declines-removing-undocumented-immigrants/.

Glazer, N. (1993). Is assimilation dead? *The Annals of the American Academy of Political Science*, *530*, 122–136.

Golfand, D. E., & Bialik-Gilad, R. (1989). Immigration reform and social work reform. *Social Work Journal*, *34*(1), 23–27.

Gonzalez-Barrera, A. R., & Krogstad, J. M. (2014). *U. S. Deportations reach record high in 2013*. Washington, DC: The Pew Research Center. Retrieved from www.

pewresearch.org/fact-tank/2014/10/02/u-s-deportations-of-immigrants-reach-record-high-in-2013/.

Gonzalez-Barrera, A. R., & Krogstad, J. M. (2016). *U. S. immigrant deportations declined in 2014, but remain near record high*. Pew Research Center. Retrieved from www.pewresearch.org/fact-tank/2016/08/31/u-s-immigrant-deportations-declined-in-2014-but-remain-near-record-high/.

Goodheart, A. (2011, April 12). *Looking at the civil war 150 years later* [Radio interview aired on NPR] Fresh Air, WHYY. Retrieved from www.npr.org/2011/04/12/135246259/looking-at-the-civil-war-150-years-later.

Goodman, A. (2016, September 7). Eminent domain? Iowans sue to stop Dakota access pipeline, say it provides no public service. *Democracy Now*. Retrieved from www.democracynow.org/2016/9/7/iowa_landowners_sue_to_stop_dakota.

Gotanda, N. (2013). A critique of "our Constitution is color-blind". In R. Delgado, & J. Stefancic (Eds.), *Critical race theory: The cutting edge* (3rd ed., pp. 35–37). Philadelphia, PN: Temple University Press.

Gratton, B., Gutmann, M., & Skop, E. (2007). Immigrants, their children, and theories of assimilation; family structure in the United States. *The History of the Family Journal, 12*(3), 203–222. Retrieved from www.ncbi.nlm.nih.gov/pmc/articles/PMC2194643/.

Guyatt, N. (2007). *Providence and the invention of the United States, 1607–1876* [Kindle for Mac]. New York: Cambridge University Press. Retrieved from Amazon.com.

Hagan, J., Castro, B., & Rodriguez, N. (2010). The effects of U. S. deportation policies on immigrant families and communities: Cross-border perspectives. *North Carolina Law Review, 88*(5), 1799–1824. Retrieved from http://scholarship.law.unc.edu/cgi/viewcontent.cgi?article=4446&context=nclr.

Hagan, J., Rodriguez, N., & Castro, B. (2011). Social effects of mass deportations by the United States government. *Ethnic and Racial Studies, 34*, 1376–1391.

Harris, C. (1993). Whiteness as Property. *Harvard Law Review. 106*(8), 1707–1791.

Heim, J. (2016, September 6). Showdown over oil pipeline becomes a national movement for Native Americans. *The Washington Post*. Retrieved from www.washingtonpost.com/national/showdown-over-oil-pipeline-becomes-a-national-movement-for-native-americans/2016/09/06/ea0cb042-7167-11e6-8533-6b0b0ded0253_story.html?utm_term=.ff222dc0c7b1.

Hernandez, K. L. (2010). *Migra! A history of the U. S. border patrol* [Kindle for Mac]. Berkeley, CA: University of California Press. Retrieved from Amazon.com.

Hing, B. (2004). *Defining America through immigration policy*. Philadelphia: Temple University Press.

Hirschman, C. (2003). The Role of Religion in the Origins and Adaptation of Immigrant Groups in the United States. Proceedings from *Conceptual and Methodological Developments in the Study of International Migration*. The Center for Migration and Development. Retrieved from faculty.washington.edu/charles/new%20PUBS/A100.pdf.

Homeland Security News Wire. (2016, September 21). *U.S.-born Mexicans: Easing integration burdens of U.S.-born children in Mexico*. Retrieved from www.homelandsecuritynewswire.com/dr20160921-easing-integration-burdens-of-u-s-born-children-in-mexico.

Howell, D (2012). *Treatment of missing data: Part I*. Retrieved from www.uvm.edu/~dhowell/StatPages/More_Stuff/Missing_Data/Missing.html.

Huntington, S. (2004a, March). The Hispanic challenge. *E-Journal of Foreign Policy,* 30–45. Retrieved from http://cyber.law.harvard.edu/blogs/gems/culturalagencyl/ SamuelHuntingtonTheHispanic C.pdf.

Huntington, S. (2004b). *Who are we? The challenges to America's national identity.* New York: Simon & Schuster Paperbacks.

ICE arrests 600 in nation wide raids after Trump's order expands criminalization of immigration. (2017, February, 13). *Democracy Now.* Retrieved from www. democracynow.org/2017/2/13/ice_arrests_600_in_nationwide_raids.

ICE. (2013). *11064.1: Facilitating parental interests in the course of civil immigration enforcement activities.* Retrieved from www.ice.gov/doclib/detention-reform/pdf/ parental_interest_directive_signed.pdf.

ICE. (2014). *Priority Enforcement Program (PEP).* Retrieved from www.ice. gov/pep.

Ignatiev, N. (1995). *How the Irish became white.* New York: Routledge

Illegal Immigration Reform and Immigrant Responsibility Act of 1996. Pub. L. No. 104-208, 110 Stat. 30009-546. (1996). Retrieved from www.uscis.gov/sites/default/ files/ocomm/ilink/0-0-0-10948.html.

Jacobson, M. F. (1998). Introduction: the fabrication of race. In *Whiteness of a different color: European immigrants and the alchemy of race* (pp. 1–12). Cambridge, MA: Harvard University Press.

Jimenez, J., Pasztor, E. M., Chambers, R. M., & Fuji, C. P. (2015). *Social policy and social Change: Toward the creation of social and economic justice* (2nd ed.). Thousand Oaks, CA: Sage Publications.

Johnson, K. (2004). The *"huddled masses" myth: Immigration and civil rights.* Philadelphia, PA: Temple University Press.

Kaiser Family Foundation. (2015). *Population distribution by race/ethnicity.* Retrieved from http://kff.org/other/state-indicator/distribution-by-raceethnicity/? currentTimeframe=0&sortModel=%7B%22colId%22:%22Location%22,%22sort %22:%22asc%22%7D.

Keeter, S., Zukin, C., Andolina, M., & Jenkins, K. (2002). *The civic and political health of a nation.* Medford, MA: The Center for Information and Research on Civic Learning and Engagement: CIRCLE. Retrieved from www.civicyouth.org/ special-report-the-2002-civic-and-political-health-of-the-nation/.

Kennedy, R. L. (2013). Racial critiques of legal academia. In R. Delgado & J. Stefancic (Eds.), *Critical race theory: The cutting edge* (3rd ed., pp. 689–704). Philadelphia, PN: Temple University Press.

Koball et al. (2015). Health and social services needs of U.S. citizen children with detained or deported immigrant parents. *The Urban Institute and the Migration Policy Institute.* Retrieved from www.urban.org/sites/default/files/ publication/71131/2000405-Health-and-Social-Service-Needs-of-US-Citizen-Children-with-Detained-or-Deported-Immigrant-Parents.pdf.

Kohen, A. (2009). The personal and the political: Forgiveness and reconciliation in restorative justice. *Critical Review of International Social and Political Philosophy, 12*(3), 339–423. doi:10.1080/13698230903127911.

Kohli, A., Markowitz, P., & Chavez, L. (2011). *Secure communities by the numbers: An analysis of demographics and new numbers.* The Chief Justice Earl Warren Institute on Law and Social Policy. University of California, Berkley Law School. Retrieved from www.law.berkeley.edu/files/Secure_Communities_by_the_Numbers.pdf.

Kohn, S. (2016, June 29). Nothing Donald Trumps says on immigration holds up. *Time.* Retrieved from http://time.com/4386240/donald-trump-immigration-arguments/.

Kosterman, R., & Feshbach, S. (1989). Toward a measure of patriotic and national-istic attitudes. *Political Psychology, 10*, 257–274.

Krogstad, J. M., Passell, J., & Cohn, V. (2016). *5 facts about illegal immigration in the U. S.* Washington, DC: The Pew Research Center. Retrieved from www.pewresearch.org/fact-tank/2016/11/03/5-facts-about-illegal-immigration-in-the-u-s/.

Layton, L. (2006). Attacks on linking: the unconscious pull to dissociate individ-uals from their social context. In L. Layton, N. Hollander, & S. Gutwill (Eds.), *Psychoanalysis, class and politics: Encounters in the clinical setting* (pp. 107–117). New York: Routledge.

Lawrence, C. R. (2013). The Id, the ego, and equal protection: Reckoning with un-conscious racism. In R. Delgado & J. Stefancic (Eds.), *Critical race theory: The cutting edge* (3rd ed., pp. 312–323). Philadelphia, PN: Temple University Press.

Lipsitz, G. (1998). *The possessive investment in Whiteness: How White people profit from identity politics.* Philadelphia: Temple University Press, 1998.

Loewenberg, P. (1991). Uses of anxiety. *Partisan Review, 3*, 514–525.

Loewenberg, P. (1995). *Fantasy and Reality in History.* New York: Oxford University Press.

Luskin, F. (2003). *Forgive for good: A proven prescription for health and happiness* (Kindle for Mac]. Retrieved from Amazon.com.

Massey, D. S., Durand, J., & Malone, N. J. (2002). *Beyond smoke and mirrors: Mexican immigration in an era of economic integration* [Kindle for Mac]. Retrieved from Amazon.com.

Massey, D. S., & Pren, K. A. (2012). Unintended consequences of US immigration policy: Explaining the post-1965 surge from Latin America. *Population and De-velopment Review, 38*(1), 1–29.

Markus, H., & Kurf, E. (1987). The dynamic self-concept. *Annual Review of Psy-chology, 36*, 299–337. Retrieved from www.annualreviews.org/doi/pdf/10.1146/annurev.ps.38.020187.001503.

McCoy, S., & Major, B. (2003). Group identification moderates emotional responses to perceived prejudice. *Personality and Social Psychology Bulletin, 29*, 1005–1017. Retrieved from https://pdfs.semanticscholar.org/a226/445442213ad2c3b0917da5dcbeffe2e15dee.pdf.

Menjivar, C., & Gomez Cervantes, A. (2016, November). The effects of parental undocumented status on families and children: Influence of parental status on the development of U.S.-born children in mixed-states families. *American Psychological Association.* Retrieved from www.apa.org/pi/families/resources/newsletter/2016/11/undocumented-status.aspx.

Meridia, N. (2017, February, 24). Trump on deportations: It's a military operation. *CNN: Politics.* Retrieved from www.cnn.com/2017/02/23/politics/donald-trump-deportation-military/.

Migration Policy Institute. (2016). *1990–2015 MPI Data Hub: Children in Immigrant Families.* Retrieved from www.migrationpolicy.org/programs/data-hub/charts/children-immigrant-families.

Miller, J., & Garran, A. (2008). *Racism in the United States: Implications for the helping professions.* Belmont, CA: Thomson Higher Education.

National Research Council and Institute of Medicine. (1998). *From Generation to Generation: The Health and Well-Being of Children in Immigrant Families.* In D. Hernandez & E. Charney (Eds.), Committee on the Health and Adjustment of Immigrant Children and Families, National Research Council and Institute of Medicine. Washington, DC: National Academy Press.

National Research Council and Institute of Medicine. (1999). *Children of immigrants: Health, adjustment, and public assistance.* Committee on the Health and Adjustment of Immigrant Children and Families. In D. Hernandez (Ed.), Board on Children Youth and Families. Washington, DC: National Academy Press.

National Immigration Law Center. (2015). *Priority enforcement program: Why 'PEP' doesn't fix S-Com's failings.* Retrieved from www.nilc.org/issues/immigration-enforcement/pepnotafix/.

Ngai, M. M. (1999). The architecture of race in American immigration law: A reexamination of the immigration act of 1924. *The Journal of American History, 86*(1), 67–92.

Ngai, M. M. (2014). *Impossible subjects: Illegal aliens and the making of modern America* (5th ed.) [Kindle for Mac]. Retrieved from Amazon.com.

Nolan, M., & Branscombe, N. (2008). Conceptions of the human self and human rights: Implications for the psychological continuity of less inclusive selves. In F. Sani (Ed.), *Self-continuity: Individual and collective perspectives* (pp. 201–212). New York: Taylor & Francis Group.

Olivas, M. A. (2013). The chronicles, my grandfather's stories, and immigration law. In R. Delgado & J. Stefancic (Eds.), *Critical race theory: The cutting edge* (3rd ed., pp. 15–24). Philadelphia, PN: Temple University Press.

Organista, P., Marin, G., & Chun, K. (2009). Chapter 4, Acculturation. In *Psychology of ethnic groups in the United States* (pp. 99–135). Thousand Oaks, CA: Sage Publications, Inc.

Oppedal, B., Roysamb, E., & Heyerdahl, S. (2005). Ethnic group, acculturation, and psychiatric problems in young immigrants. *Journal of Child Psychology and Psychiatry, 46*(6), 646–660. Retrieved from www.ncbi.nlm.nih.gov/pubmed/15877769.

Oyserman, D. (2004). Self-concept and identity. In B. Brewer & M. Hewstone (Eds.), *Self and social identity* (pp. 5–24). Malden, MA: Blackwell Publishing.

Pager, T. (2017, March 14). Amid Trump's immigration crackdown, there's fear on farms. *The Boston Globe.* Retrieved from www.bostonglobe.com/news/nation/2017/03/13/immigration-crackdown-strains-farms-nationwide/Hr9oqoJ1dENI3ekKw3HHdO/story.html.

Parker, I. (1992). Discovering discourses, tackling texts. In *Discourse dynamics: Critical analysis for social and individual psychology* (pp. 3–22). London: Routledge.

Passel, J. S., Cohn, D., & Gonzalez-Barrera, A. (2012). *Net migration from Mexico falls to zero and perhaps less.* Washington, DC: Pew Research Center. Retrieved from www.pewhispanic.org/2012/04/23/ii-migration-between-the-u-s-and-mexico/.

Payne, E., Martinez, M. R., & Yan, H. (2014). Showdown over immigration: 'This is an invasion'. *CNN.com.* Retrieved from www.cnn.com/2014/07/03/us/california-immigrant-transfers/.

Peralta, E. (2015, November 11). *It came up in the debate: Here are 3 things to know about 'Operation Wetback".* Northeastern Public Radio. Retrieved from www.npr.org/sections/thetwo-way/2015/11/11/455613993/it-came-up-in-the-debate-here-are-3-things-to-know-about-operation-wetback.

Pinsky, S. (2014, May 12). *ICE's new policy on protecting parental rights.* Retrieved from www.socialworkhelper.com/2014/05/12/ices-new-policy-protecting-parental-rights/.

Porter v. Hall 34 Ariz. 308 (Ariz. 1928). Retrieved from https://casetext.com/case/porter-v-hall.

Portes, A., & Bach, R. (1985). *Latin journey: Cuban and Mexican immigrants in the United States.* Berkley, CA: University of California Press.

Portes, A., & Zhou, M. (1993). The New Second Generation: Segmented Assimilation and Its Variants. *Annals of the American Academy of Political Social Science, 530*, 75–98.

Portes, A., & Zhou, M. (1994). Should immigrants assimilate? *Public Interest, 11*(6), 18–33.

Portes, A., & Rubén G. R. (2012). *Children of Immigrants Longitudinal Study (CILS), 1991–2006.* ICPSR 20520-v2. Ann Arbor, MI: Inter-university Consortium for Political and Social Research [distributor], 2012-01-23. doi:10.3886/ICPSR 20520.v2.

Portes, A., & Rumbaut, R. (2001). *Legacies: The story of the immigrant second generation.* Berkley, CA: University of California Press.

Portes, A., & Rumbaut, R. (2005). Introduction: The Second Generation and the Children of Immigrants Longitudinal Study. *Ethnic and Racial Studies, 28*(6), 983–999.

Portes, A., Fernandez-Kelly, P., & Haller, W. (2005). Segmented assimilation on the ground: The new second generation in early adulthood. *Ethnic and Racial Studies, 28*(6), 1000–1040.

Portes, A., & Rumbaut, R. (2006). *A portrait: Immigrant America* (3rd ed.). Berkley, CA: University of California Press.

Portes, A., & Rumbaut, R. (2014). *A portrait: Immigrant America* (4th ed.). Berkley, CA: University of California Press.

Preston, J (2011a, Oct. 18) Latinos said to bear the weight of a deportation program. *The New York Times.* Retrieved from www.nytimes.com/2011/10/19/us/latinos-said-to-bear-weight-of-deportation-program.html?ref=juliapreston.

Preston, J (2011b, Jan. 5) State lawmakers outline plan to end birthright citizenship, drawing outcry. *The New York Times.* Retrieved from www.nytimes.com/2011/01/06/us/06immig.html.

Putnam, R. (1995). Bowling alone: America's declining social capital. *Journal of Democracy, 6*(1), 65–78. Retrieved from www.directory-online.com/Rotary/Accounts/6970/Downloads/4381/Bowling%20Alone%20Article.pdf.

Putnam, R. (2000). *Bowling alone: The collapse and revival of American community.* New York: Simon & Schuster.

Reisigl, M., & Wodak, R. (2001). *Discourses and discrimination: Rhetorics of racism and anti-Semitism.* New York: Routledge.

Renshon, S. (2000). American character and national identity: The dilemmas of cultural diversity. In S. Renshon & J. Duckitt (Eds.), *Political psychology: Cultural and crosscultural foundations* (pp. 285–310). New York: New York University Press.

Roedinger, D. R. (2006). *Working toward Whiteness: How America's immigrants became white. The strange journey from Ellis Island to the suburbs* [Kindle for Mac]. Retrieved from Amazon.com.

Rogler, L., Cortes, D., & Malgady, R. G. (1991). Acculturation and mental health status among Hispanics: Convergence and new directions for research. *American Psychologist, 46*, 585–597. http://psycnet.apa.org/doi/10.1037/0003-066X.46.6.585.

Rogers-Sirin, L., Ryce, P., & Sirin, S. (2014). Acculturation, acculturative stress, and cultural mismatch and their influences on immigrant and adolescents' well being. In *Global perspectives on well-being in immigrant families* (pp. 11–30). New York: Springer.

Rollings, W. H. (2004). Citizenship and suffrage: The Native American struggle for civil rights in the American West, 1830–1965. *Nevada Law Journal, 5*, 126–140. Retrieved from http://scholars.law.unlv.edu/nlj/vol5/iss1/8.

Rosaldo, R. (1997). Cultural citizenship, inequality, and multiculturalism. In R. Benmayor & W. Flores (Eds.), *Latino cultural citizenship* (pp. 27–38). Boston, MA: Beacon Press.

Rosenblum, M. R. (2015). *Understanding the potential impact of executive action on immigration enforcement.* Washington, DC: Migration Policy Institute. Retrieved from www.migrationpolicy.org/research/understanding-potential-impact-executive-action-immigration-enforcement.

Ross, M. (2007). *Cultural contestation and ethnic conflict.* New York: Cambridge University Press.

Salo, J. (2015, September 16). GOP immigrant debate: 'Immigration without assimilation is invasion'. *International Business Times.* Retrieved from www.ibtimes.com/gop-immigrant-debate-immigration-without-assimilation-invasion-2098894.

Sani, F., Bowe, M., & Herrera, M. (2008). Perceived collective continuity: seeing groups as temporarily enduring entities. In F. Sani (Ed.), *Self-continuity: Individual and collective perspectives* (pp. 159–172). New York: Taylor & Francis Group.

Sarbin, T. (2000). Worldmaking, self and identity. *Culture and Psychology, 6*(2), 253–258.

Scheibe, K. (1995). *Self studies: The psychology of self and identity.* Westport, CT: Praeger Publishers.

Schafer, J., & Graham, J. (2002). Missing data: our view of the state of the art. *Psychological Methods, 7*(2), 147–177. http://psycnet.apa.org/doi/10.1037/1082-989X.7.2.147.

Schwatrz, S., Unger, J., Zamboanga, B., & Szapocznik, J. (2010). Rethinking the concept of acculturation: Implications for theory and research. *American Psychology, 65*(4), 237–251. doi:10.1037/a0019330.

Shane, P. (2016, June 28). The U.S. Supreme Court's Big Immigration Case Wasn't About Presidential Power. *The Atlantic.* Retrieved from www.theatlantic.com/politics/archive/ 2016/06/us-v-texas-wasnt-really-about-presidential-power/489047.

Shklar, J. (1991). *American citizenship—the quest for inclusion.* Cambridge, MA: Harvard University Press.

Sidanius, J., Feshback, S., Levin, S., & Pratto, F. (1997). The interface between ethnic and national attachment: Ethnic pluralism or social dominance? *Public Opinion Quarterly, 61*(1), 102–133. doi10.1086/297789.

Simon, B., Aufderheide, B., & Kampmeier, C. (2004). The social psychology of minority-majority relations. In B. Brewer & M. Hewstone (Eds.), *Self and social identity* (pp. 278–297). Malden, MA: Blackwell Publishing.

Simon, R. (1997). *In the golden land: a century of Russian and Soviet Jewish immigration in America.* Westport, CT: Praeger Publisher.

Sorenson, S., & Jacqueline, M. (1988). Prevalence of suicide attempts in a Mexican-American population: Prevention implications of immigration and cultural issues. *Suicide and Life-Threatening Behavior, 18,* 322–333. doi:10.1111/j.1943-278X.1988.tb00170.x

Staff, H. (2015, May 1). Anti-immigrant movement renews assault on the 14th amendment. *SPLC, Southern Poverty Law Center.* Retrieved from www.splcenter.org/hatewatch/2015/05/01/anti-immigrant-movement-renews-assault-14th-amendment.

St. Clair, M. (2004). *Object relations and self-psychology: an introduction* (4th ed.). Belmont, CA: Thomson: Brooks/Cole.

Stepler, R., & Brown, A. (2016). *Statistical portrait of Hispanics in the United States.* Washington, DC: Pew Research Center. Retrieved from www.pewhispanic.org/2016/04/19/statistical-portrait-of-hispanics-in-the-united-states-key-charts/.

Stern, P. (1995). Why do people sacrifice for their nations? *Political Psychology,* *16*(2), 217–235. doi:10.2307/3791830.

Stryker, S., & Serpe, R. T. (1982). Commitment, identity salience and role behavior. In W. Ickes & E. S. Knowles (Eds.), *Personality, roles and social behavior* (pp. 199–218). New York: Springer-Verlag.

Spiro, P. (2008). *Beyond citizenship: American identity after globalization.* New York: Oxford University Press.

Swain, C. (2002). *The new white nationalism in America: its challenge to integration.* New York: Cambridge University Press.

Swain, C. (2007). *Debating immigration.* New York: Cambridge University Press.

Szapocznik, J., & Kurtines, W. (1989). *Breakthroughs in family therapy with drug abusing and problem youth.* New York: Springer.

Tajfel, H. (1981). *Human groups & social categories: Studies in social psychology.* New York: Cambridge University press.

Tajfel, H. (1982). Introduction. In H. Tajfel (Ed.), *Social identity and intergroup relations* (pp. 1–11). New York: Cambridge University Press.

Tani, M. (2015, September 17). Donald Trump and other GOP candidates want to radically change a 150-year-old cornerstone of American citizenship. *The Business Insider.* www.businessinsider.com/donald-trump-birthright-citizenship-14th-amendment-debate-2015-8.

Taylor, P., Lopez, H., Martinez, J., & Velasco, G. (2012). II. Identity, pan-ethnicity and race. In *When Labels Don't Fit: Hispanic and their Views of Identity.* Pew Research Center. Retrieved from www.pewhispanic.org/2012/04/04/ii-identity-pan-ethnicity-and-race/.

The Urban Institute. (2010). *Children of immigrants: Data tool.* Retrieved from http://datatool.urban.org/charts/datatool/pages.cfm.

The 190th General Court of the Commonwealth of Massachusetts. (n. d.). Massachusetts General Laws, Title XV, Chapter 94 C, Section 32 E. Retrieved from https://malegislature.gov/Laws/GeneralLaws/PartI/TitleXV/Chapter94C/Section32E.

TRAC. (2016). *Many unrepresented families quickly ordered deported.* Retrieved from http://trac.syr.edu/whatsnew/email.161018.html.

Tutu, D. (1999). *No future without forgiveness* [Kindle for Mac]. Retrieved from Amazon.com.

U.S. Chamber of Commerce, Labor, Immigration and Employment Benefits Division. (2016). *Myths and facts about immigration.* Retrieved from www.uschamber.com/sites/default/files/documents/files/022851_mythsfacts_2016_report_final.pdf.

U. S. Census Bureau. *Office of management and budget: Revisions to the Standards for the Classification of Federal Data on Race and Ethnicity.* Retrieved from https://nces.ed.gov/programs/handbook/data/pdf/Appendix_A.pdf.

U. S: Drug deportations tearing families apart. (2015, June 16). New York: *Human Rights Watch.* Retrieved from www.hrw.org/news/2015/06/16/us-drug-deportations-tearing-families-apart.

Van Dijk, T. A. (1997). What is political discourse analysis? In J. Blommaert & C. Bulcaen (Eds.), *Political linguistics* (pp. 11–52). Amsterdam: Benjamins.

Van Dijk, T. (2000). Ideologies, racism, discourse: Debates on immigration and ethnic issues. In J. Wal & M. Verkuyten (Eds.), *Comparative perspectives on racism* (pp. 91–116). Aldershot: Ashgate Publishing, Limited.

Van Dijk, T. A. (2001). Critical discourse analysis. In D. Tannen, D. Schiffrin, & H. Hamilton (Eds.), *Handbook of discourse analysis* (pp. 352–371). Oxford: Blackwell.

Van Dijk, T. (2002). Political discourse and ideology. In C. U. Lorda & M. Ribas (Eds.), *Anàlisis del discurso político* (pp. 15–34). Barcelona: Universitat Pompeu Fabra. IULA.

Vargas, Z. (2011). *Crucible of Struggle: A history of Mexican Americans from Colonial Times to present era.* New York: Oxford University Press.

Volkan, V. (1985). The need to have enemies and allies: A developmental approach [Special issue]. *Political Psychology, 6*(2), 219–247.

Volkan, V. (1988). *The need to have enemies and allies: From clinical practice to international relationships.* Northvale, NJ: Jason Aronson.

Volkan, V. (1998). Ethnicity and nationalism: A psychoanalytic perspective. *Applied Psychology, 47*(1), 45–57.

Volkan, V. D., Ast, G., & Greer, W. K. (2002). *Third reich in the mind: Transgenerational transmissions and its consequences.* New York: Routledge.

Volkan, V. (2009a). *Large-group identity, international relations and psychoanalysis.* Retrieved from http://vamikvolkan.com/Large-group-Identity%2C-International-Relations-and-Psychoanalysis.php.

Volkan, V. (2009b). Not Letting go: From individual perennial mourners to societies with entitlement ideologies. In L. Glocer Fiorini, T. Bokanowski, & S. Lewkowicz (Eds.), *On Freud's "Mourning and Melancholia"* (pp. 90–109). London: Karnac.

Volkan, V. (2013). *Enemies on the Couch: A Psychopolitical Journey Through War and Peace.* Durham, NC: Pitchstone Publishing.

Wade, T., & Scheyder, E. (2016, October 24). Dekota access pipeline opponents occupy land, citing 1852 treaty. *Reuters.* Retrieved from www.reuters.com/article/us-usa-pipeline-dakotaaccess-idUSKCN12O2FN.

Wadsworth, T., & Kubrin, C. (2007). Hispanic suicide in U. S. metropolitan areas: Examining the effects of immigration, assimilation and disadvantage. *American Journal of Sociology, 112*(6), 1848–1885. Retrieved from www.jstor.org/stable/10.1086/512711.

Wessler, F. S. (2011). *Shattered families: The perilous intersection of immigration enforcement and the child welfare system.* New York: Applied Research Center. Retrieved from www.atlanticphilanthropies.org/app/uploads/2015/09/ARC_Report_Shattered_Families_FULL_REPORT_Nov2011Release.pdf.

Werner, H., & Kaplan, B. (1963). *Symbol formation: An organismic-developmental approach to the psychology of language.* New York: John Wiley & Sons, Inc.

Wakefield, J., Hopkins, N., Clockburn, C., Shek, K., Muirhead, A., Reicher, S., & Rijswijk, W. (2011). The impact of adopting ethnic or civic conceptions of national belonging for others' treatment. *Personality and Social Psychology Bulletin, 20*(10), 1–12. doi:10.1177/0146167211416131.

Wallerstein, I. (2000). *The essential Wallerstein.* New York: The New Press.

Wallerstein, I. (2003). *The decline of American power.* New York: The New Press.

Winnicott, D. (1965).The maturational process and the facilitating environment: Studies in the theory of emotional development. In *The International Psycho-Analytical Library, Series* (Vol. 64). London: The Hogarth Press and the Institute of Psycho-Analysis. Retrieved from http://search.ebscohost.com.libproxy.smith.edu:2048/login.aspx?direct=true&db=pph&AN=IPL.064.0001A&site=ehost-live.

Winnicott, D. (1967). The location of cultural experience. *International Journal of Psycho-Analysis, 48,* 368–372.

Wodak, R., Cillia, R., Reisigl, M., & Liebhart, K. (2009). *The discursive construction of national identity* (2nd ed.). Edinburgh: Edinburgh University Press.

Wodak, R. (2015). *The politics of fear: What right-wing populist discourses mean.* Thousand Oaks, CA: Sage Publications.

Wolchok, C. L. (1997). Demands and anxiety: The effects of the new immigration law. *Human Rights Journal, 24*(2), 12. Retrieved from http://heinonline.org/HOL/LandingPage?handle=hein.journals/huri24&div=23&id=&pag=e.

Workers World. (2006, November 22). *A native view of immigration.* Retrieved from www.workers.org/2006/us/native-immigration-1130/.

Wray, M. (2006). *Not quite White: White trash and the boundaries of Whiteness* [Nook Book]. Retrieved from: Barnesandnoble.com

Yip, T. (2005). Sources of situational variation in ethnic identity and psychological well-being: A Palm Pilot study of Chinese American students. *Personality and Social Psychology Bulletin, 31*, 1603–1616. doi: 10.1177/0146167205277094.

Yoshikawa, H. (2011). Immigrants raising citizens: Undocumented parents and their young children [Kindle Book]. New York: Russell Sage Foundation. Retrieved from Amazon.com.

Zane, N., & Mak, W. (2003). Major approaches to the measurement of acculturation among ethnic minority populations: A content analysis and an alternative empirical strategy. In K. Chun, P. Organista, & G. Marín (Eds.), *Acculturation: Advances in theory, measurement, and applied research* (pp. 39–60). Washington, DC: American Psychological Association.

Zayas, L. H., Aguilar-Gaxiola, S., Yoon, H. & Guillermina, N. (2015). The distress of citizen-children with detained and deported parents. *Journal of Child and Family Studies, 24*(11), 3233–3223. doi:10.1007/s10826-015-0124-8.

Zehr, H. (2005). *Changing lenses: Restorative justice for our time [Kindle for Mac].* Harringsonburg, VA: Herald Press. Retrieved from Amazon.com.

Zinn, H. (2003). *A people's history of the United States.* New York: Harper Collins Publisher.

Zong, J., & Batalova, J. (2016). *Frequently requested statistics on immigrants and immigration in the United States.* Washington, DC: Migration Policy Institute. Retrieved from www.migrationpolicy.org/article/frequently-requested-statistics-immigrants-and-immigration-united-states.

# Appendix A

**CILS Survey Questionnaires, 1991, 1995, 2001**

The questionnaires used for this secondary study were part of the CILS study conducted by:

Portes, Alejandro, and Rubén G. Rumbaut. Children of Immigrants Longitudinal Study (CILS), 1991–2006. ICPSR 20520-v2. Ann Arbor, MI: Inter-university Consortium for Political and Social Research [distributor], January 23, 2012. doi:10.3886/ICPSR 20520.v2.

The original CILS surveys and data sets used in this secondary study can be found with the doi provided above.

# Appendix B

**A comparison and discussion of the original Perception of Society and Discrimination Index (PSDI) and the CILS PSDI**

The original PSDI items (Portes & Bach, 1985) were:

1   There is racial discrimination in economic opportunity in the U.S.
2   American way of life weakens family ties
3   Relations between Mexicans/Cubans and Anglo-Americans are mostly cold
4   Relations between Mexicans/Cubans and Anglo-Americans are mostly distant
5   Relations between Mexicans/Cubans and Anglo-Americans are mostly hostile
6   Anglo-Americans discriminate against Mexicans/Cubans
7   In relation to Mexicans/Cubans, Anglo-Americans regard themselves as superior (p. 284)

When the original PSDI items are compared with those in the CILS PSDI, slight variations, albeit minimal, can be observed between the corresponding first two index items. Items 3 through 5, in the original PSDI index, were substantially changed in the CILS, PSDI. These items were collapsed and reworded into a single item, represented by question 81, in the 1991 and 1995 CILS surveys, reading as follows: "There is much conflict between different racial and ethnic groups in the U.S." Item 6, of the original PSDI index, was eliminated from the CILS PSDI, i.e. "Anglo-Americans discriminate against Mexican/Cubans"; and, substituted instead by an item pertaining to economic opportunity, reflected by question 82, "Non-whites have as many opportunities to get ahead economically as whites in the U.S.," 1991 and 1995, CILS surveys. Item 7, of the original PSDI, was included with only slight variations in the 1991 and 1995 CILS PSDI, as question 84, "Americans generally feel superior to foreigners." Lastly, question 83, "There is no better country to live in than the United States," included in the 1991 and 1995, CILS PSDI was not an original item of the PSDI (Portes & Bach, 1985). Analyses were performed to examine how the questions included in the CILS affected the index.

# Appendix C

## Construction and coding of measures

### Demographic measures

Parental demographic categories: CILS survey 1991

1    Question 9: In what country was your father born?
     Question 15: In what country was your mother born?
2    Father's and mother's current citizenship status:
     Question 11: (If father born in a foreign country) Is your father now a U.S. citizen?
     Question 17: (If mother born in a foreign country) Is your mother now a U.S. citizen?
3    Father's and mother's level of education:
     Question 36: What is the highest level of education that he completed?
     Question 41: What is the highest level of education that she completed?
4    Family's housing situation:
     Question 42: Do your parents (or adult guardians) own or rent the house or apartment where you now live?

Children demographic categories: CILS surveys 1991 and 1995

5    Age:
     Question 19: How old are you?
6    Number of years lived in the United States:
     Questions 22: How long have you lived in the United States?
7    Children's possible dual citizenship or nationality:
     Question 23: Are you a U.S. citizen?
     Question 41: What is your citizenship status? (2001 survey)

## Non-demographic measures and operational definitions

### Explicit, Ethnic Identity Importance Index

The Explicit, Ethnic Identity Importance Index was operationalized as follows:
   Question 78: How do you identify yourself? (CILS survey 1991)
   Question 78 (a): How do you identify yourself? (CILS survey 1995)
   Question 78 (b): And how important is this identity to you, that is, what you call yourself? (CILS Survey 1995)
   Question 33: How do you identify, that is, what do you call yourself? (CILS survey 2001)
   Question 34: How important is this identity to you? (CILS survey 2001)

### Racial identification

The questions used were part of the 1995 and 2001 CILS surveys:
   Question 123: Which of the races listed do you consider yourself to be? (CILS survey 1995)
   Question 36: Which of the following race categories listed do you consider yourself to be? (CILS survey 2001)

### Sociopolitical White Nativism

This theoretical construct was measured though the Experiences of Prejudice Index and the Perceived Sociopolitical White Nativism Index, which will be subsequently described.

1   Experience of Prejudice Index
    The questions used as part of this index were:
    Question 85: Have you felt discriminated against? (CILS surveys 1991 and 1995)
    Question 86: And by whom did you feel discriminated? (CILS survey 1991 and 1995)
    Question 35: Have you ever felt discriminated against because of your race or ethnicity? (CILS survey 2001)
2   Perceived Sociopolitical White Nativism
    This index was operationalized using questions from the 1991 and 1995 CILS surveys, as no equivalent questions could be found in the 2001 CILS survey questionnaire. The questions comprising the 1991 and 1995 index were as follows:
    Question 79: There is racial discrimination in economic opportunities in the U.S.
    Question 80: The American way of life weakens the family
    Question 81: There is much conflict between different racial and ethnic groups in the U.S.

Question 82: Non-whites have as many opportunities to get ahead economically as whites in the U.S.

Question 83: There is no better country to live in than the United States

Question 84: Americans generally feel superior to foreigners

The questions selected were identified in the Variable Naming Conventions form provided by the Inter-University Consortium for Political and Social Research as being part of the Portes and Bach's Perception of Society and Discrimination Index, PSDI (1985).[1] A review of the original PSDI index[2] revealed some significant changes had been made to the PDSI items when they were introduced in the CILS surveys; for a discussion of these changes and their implications please refer to Appendix B. Despite some of the differences found when both PSDIs were compared, there were a number of similarities that made the CILS PSDI comparable to the original PSDI developed by Portes and Bach (1985), and thus an appropriate measure and operational construct to use for this study, given its ability to capture the children's perception of the White Nativism present in their social and political context.

It is important to note that the questions comprising the Sociopolitical White Nativism Index were not present in the 2001 survey. To address the absence of this data the following procedures were used:

1  A univariate imputation sampling method based on multiple regressions was used:

    a  First, Sociopolitical White Nativism was predicted for 1995 using White Nativism data obtained in 1991, in conjunction with the revised Experience of Prejudice Index for 1991, 1995, 2001. For further information please review the Experience of Prejudice Index section.

    b  Using these predicted values as the new dependent variable, a second regression model was calculated for White Nativism in 1991 and 1995, including the results of the revised Experience of Prejudice Index for 1991, 1995 and 2001.

2  For those models requiring the 2001, Sociopolitical White Nativism data, results were reported in two ways:

    a  First, each model was computed using a simple carry forward imputation method, in which 1995 values were used in place of the 2001 values; then,

    b  each model was recalculated using the multiple imputation method described above.

### National Belonging Index

This index was comprised of two dimensions: patriotism and civic engagement. Civic engagement was in turn comprised by religious participation and electoral participation. The questions included in the national belonging index were only included in the 2001 CILS survey.

## Patriotism

Patriotism was measured by one question:

Question 47: which feels most like "home" to you? (CILS survey 2001)

Given that this study sought to explore whether there was a relationship between the increasing White Nativist sociopolitical discourse and the ability of American-born, children of Mexican parents, to establish a sense of national belonging, question 47, with its focus on "which feels most like home to you?" seemed to capture two central aspects of national belonging: (1) the child's affective tie to the United States; and (2) the child's belief that the nation can indeed function as a family home, providing a safe base from which to explore the world and a safe base to return to for nurturance and protection (Bowlby, 1988).

## Civic engagement

To measure civic engagement along its two components, religious and electoral participation, the following questions from the 2001 CILS survey were selected:

Question 39: What is your current religion?

Question 40: About how often do you attend religious services?

Question 42: Are you currently registered to vote?

Question 43: What is your political party preference or affiliation?

Questions 39 and 40 were selected as indicators of community participation, since they are consistent with Putnam's (1995 and 2000), Crowley's, (n.d.), and Flanagan, Levine and Setterson's (2009) definitions of community participation, in which religious participation was identified as an operational indicator.

Questions 42 and 43 were selected as indicators of electoral participation, consistent with Putnam (1995, 2000), Crowley (n.d.) and Flanagan et al. (2009).

## Acculturation Strategies Index

The Acculturation Strategies Index was comprised by the following subscales: Linguistic Assimilation: English Acquisition Scale; Parental Native Language Acquisition Scale; Linguistic Preference; Culture, Values and Behavior Scale; and Ethnic Interaction Scale, which are all described below.

## Linguistic Assimilation: English Acquisition Scale

The following questions were used to obtain this measure:

Question 24: How well do you speak English? (CILS survey 1991 and 1995)

Question 25: How well do you understand English? (CILS 1991 and 1995)

Question 26: How well do you read English? (CILS 1991 and 1995)

Question 27: How well do you write English? (CILS 1991 and 1995)

Question 29: How well do you (a) speak, (b) understand, (c) read and (d) write in English? (CILS 2001)

To facilitate data analysis, answers provided by each child along each of the selected questions were added and divided by four, to obtain a mean score. The score was rounded up to obtain a whole number and ensure consistency with the rating scale used in the CILS where values ranged from 1 to 4.

*Parental Native Language Acquisition Scale*

The following questions comprised this scale:

Question 49: Do you know a language other than English? (CILS 1991 and 1995)

Question 50: What language is that? (CILS 1991 and 1995)

Question 51: How well do you speak that language? (CILS 1991 and 1995)

Question 52: How well do you understand that language? (CILS 1991 and 1995)

Question 53: How well do you read that language? (CILS 1991and 1995)

Question 54: How well do you write that language? (CILS 1991 and 1995)

Question 27: Do you know a language other than English? (CILS 2001)

Question 27a: If yes, what language is that? (CILS 2001)

Question 28: How well do you (a) speak, (b) understand, (c) read, and (d) write this non-English language? (CILS 2001)

This question was divided into 4 different subcategories, each measuring the identified language competency.

To obtain a single numerical measure of Parental Native Language Acquisition the following re-coding methodology was applied:

For 1991 and 1995:

For questions 49 and 50: If yes in question 49 and Spanish in question 50, a value of 1 was assigned; if no in question 49 and/or another language in Question 50 (other than Spanish) a value of 0 was assigned. Thus, each child had a total aggregate score of 1 or 0 for questions 49 and 50.

For Questions 51–54 (inclusive): the numerical values selected by each child in these four questions were added, and then divided by four, to provide a mean score. Results were rounded up to ensure consistency with the original scale used in the CILS.

The total numerical score of Parental Native Language Acquisition, for 1991 and 1995, was calculated for each child by adding the aggregate numerical score for questions 49 and 50 and the child's mean score to questions 51–54. The final numerical score ranged between 1 through 5.

For 2001:

For questions 27 and 27a: If yes in question 27 and Spanish in question 27a, a value of 1 was assigned; if no in question 27 and/or another language in Question 27a (other than Spanish) a value of 0 was assigned. Thus, each child had a total aggregate score of 1 or 0 for questions 27 and 27a.

For Question 28a, b, c and d: the numerical values selected by each child were added, and then divided by four, to provide a mean score. Results were rounded up to ensure consistency with the original scale used in the CILS.

The total numerical score of Parental Native Language Acquisition for 2001 was calculated for each child by adding the aggregate numerical score for questions 27 and 27a, and the child's mean score to questions 51–54. The final numerical score ranged between 1 through 5.

*Linguistic Preference*

The following questions comprised this measure:

Question 59: In what language do you prefer to speak most of the time? (CILS 1991 and 1995) This question was designed as a nominal level variable, where 1 = Spanish; given the number of languages identified under this question, corresponding languages and codes will not be included here, but can be provided upon request.

Question 31: In what language do you prefer to speak most of the time? (CILS 2001)

Results obtained in Question 59 were re-coded into four categories to facilitate their comparison with the results of Question 31.

*Culture, Values and Behavior Scale*

The following questions comprised this scale:

For 1991 and 1995:

Question 98: How often do you prefer American ways of doing things? (CILS 1991 and 1995)

For 2001:

Questions 30c and 32 were used to design a new variable, named culture, values and behavior.

Question 30c: In what language do you speak with your children? (CILS 2001)

Question 32: In what language do you hope to raise your children? (CILS 2001)

New culture, value and behavior variable: since not all respondents were parents in 2001, a new variable was developed, combining the answers to question 30c and 32. To do so, a cross tabulation of both variables was computed.

Cross tabulation results were then recoded using a coding map, to match specific response combinations to the codes used in question 98, CILS surveys 1991 and 1995, thus ensuring coding consistency between 2001 and previous culture, values and behavior results obtained in 1991 and 1995. Codes used where 1 = all of the time; 2 = most of the time; 3 = sometimes; and, 4 = never.

*Ethnic Interaction Scale*

As discussed in segmented assimilation, structural barriers embedded in social policy can hinder the upward integration of second immigration immigrant youth, instead propelling them into a downward assimilation path, furthering identification with other U.S. marginalized and reactive subgroups (Berry, 2003; Garza et al., 1996; Portes & Rumbaut, 1996; Sidanius et al., 1997). To measure the level of integration across ethnic groups, including the White dominant group, the Ethnic Interaction Scale was developed. The following questions were used to develop this scale:

Question 73: How many of these close friends have parents who came from foreign countries, that is, who were not born in the United States? (CILS 1991 and 1995)

Question 30d: In what language do you speak with your closest friends?

To compare the 1991 and 1995 data to the 2001 data, question 30d was recoded using the same coding values used in question 73, 1991 and 1995 CILS surveys. The 30d codes used were as follows: 1 and 2 were recoded as 1 = none; 3 was recoded as 2 = some; and, codes 4 and 5 were recoded as 3 = many or most.

Once each subscale was calculated, a coding map was developed to assign score combinations to specific acculturation strategies using Berry's conceptual definitions. Berry (2003) defined these categories as follows:

> From the point of view of the non-dominant groups…when individuals do not wish to maintain their cultural identity and seek daily interactions with other cultures, they are using the assimilation strategy. In contrast, when individuals place a value on holding on to their original culture and at the same time wish to avoid interacting with others, they are using the separation alternative. When people have an interest in maintaining their original culture during daily interactions with other groups, they use the integration strategy… Finally the marginalization strategy is used when there is little possibility of or interest in cultural maintenance and little interest in having relationships with others.
>
> (p. 24)

Berry's four main acculturation strategies were operationalized as follows:

1   Assimilation: Relationships with other groups are sought + maintenance of heritage culture decreases.
2   Integration: Relationships with other groups are sought + maintenance of heritage culture is sought.
3   Separation: Relationships with other groups are not sought as much + maintenance of heritage culture is sought.
4   Marginalization: Relationships with other groups are not sought + maintenance of heritage culture is not sought.

However, in the coding process, it became apparent that the use of the five scales was confounding the acculturation strategies; thus, the final acculturation index was revised and only three of the five scales were included in the final index: Linguistic Preference, as this measure was able to identify both English acquisition and acquisition/retention of parental native language; the Ethnic Interaction Scale; and, the Culture, Values and Behavior Scale.

*Exceptions to the Coding Map*

When particular scale scores were used to identify the acculturation categories used by the children in the study, a number of coding combinations overlapped with two possible acculturation categories. This coding assignment difficulty had also been found by researchers such as Schwatrz, Unger, Zamboanga, and Szapocznik (2010), and Organista, Marin, and Chun (2010), who posited that while Berry's acculturation model offers a more complex understanding of acculturation, its applicability to research studies has been difficult, and has led to the questioning of its usefulness in evaluating acculturation as a variable. Schwatrz et al. (2010) discussed some of the difficulties encountered when operationalizing Berry's acculturation model (2003), stating that the assignment of individuals into one of the model's four categories requires the establishment and use of "a priori cut points... [which are] arbitrary" (p. 241) and sample dependent. Furthermore, Schwatrz et al. (2010), as well as Organista et al. (2010) also stated that "...the use of a priori classification rules assumes that all four categories exist and are equally valid... [although] the validity of marginalization as an approach to acculturation has been questioned" (p. 241). However, Berry's model (2003) has been widely used as it allows for a more nuanced understanding of acculturation, in which the acculturation strategy used by an individual is understood as a reflection of individual characteristics and their interaction with the individuals' environment, such as the sociopolitical climate of the host country in regards to the individual's ethnic or racial group.

Since operationalization difficulties, as described by Schwatrz et al. (2010) and Organista et al. (2010) were encountered in this study, the coding process was further reviewed, identifying the coding combinations that could belong to one or more acculturation categories. These coding combinations were assigned to an a priori category, informed by Berry's theoretical conceptualization. A priori coding combinations were applied consistently throughout the analysis. It is also important to note that further analysis of the sample's acculturation strategies yielded a number of coding combinations that didn't completely reflect a unique acculturation strategy, but rather exhibited aspects of two possible strategies. As a result, for the purpose of this study, and to reflect a more nuanced understanding of the acculturation strategies reported by the children in the three samples, the number of possible acculturation strategies was expanded as follows: assimilation = A; assimilation/separation = A/S; integration = I; integration/assimilation = I/A; integration/separation = I/S; marginalization = M; and, separation = S.

# Notes

1 The PSDI as defined by Portes and Bach (1985), is a "...unit-weighted sum of seven items tapping the immigrants' views on the existence of discrimination in the United States, on how the American way of life affects the family, and on the relationships between Anglo–Americans and their own ethnic group" (p. 283). The six PSDI items were presented in this section, and in Appendix B. The components of the original 1985, PSDI "...were selected by factor analysis using principal components extraction with iterations" (Portes & Bach, 1985, p. 283).

2 The questions selected from the CILS surveys of 1991 and 1995, although identified in the Variable Naming Conventions form provided by the Inter-University Consortium for Political and Social Research, as part of the Portes and Bach's Perception of Society and Discrimination Index, PSDI (1985), are not actually part of the PSDI (Portes & Bach, 1985). Detailed examination of the PSDI, which was developed from data obtained in an eight-year longitudinal study of Cuban and Mexican immigrants conducted in the 1970s, instead revealed a confusion between the PSDI, seven item index, and an associated measure, discussed as "actual experiences of discrimination suffered in the United States..." (Portes & Bach, 1985, p. 283) by Cuban and Mexican immigrants. This measure of "actual experiences of discrimination" was used by Portes and Bach (1985) as a means by which to provide construct validity to the PSDI; hence, a correlation coefficient was calculated, with the underlying assumption that "the more frequent the personal confrontations with discrimination, the more negative the immigrants' perceptions should be" (p. 283). The results indicated a positive and significant correlation (Portes & Bach, 1985).

# Index

Made in United States
North Haven, CT
19 January 2022

14997854R00135